ALL THE EMPEROR'S MEN

ALL THE EMPEROR'S MEN
Kurosawa's Pearl Harbor

HIROSHI TASOGAWA

APPLAUSE
THEATRE & CINEMA BOOKS
An Imprint of Hal Leonard Corporation

Published in 2012 by Applause Theatre & Cinema Books
An Imprint of Hal Leonard Corporation
7777 West Bluemound Road
Milwaukee, WI 53213

Trade Book Division Editorial Offices
33 Plymouth St., Montclair, NJ 07042

Printed in the United States of America

Book design by Kazuhiko Miki

Library of Congress Cataloging-in-Publication Data

Tasogawa, Hiroshi, 1934-
  All the emperor's men : Kurosawa's Pearl Harbor / Hiroshi Tasogawa.
     p. cm.
  Includes index.
  ISBN 978-1-55783-850-6
  1. Tora! Tora! Tora! (Motion picture) 2. Kurosawa, Akira, 1910-1998--Criticism and
     interpretation. I. Title.
  PN1997.T63T38 2012
  791.43'72--dc23
                              2012033787

www.applausebooks.com

CONTENTS

FOREWORD

Elmo Williams

Akira Kurosawa, feared and revered as the 'Emperor' of Japanese film-dom, was a man of exceptional talent—an enigma—a mystic—a man who left his stamp on many motion pictures to give the vast film-going public escape, entertainment, and education.

Long before *Tora! Tora! Tora!* became a part of my life, I was a fan of Kurosawa's. Fate would bring us together in a promising union but one that would end on a tragic note. Although it was my unpleasant duty to remove him as director of the Japanese part of *Tora! Tora! Tora!* I kept intact my admiration for his creative genius as a filmmaker. I rank him with other legendary directors of the twentieth century like John Ford, René Clair, William Wyler, Orson Welles, David Lean, Federico Fellini and Ingmar Bergman. Firing him filled me with an anguish I cannot describe.

Hiroshi Tasogawa, the author of this book, *All the Emperor's Men: Kurosawa's Pearl Harbor*, has left no stone unturned in his relentless research into the reasons for Kurosawa's dismissal. As I was the producer of *Tora! Tora! Tora!*, Tasogawa spent many hours in my Oregon home discussing the entire experience. We talked at length in trying to make some sense of it. Like a precious diamond, there are so many glittering facets to the story that it is difficult to know where to start. Readers of this book will find and decide for themselves.

I feel it basic to a reader's understanding that everyone recognize that making motion pictures is a business. A film requires creative talent and superb imagination but it is still a business. Without the investment of large sums of money there would be no movies. There has always been an uneasy alliance between the creative entity and the financial entity. The creator wants unfettered freedom but the bank insists on control. Producers stand in between in a cold sweat. When Twentieth Century-Fox assigned me to be the producer of *Tora! Tora! Tora!*, it was my responsibility to make the venture successful and I did my best.

Once a screenplay has been approved, experts make up a budget and a schedule based on experience and knowledge of how the creative partner works. In the case of *Tora! Tora! Tora!*, the creator was Kurosawa. Before the cameras turned there were many meetings in which the producer, the director, and sometimes the writers each expressed his or her concept. Kurosawa and I described our intent to make the film about Japan's attack on Pearl Harbor as factual as possible by telling both sides of the story. On a grander scale, both of us stressed the importance of letting truth guide us in the production so that when we finished the American and the Japanese peoples would be united in friendship as never before.

While I was supervising the writing of the screenplay with Darryl Zanuck's help, I agreed to give Kurosawa directorial freedom of expression so long as he stuck to the facts. He was given the right to express Japanese views while he supervised the writing of his part of the production. With this background you would think there would be no great problems. Not so. Kurosawa was a master of surprises.

The first one came when I tried to get the American director (Richard Fleischer) and Kurosawa together to decide how to integrate the two separate parts of the production. I flew the two men to Honolulu and even though both were booked into the same hotel, the meeting never took place. It turned out that Kurosawa felt Fleischer was not his equal in stature as a director.

The second surprise was Kurosawa's choice for each of the key roles when it came to casting. Without consulting me, Kurosawa chose non-professional actors for major roles: former Imperial Navy officers who had become successful business executives. This unorthodox casting was the source of rumors in Hollywood that Kurosawa was currying favor with the industrialists, making them screen stars so they would assume some of the financing of his future films.

8

It was my opinion that Kurosawa, unable to get desired performances from his non-professional actors, had slipped into an untenable position when the filming started. I know from experience that it was not unusual for a director to use abusive language to get an actor to perform but in this case the business executives would not tolerate such treatment. They were either superior or at least equal to Kurosawa in social stature.

Those examples of Kurosawa's surprises were evidence of his inability to fulfill the dictates of the agreed schedule and budget. After three weeks of shooting, Kurosawa had produced only six minutes of usable film at a cost of well over a million dollars. My job was to explain this to Fox Studio executives in my daily reports and to listen to their tirades afterward. In their eyes I had lost control of Kurosawa.

As time went on, Kurosawa drifted more and more behind schedule at a mounting cost to Fox until I was ordered to correct the situation. Darryl Zanuck and his son Richard Zanuck told me to fire Kurosawa, to scrap the rest of the planned production in Japan, and to move the operation to Hawaii to complete the film. Those orders so stupefied me that I put up a big argument for continuing with a new Japanese director in Japan. Among other things, I pointed out that all of the sets—including the full-scale battleship *Nagato* and carrier *Akagi* built on the seashore in southwestern Japan—had been paid for. All my pleading had no effect on the Zanucks who told me to do as I was told. I then shocked them by threatening to resign. As Darryl Zanuck had faith in me due to my work as his associate on *The Longest Day*, he countermanded the order and asked me to continue after firing Kurosawa. This account brings us full circle to my earlier statement about the traumatic dismissal of this great filmmaker.

This book is a meticulously documented study of all that happened and why those things happened. It is a stirring account of the American and Japanese sides of the story, rich in detail and fair in its appraisals.

It was fascinating reading as I relived some of the happy and unhappy memories of making *Tora! Tora! Tora!* that consumed five turbulent years of my life. Once again, I was saddened by my inability to make

Kurosawa a friend and by my failure to share his concept and his grand ambition for making the epic film as portrayed in this book. Nonetheless, it is good to have now been apprised of Kurosawa's joys and sorrows.

In the gestation period of *Tora! Tora! Tora!* I spent many hours with the late Professor Gordon W. Prange, who generously gave me his thoughts on his decades of research of Japan's Pearl Harbor attack and its historical significance. I will never forget his summation: "There were no Pearl Harbor villains; there were no Pearl Harbor scapegoats; they all made mistakes." I believe the same is true with the *Tora! Tora! Tora!* fiasco. There were no villains; we all made mistakes.

In a joint announcement of the film project in April 1967, Kurosawa and I emphasized that it would be "neither a record of victory nor a record of defeat." We said: "No attempt will be made to place blame on individuals of either side…(the film) will show how tragic misunderstandings can grow between two nations, and how misunderstandings… can combine with an unpredictable chain of coincidence to produce a disaster…" In retrospect, it was indeed an unintended prophecy of what was to follow.

—Elmo Williams, Brookings, Oregon, USA 2012

ALL THE EMPEROR'S MEN

INTRODUCTION

Peter Cowie

The French word *patrimoine* is difficult to translate precisely into English. "Heritage" is the closest equivalent, and it's a term that should be applied to Akira Kurosawa. I believe, as a film historian, critic, and author of books on the cinema, that he was, and remains, a national treasure for Japan, his films constituting a legacy that will inspire future generations. He belongs in the pantheon of international moviemakers, alongside such contemporaries as Fellini and Bergman who flourished in that glorious vintage of the 1950s and 1960s.

For some critics and intellectuals, Kurosawa was not in the same league as his compatriots Kenji Mizoguchi and Yasujiro Ozu. In part, because he was not so "Japanese" as them, whatever that means. In part, because his work was forthright and often tumultuous. In part, too, because he admired Occidental filmmakers like John Ford, and composers like Schubert, Ravel, and Offenbach. If, in musical terms, Ozu was the Chopin of Japanese cinema, and Mizoguchi its Haydn, Kurosawa assumed the mantle of Beethoven, tackling the giant themes of life, and rendering on screen, without inhibition, his own fears and aspirations.

His range was extraordinary. He seemed equally at home when filming an intimate chamber-drama like *Ikiru* as he was when tramping the dusty slopes of his beloved Mount Fuji and giving orders to hundreds of extra in epics like *Kagemusha* or *Ran*. He could tear aside the veil of hypocrisy and pseudo-respectability that vitiated so much of Japanese corporate life, in films like *The Bad Sleep Well* and *High and Low*. He could confront the appalling legacy of the nuclear attack on Hiroshima and Nagasaki, in works as poignant as *Dreams* and *Rhapsody in August*.

He could bring alive, as no other filmmaker has done so successfully, the turbulent middle ages of Japanese history, when the *samurai* wandered the land in search of food and recognition.

Kurosawa also had the courage to analyze emotions. His characters are passionate, and eager to escape the bounds and codes of behavior imposed upon them by society. This explains why Kurosawa admired Shakespeare's flawed "giants" like *Macbeth* and *King Lear*. This explains, also, why he seized on the effervescent talent of the young Toshiro Mifune, and created role after role for him. Mifune expressed the anger and frustration, as well as the heroic dimension, in Kurosawa's own personality, just as the master's other loyal actor, Takashi Shimura, embodied his reticence and his rational approach to life.

Despite the host of awards and honors bestowed upon him, Kurosawa suffered periods of rejection and profound depression. From 1965, when *Red Beard* appeared, until the end of his career with *Madadayo* in 1993, each of his remaining films was financed with enormous difficulty.

The great merit of Hiroshi Tasogawa's new book lies in its investigation of a traumatic passage in Kurosawa's life, *Tora! Tora! Tora!*, when he was eventually fired by Twentieth Century-Fox in 1968. The author's research is so meticulous that the narrative possesses the same verve as an action movie by Kurosawa himself. Underlying it all like a matrix is the struggle between two views of the world, between Hollywood executives like Darryl F. Zanuck and the head of Fox's European production arm, Elmo Williams, and Akira Kurosawa, who wanted *Tora! Tora! Tora!* to emerge as a tragedy, and not as a "show." Those who have read Kurosawa's *Something Like an Autobiography* will recall that he had been traumatized by cataclysmic events such as the Kanto Earthquake of 1923, and then the destruction of Hiroshima and Nagasaki in 1945. He could not be expected to abandon, at the behest of Hollywood, his personal, painful vision of modern history.

To this extent, *All the Emperor's Men: Akira Kurosawa's Pearl Harbor* represents a valuable addition to the Kurosawa bibliography. By including so many extracts from Kurosawa's letters and personal records, and so many tantalising extracts from the scenario for *Tora! Tora! Tora!*, Tasogawa-san brings to life what might have been one of the finest war films ever made. He is uniquely qualified to address us on the subject, for it was he who acted as interpreter and translator for Kurosawa for some two years during the gestation of *Tora! Tora! Tora!*, and translated no fewer than 27 versions of the screenplay!

The history of Hollywood is littered with projects abandoned by European and Asian directors. Kurosawa would dearly have loved to shoot a movie in America, and although he spoke little English, might well have succeeded to the same degree as he did with *Dersu Uzala*, shot in Russian in the steppes of Siberia. He preserved his integrity, however, or perhaps more precisely his sensitivity, at the expense of projects such as *Tora! Tora! Tora!* and *The Runaway Train* that might have brought him large sums of money and recognition in Hollywood's corridors of power.

I met him only once. It was during the Indian Film Festival in New Delhi in 1977. Satyajit Ray, the prominent Indian director and writer, had persuaded had persuaded both Kurosawa and Antonioni to attend, and to see all three men strolling through the purlieus of the Taj Mahal in the numinous dawn was memorable indeed. A day or so later, we were introduced during a cocktail reception. One was struck immediately not only by Kurosawa's height, but by his "stature," by the noble way with which he held himself. His dark glasses, which he seemed to wear at any time of day (he suffered from fragile eyes), gave him a detached, mysterious aura. He was not arrogant or disdainful, but his amiability was tempered by a dignified formality no doubt natural in a man descended from *samurai* ancestors. Impeccably dressed, often in western suits and discreet tweed jackets, Kurosawa more than lived up to the sobriquet "Master" (*sensei*). Sometimes suicide beckoned him, and yet he always recovered, even apologizing to his family and close associates, and preferring to continue the struggle until the very end, like Mifune's Kikuchiyo in *Seven Samurai* or Shimura's Watanabe in *Ikiru*.

His *Weltanschauung* seems best summed up by the lines of the 19th century British poet Arthur Hugh Clough:

> Say not the struggle naught availeth,
> The labour and the wounds are vain,
> The enemy faints not, nor faileth,
> And as things have been they remain.

—Peter Cowie, Blonay, Switzerland, 2012

PROLOGUE

07:55 December 7, 1941, Honolulu, Hawaii:

All but a few on the United States naval station at Pearl Harbor were asleep on this Sunday morning. The sun rose and Japanese warplanes appeared over the North Shore of Oahu, the island on which the Pearl Harbor base was situated. Minutes later, the planes swooped down like a cloud of locusts on the base, airfields nearby, and warships in the anchorage. Bombs fell, 2400 Americans perished, including 1177 in the sunken battleship *Arizona*. The Japanese lost 65 aviators and submariners in the attack. The world came apart. The American giant awoke and started to fight back.

That is how World War II started between Japan and America. "All warfare is based on deception," said the famous Chinese strategist Sun Tzu 2500 years ago. Surprise attack has not been rare in wars ancient or modern; some have been successful, others fatal to the aggressor.

Seven decades after the attack on Pearl Harbor, both Japanese and American historians say the assault constituted tactical brilliance but strategic blunder. President Franklin Delano Roosevelt rallied the Americans with his emotional "Day of Infamy" speech to Congress and led them to retaliate, launching a long campaign that devastated and finally defeated Japan. The war that began at Pearl Harbor ended in Japan's surrender aboard the battleship *Missouri* in Tokyo Bay on September 2, 1945. Today, the battleship *Arizona* that took a direct hit in her powder magazine remains on the bottom of Pearl Harbor while the *Missouri* is berthed 200 meters downstream, marking the beginning and the end of that bitter conflict.

13:30 April 28, 1967, Tokyo:

Akira Kurosawa, a national icon in Japan and a movie director dubbed "master of cinema" and "emperor," spoke about his grand ambition. Through a definitive, epic movie about Pearl Harbor, Kurosawa would seek to vindicate the honor of Japan and remove the stigma for having launched a treacherous "sneak attack." He said he would present a fresh and universal perspective incorporating both American and Japanese points of view and bring a new light to the history of the war between them. He would change the world for the better for posterity.

At a news conference in Tokyo, he declared his intention to produce a Twentieth Century-Fox film titled *Tora! Tora! Tora!* (*Tiger! Tiger! Tiger!*), the coded message meaning "surprise has been achieved," and said: "This movie will be a record of neither victory nor defeat but of misunderstandings and miscalculations and the waste of excellent capability and energy. As such, it will embrace the typical elements of tragedy. I want to look straight into what it might mean to be a human being at a time of war."

On that occasion and many others, Kurosawa mused in public about his objectives and may thus have set for himself a "mission impossible."

"After this movie, no one will again be able to say that Pearl Harbor was a sneak attack," he asserted. "This is neither documentary nor spectacle. It is nothing short of tragedy. It will be, in the end, a scary, scary tale."

"This is a good chance to explain to the world what the Japanese are truly like and to demonstrate our traditional trait of integrity," he contended. "By all means, I will make a movie that will carry weight and leave its mark in cinema history. Who needs a movie that will become obsolete in one or two hundred years?"

15:00 December 24, 1968, Kyoto:

Elmo Williams, a senior producer at Twentieth Century-Fox, walked with a heavy step along the corridor of the Kyoto Hotel. He was heading to the suite where Akira Kurosawa was staying, saying to himself, "I have to tell Kurosawa today. I have to tell him he is being dismissed."

For nearly two years, with the staunch support of Darryl F. Zanuck, the Chief Executive Officer of Twentieth Century-Fox, the prominent studio in Hollywood, Williams and Kurosawa had shared the dream of making a great movie that would go down in history. They had toiled day and night. After rewriting the screenplay 27 times, everything was ready and the principal photography had begun with everybody's blessing at a studio in the ancient city of Kyoto, Japan.

Then something unexpected happened. The filming came to a standstill and the staff blamed Kurosawa for the confusion. Many said he was not well. Others were more outspoken and said Kurosawa was out of his mind, a madman. After painful consultations with Zanuck, Williams decided that Kurosawa should go. On Christmas Eve, 1968, Kurosawa was abruptly dismissed as director just three weeks after he started filming *Tora! Tora! Tora!*

"Must it all end like this?" Williams had asked himself, he said later. In the hotel lobby was a big Christmas tree, even though Japanese do not celebrate Christmas like Americans. On it twinkled many colorful miniature bulbs. Looking back, Williams said it was "really a surreal sight" and everything seemed to him like a bad dream.

When Kurosawa came into the hotel room, he was wearing dark glasses so Williams could not read his eyes. Kurosawa looked tense, ill at ease, even haggard. When he saw Elmo, he nodded slightly and took a chair. An interpreter sat beside him.

A week previously, Kurosawa had been examined by a doctor, and Williams opened the conversation by referring to the doctor's diagnosis. Kurosawa needed at least four weeks of rest and medical treatment. Williams advised him to return to Tokyo and enter a hospital at once. Then he said the filming was already behind schedule and any further delay would jeopardize the entire production. Consequently, Fox had decided to replace Kurosawa. Williams stressed that the decision was final.

Kurosawa listened impassively to the interpreter and remained silent for a minute. Then he slowly stood up, muttered some words, and left.

The interpreter stared in blank amazement. When the interpreter explained what Kurosawa had said, Williams too was shocked: "If you all insist on dismissing me, I will commit *hara-kiri* and die." (*Hara-kiri*, or *seppuku*, is ritual suicide by disembowelment, practiced in feudal Japan to protect the honor of a *samurai* warrior.)

For a moment, Williams said later, in his mind's eye he saw Kurosawa covered with blood and shuddered in horror. But he quickly regained his composure, thinking Kurosawa was bluffing. Williams had often been confused by Kurosawa's bluffs. He gave the interpreter a message for Kurosawa and left the room. The message was: "I informed you of Twentieth Century-Fox's decision to dismiss you. You are free to do whatever you want from now on."

Akira Kurosawa's Pearl Harbor:

This is the story of the grand failure of a great filmmaker, why Akira Kurosawa suffered the greatest humiliation of his life and how his ambition to make the definitive Pearl Harbor epic movie ended in a fiasco. More than that, it is a tale of a clash between Japanese and American personalities, a clash of differences in the ways of making movies, and in the broadest sense, a clash between cultures.

On a personal level, what constituted Kurosawa's "strange" or "erratic" behavior during the shoot that baffled those around him and even led to rumors that he had lost his mind? Why did Kurosawa go through such a tortuous time in preparing for the production of the film? What went wrong and why did it go wrong, which has remained a mystery for more than 40 years? What were the key factors that led to the worst crisis in the life of Kurosawa and a nightmare for Twentieth Century-Fox? And the big question: what was Kurosawa trying to impart to us with his Pearl Harbor story, which ultimately vanished like a mirage?

Based on verifiable facts from the perspectives of Japan and America, this book is an effort to tell the story of Akira Kurosawa's Pearl Harbor.

CHAPTER 1

EXTRAORDINARY MEN

A Flash of Inspiration

The Twentieth Century-Fox headquarters building was situated on West Fifty-Sixth Street in the New York City borough of Manhattan. An age-darkened red-brick structure, at first glance its elegance brought to mind an old European fortress. There, in the summer of 1966, the idea for *Tora! Tora! Tora!* was born in the president's office overlooking the wide green expanse of Central Park. With that park as a backdrop, President Darryl F. Zanuck lit a cigar, sank back in his huge leather chair, and tried to come up with an idea for his company's next big hit.

Looking down at the list of books to which Fox had acquired rights, his eyes stopped at *The Broken Seal*, a non-fiction spy tale about code breaking just before the outbreak of war between the United States and Japan. It had been written by Ladislas Farago, who had worked for U.S. Naval Intelligence for four years during World War II. The book contended that, from long before the start of what the Japanese call the Pacific War, American intelligence had broken the codes used for Japanese diplomatic telegrams and the confidential messages of the Imperial Japanese Navy so that, Farago contended, President Franklin Delano Roosevelt knew of the impending Japanese attack five hours before the first bomb fell on Pearl Harbor. Several screenwriters had already tried to turn this book into a movie plot but had given up because it was too controversial to deal with Farago's White House conspiracy theory.

After reading the book, Zanuck had an instinctive feeling: This is it. We can do it! From that point, he moved quickly. Summoning a

EXTRAORDINARY MEN

secretary, he put both feet up on his desk and, cigar in hand, dictated a telegram to his son, Richard Zanuck, who was head of production at the Fox studio in Los Angeles. Saying this had the ingredients of a hit on a par with *The Longest Day*, a huge breakthrough that in one stroke had revived Fox finances four years earlier, Darryl told Richard to move forward immediately with development and to prepare a treatment, or basic narrative about what the movie would show, as soon as possible. He was determined to make lightning strike twice.

After dictating the telegram, Zanuck called London to explain his ideas to Elmo Williams, a close friend in charge of Fox's British branch and head of production in Europe. He told Williams to put together a rough plan for making the film and asked him to serve as producer when the project got on track. Serving as Zanuck's right-hand man, Williams had been involved in *The Longest Day* from planning to completion and was the person who worked hardest to make that movie a great success. Zanuck placed tremendous trust in Williams's character and abilities. Put simply, what Zanuck wanted was to use the same techniques to make a Pacific version of *The Longest Day*.

Path of a Film Mogul

Zanuck at the time was 64 years old. He always wore a pair of dark sunglasses and nearly always had an outsized cigar in his mouth. Sporting a carefully trimmed mustache, his face conveyed a sense of dignity and he spoke slowly and thoughtfully. It has been said that he was always playing the role of the VIP.

Williams told the author that he had seen strong similarities between Akira Kurosawa and Zanuck. "Both like to put on airs and impress people. Maybe that's why they wear dark glasses all the time. Kurosawa is taller but Darryl's glasses are larger. Both are heavy smokers. Kurosawa chain-smokes plain cigarettes. Darryl always has a foot-long Havana cigar dangling from his teeth. So Darryl is one step ahead in the smoking duel," he recalled with a laugh in his house on the Oregon coast more than thirty years after Kurosawa's firing as director of *Tora!*

ALL THE EMPEROR'S MEN

Tora! Tora! "Both are gruff and unapproachable to strangers. Sometimes they look formidable, but in truth they are hungry for company. Both hate to be alone. Tough outside. Sensitive inside. That explains why they smoked a lot. Maybe they needed a smokescreen," he added.

Zanuck was legendary. He took Hollywood by storm with his sensational working style and he lived a turbulent life full of ups and downs. Ranked with Cecil B. DeMille and David O. Selznick as the industry's most important producers, he was called the last tycoon of the American movie industry. From the silent film era onward, Zanuck was involved in the production of more than 600 movies as a screenwriter, director, editor, and producer. Among them were *The Grapes of Wrath*, *How Green Was My Valley*, and *My Darling Clementine*, directed by John Ford, whom Kurosawa admired and considered a master and mentor. Partly because of the friendship with Ford, Zanuck was held in considerable esteem by Kurosawa. "Zanuck is a good guy. He knows movies," Kurosawa once said. He called Zanuck an "extraordinary man."

Zanuck was seven and a half years Kurosawa's senior. An American born in Nebraska in 1902, his father was of Swiss descent and his mother came from British stock. The family was poor. After dropping out of high school, Zanuck enlisted in the Army. He was only fifteen at the time but got in by claiming he would be seventeen on his next birthday. He fought in World War I as a private in the forces sent to the Belgian front. His discharge came before he turned seventeen as he was injured, although not wounded in action, while on the German front in 1918. After that, Zanuck moved around looking for work. He tried working in a shipyard and a sewing factory and used the boxing skills he had acquired in the Army. He even fought as a pro boxer in preliminary bouts at a run-down gym.

Despite the hard times, Zanuck never gave up the dream of writing for a living someday. When he could find free time, he sat in his room in a cheap apartment and pounded out a novel or screenplay on his battered Underwood typewriter. Far away, young Akira Kurosawa in another cheap rooming house lay on thin futon bedding scribbling a screenplay using a worn-out pencil, coarse paper, and the light of a bare bulb.

A Turning Point

In 1924, twenty-two-year-old Zanuck's dream began to be realized when he was hired as a scriptwriter by Warner Brothers. The silent adventure movies he wrote for canine star Rin Tin Tin became major hits and Zanuck started to make his name in Hollywood. He was soon able to try his hand at movie production. Zanuck was one of the trailblazers who established the Hollywood studio system in which a producer controlled everything in the film production.

The movie acumen of young Zanuck, then twenty-seven, was recognized in 1929 with a promotion to head of production at Warner Brothers. About this time, he grew a mustache and began wearing dark sunglasses and smoking cigars, perhaps as a tactic to look older than his years.

Zanuck took another ambitious step in 1933 when he left Warner Brothers to form Twentieth Century Pictures. After the 1935 merger with the Fox Film Corporation, he was named vice president and head of production of the Twentieth Century-Fox Film Corporation. By this time, Zanuck married Virginia Fox, who had been a popular actress in the silent film era, and fathered three children, two girls and son Richard, with her. To onlookers it seemed to be a happy family but Zanuck was apparently not satisfied. Paying little heed to family, he was soon devoting his energy and passion to work and uninhibited love affairs.

In 1956, evidently tired of family, tired of Hollywood, and tired of women, fifty-three-year-old Zanuck separated from his wife and, leaving his family behind, moved to Paris, where he founded an independent production company. Things did not go as he had hoped, however, with his company under contract to Twentieth Century-Fox producing a series of failures. Drinking heavily after the collapse of an intense affair with French singer and actress Juliette Gréco, in 1960 Zanuck was felled by a mild stroke. He was treated by doctors and nurses in his Paris apartment but did not enter a hospital. But he was out of action for several weeks as he recovered and often lay crushed and despondent on his bed.

In the depths of Zanuck's despair, Elmo Williams arrived to visit him in his lonely sickroom. Zanuck was so happy to see his old friend that he looked like he might cry. When Williams asked if there was anything he could do to help, Zanuck handed him several screenplays and asked him to see if they had any potential. Visiting Zanuck again two days later, Williams reported that not one of the screenplays was usable. Hearing this, Zanuck pointed to a fat book on the table beside his bed and said, "Maybe there is a film in it. Would you take it and read it and see what you think?" That book was *The Longest Day* by Cornelius Ryan. The movie rights had come to Zanuck as collateral for money he had lent to a friend who was a French producer.

Williams read it and was floored by the book. "That's a helluva book. It will take an awful lot of guts to make [a movie out of] it," he reported to Zanuck. An exciting moment-by-moment account of the Allies' daring D-Day invasion of Normandy in Nazi-occupied France, the events would require a large production budget to recreate the book on film. Even so, both Zanuck and Williams were seduced by this reckless gamble of a movie. Williams tossed aside all his other work to devote himself to the project as associate producer. Convalescing from the stroke and regaining strength, energy, and confidence, Zanuck made a near-miraculous recovery. Staking everything on this movie, he worked passionately, denying himself sleep. Fox was reluctant to go ahead with the project but Zanuck was undaunted. He poured in his own funds to push production forward.

In 1962, *The Longest Day* was done. Instead of the usual single-thread war movie plot, it was structured to merge multiple threads. With an unusual collection of more than twenty top stars from America, Britain, France, and Germany, it was a spectacle on a staggering scale.

There were three directors: Andrew Marton for American scenes, Ken Annakin for British scenes, and Bernhard Wicki for German scenes. Williams served as coordinator of battle episodes. That this movie, which covered a wide ground with a large cast of characters, hung together as a war epic was due to the capabilities of Zanuck and Williams, who had strong editing skills honed through experience.

Williams explained later: "Darryl loved France and French women all his life. And France loved Darryl." Williams in his poor younger days had moved to London after abandoning plans to attend college. There he struggled to learn film editing and for many years worked on movie production in England. So both men had an intimate knowledge of Europe as well as many friends there. This proved to be an enormous help in making the war movie.

A European sensibility not found in Hollywood movie people was reflected in the dialogue of *The Longest Day*. The three languages—English, German, and French—were spoken by the actors in their own languages. For the English parts, the American and British actors spoke with their own accents. Fox made an all-English dubbed version but the world premieres in Paris, London, and New York used the original language version subtitled for each country. The movie proved to be more popular than expected and was well received by the critics. Emboldened by this, Zanuck pushed through the decision to use the original language version in the general release.

With the success of *The Longest Day*, Zanuck was awarded a seat on the Fox board of directors and started an intense struggle to gain control of the company. He won the president's seat by evicting Spyros Skouras, who had incurred huge financial losses on *Cleopatra*, the epic movie with Elizabeth Taylor as Cleopatra and Richard Burton as Mark Antony. The movie was an epic investment, generated epic gossip, but ultimately was an epic flop for Twentieth Century-Fox. In contrast, *The Longest Day* became a record-breaking hit throughout the world and enabled Twentieth Century-Fox to survive a financial crisis. For Zanuck, the movie reflected lifelong glory for him as he fought his way back from the brink of destruction to experience the greatest success of his life in cinema. Moreover, Williams had enhanced the trust of Zanuck and was subsequently put in charge of Fox's British subsidiary and appointed head of production in Europe. Thus, when the time came to make the Pearl Harbor epic as the Pacific version of *The Longest Day*, it was only

Director Akira Kurosawa and Elmo Williams, producer of 20th Century-Fox, jointly announced the making of Tora! Tora! Tora! *at Tokyo Prince Hotel on April 28, 1967. (Photo courtesy of Jiji Press)*

natural that Zanuck would, without hesitation, entrust the project to Elmo Williams.

"You never forget where you were when you heard the Pearl Harbor news. But that does not mean you know the exact historical facts beyond personal recollections. Darryl and myself were no exception. We knew nothing," Williams recalled. His hard study had begun when he was asked by Zanuck to turn his attention to the Pearl Harbor project.

For many Americans in 1966, the Imperial Japanese Navy attack on the U.S. Navy base at Pearl Harbor in Hawaii twenty-five years earlier had been the truly unforgettable news of that era. Pearl Harbor Day, December 7, 1941, held strong personal memories for Williams. Twenty-eight years old at the time, he and his new wife Lorraine had moved that very day from a small Los Angeles apartment to the single-family home they had managed to buy in North Hollywood. The next day they heard on the radio President Roosevelt give his historic

EXTRAORDINARY MEN

speech to a joint session of Congress. The president opened his address: "Yesterday, December Seventh, Nineteen Forty-One—a date which will live in infamy—the United States of America was suddenly and deliberately attacked by naval and air forces of the Empire of Japan." That later became known as the "Day of Infamy Speech."

The twenty-fifth anniversary of Pearl Harbor saw the publication of many books and academic papers about the attack, and American television networks vied with one another in presenting special programs. There was no shortage of living witnesses and people were still trying to dig up facts. For Pearl Harbor Day that year, President Lyndon Baines Johnson ordered that flags over federal offices be flown at half-mast in remembrance of the victims.

At this time, it did not take long for Williams to meet Gordon W. Prange, a University of Maryland history professor who would come to be considered to be a leading authority in research on the Pearl Harbor attack. Williams asked Prange, who had been the chief historian on General Douglas MacArthur's staff during the Allied Occupation of postwar Japan, to assist on the movie project, and the professor readily promised to provide materials. Before the start of the project, Williams had never heard of Prange and neither had Zanuck or his son Richard as Prange's research on Pearl Harbor had not yet been published in book form. His work began to appear in public in 1963, when the *Reader's Digest* published two articles based on his research. A year later, the Japanese edition of *Reader's Digest* published four installments of Prange's work. In 1966, Fox purchased the movie rights of Prange's unpublished manuscript entitled *TORA TORA TORA*. Prange died of cancer at the age of 70 in 1980 but his co-workers saw to it that his definitive work on Pearl Harbor was published the following year as *At Dawn We Slept*, which became a best-seller. The Japanese version of that book was published in three volumes by Kodansha in 1986-1987.

When Fox purchased the movie rights to Prange's unpublished 530-page manuscript, the title *TORA TORA TORA* on the manuscript came with it and ended up as the title of the movie. The credits of the Twentieth Century-Fox movie *Tora! Tora! Tora!* that premiered in September

1970 stated that it was based on two works: Farago's *The Broken Seal* and Prange's *TORA TORA TORA*, although Prange never published a book with that title.

Capturing Kurosawa

Zanuck planned to use the same techniques as those of *The Longest Day* for the Pearl Harbor epic. This would involve considering the Pearl Harbor attack from both American and Japanese perspectives and then combining the American and Japanese scenes into a single well-balanced movie. To achieve this goal, it was necessary to select a suitable screenwriter and director for the Japanese scenes. When asked his opinion, Williams recommended director Akira Kurosawa as someone who could do both. He was astonished when Zanuck responded with "Kurosawa? Who's that?" and a puzzled look. His son Richard just shook his head in silence.

The work that had brought Kurosawa to Williams's attention was the 1950 production of *Rashomon*. After taking the top prize at the 1951 Venice Film Festival, it received an Academy Honorary Award as the most outstanding foreign language film in 1952. In the same year, Williams received an Academy Award for his editing of the movie *High Noon*. Ordinarily the two might have seen each other give speeches on stage at the 1952 ceremony but Kurosawa did not attend.

The Kurosawa work for which Williams had the most enduring affection was *Ikiru (To Live)*. He considered it too quiet a picture, however, to use as an example of the director's work so he presented a double feature of *Seven Samurai* and *Rashomon* to Darryl and Richard in a Fox screening room. Both Zanuck and his son greatly enjoyed the showing and readily agreed to hire Kurosawa. When Williams told Zanuck that Kurosawa held Zanuck's close friend, director John Ford, in great esteem, considering him a master of the art and a mentor, Zanuck ordered: "A top film needs a top director. OK. Go and get Kurosawa."

In late November 1966, producer Tetsuo Aoyagi glanced through the mail after arriving at the Kurosawa Productions office on the fourth floor of the Tokyo Prince Hotel. In Japan, entrepreneurs sometimes set up temporary offices in a hotel for convenience and as a status symbol. Some Japanese are superstitious about the number four as, in Japanese, it is pronounced in the same way as the word "death." Kurosawa didn't care. Aoyagi's eye stopped on an airmail envelope with a Los Angeles postmark dated November 15. The envelope was addressed to Akira Kurosawa and the name on the return address was Elmo Williams. Assigned by Kurosawa to handle all overseas communications, Aoyagi immediately tore the envelope open. He said later his heart beat faster as he read the enclosed letter.

Dear Mr. Kurosawa:

For a number of years, I have admired your numerous cinematic achievements. As a dedicated filmmaker and as a producer I have long hoped that some day fate would afford me the chance to work with you. At long last I have found a project that makes this possible.

Five years ago Mr. Darryl F. Zanuck made me his Associate Producer on "THE LONGEST DAY." The film, as you know, enjoyed enormous success throughout the world. Now it is my intention to make a worthy successor to it by focusing my cameras on the dramatic story of "Pearl Harbor."

Utilizing the techniques developed on "THE LONGEST DAY," I intend to make the American part of this film in the United States and in Hawaii with a top Hollywood director at the helm. The Japanese part of this production is to be made in Japan, using Japanese actors speaking in their own language. It is imperative that this work be done by a Japanese director of your stature.

This film is to be as factual as I can make it, showing both the Japanese and the American points of view in each of the numerous incidents leading up to the Pearl Harbor incident of December 7, 1941. The title of this production is "TORA TORA TORA."

We have already started our search for period aircraft and other equipment. Mr. Larry Forrester is currently developing the screenplay based on factual material brought to him by a staff doing research. Several artists are busy at work translating Mr. Forrester's work into a story board. All of the care, all the planning, all of the scope, all of the attention that went into the making of "THE LONGEST DAY" will go into the production of "TORA TORA TORA."

If the idea of working on a subject of this importance appeals to you, then let us arrange to discuss the project in person. As I am anxious to do some research in Japan, I should be pleased to meet you in Tokyo. I feel sure that we can both benefit by working together in bringing to the screen one of history's most dramatic moments.

Sincerely,

Elmo Williams (signed)

Carrying the letter with him, Aoyagi hurried out to Kurosawa's home in fashionable Setagaya Ward. After hearing an explanation of the letter's content, Kurosawa was slow to react. Nevertheless, he decided at least to meet with Williams and hear the details of the proposal when Williams visited Tokyo. The next morning, Kurosawa sent a telegram to Williams:

RECEIVED YOUR LETTER DATED NOVEMBER FIF-
TEENTH STOP YOUR OFFER IS MOST INTERESTING
STOP TALKS IN TOKYO PREFERRED STOP DEFINITE
DATE PENDING MUTUAL CONSENT STOP KUROSAWA

It was December 8, 1966 (December 7, American time), by curious coincidence the same day the Imperial Japanese Navy attacked Pearl Harbor, when Williams, accompanied by his secretary, Christa Streichert, knocked on the door of Room 484 at the Tokyo Prince Hotel at the appointed hour of 3 P.M.

Aoyagi opened the door and invited them in. Wearing a dark suit and dark sunglasses, Kurosawa stood up slowly from the sofa. He shook hands with Williams and nodded to Streichert, welcoming them with a big smile. Recalling his impression of Kurosawa at that first meeting, Williams later said that Kurosawa had a sharp, masculine look, and he was much taller than expected so he didn't really seem Asian.

Sitting across from Kurosawa, Williams immediately began to explain the goals of the project. Aoyagi translated Williams's comments to Kurosawa. Streichert recalled that, as Aoyagi warmed to his task, he stood up and paced back and forth between Kurosawa and Williams, sometimes speaking loudly and gesticulating actively.

Williams's explanation was concise and articulate. Zanuck wanted to make a movie that would re-examine the great historical confrontation that had occurred between the two countries focusing on the Pearl Harbor attack from both the American and Japanese perspectives. He indicated they would gather all the facts that had come to light by that time—considering questions such as: Why did it happen? How was it planned? How was it executed? And, why couldn't it have been prevented? He pledged that they would accurately and faithfully make the film conforming to those facts. The production would maintain a point of view that did not lean to either the American side or the Japanese side.

To achieve these objectives, Williams said it was crucial to have the full cooperation of the Japanese and he strongly hoped that Kurosawa would participate. He explained preparations that Fox had made so far and the steps that would be taken as the production moved forward. Finally, he communicated Zanuck's determination to complete the picture.

Kurosawa listened to the explanation in silence, nodding occasionally. Then he said, softly: "So you also expect me to write the screenplay."

"That's exactly what I want. Please write the screenplay for the Japanese sequence on the assumption you film it," Williams answered.

When the meeting was over, Kurosawa shook hands with Williams and left the room. After walking to the door with Kurosawa, Aoyagi returned to the sofa. Looking serious, he paused to take a breath and then stated emphatically to Williams, "Kurosawa will certainly do it."

After that Aoyagi talked on in almost a monologue. He said Kurosawa was a true artist who lived in his own world. As a pure and sensitive artist, he was not good with contract and monetary matters, so the practical business aspects for this project would be in the hands of Aoyagi himself. According to Aoyagi, Kurosawa was a friend of his family and, although they were not related by blood, Kurosawa was virtually a family member. The director thinks of me as a son, Aoyagi explained, adding that since he had full authority to handle the public relations of Kurosawa Productions, he would be the contact person for all communications. Williams's secretary, Christa Streichert, remembered the relatively short Aoyagi as cutting a fine and impressive figure in his well-fitted designer suit. He reminded her of the sharp businessmen she often saw on Madison Avenue in New York.

From that moment on Aoyagi became the most important source for Williams since all information concerning Kurosawa was delivered to him via Aoyagi. In subsequent Fox documents and communications, Williams frequently referred to Aoyagi as "Kurosawa's manager." It seems clear that Aoyagi was seen as the key person who had sole command of the schedule, contracts, public relations, and other aspects of Kurosawa's work.

This framework would lead to problems in the future.

Born in 1934, Aoyagi was then thirty-two years old, twenty-four years younger than Kurosawa. He used the nickname Tetsu in English conversation, asking people to call him that. In English letters and other documents, he used the name Tetsu Aoyagi and signed his name that way. He was considered an outsider in the Japanese movie world, however, and to this day he remains something of an enigma with a reputation that is neither good nor bad. He was ostracized as a "villain" by the Japanese film industry after *Tora! Tora! Tora!* turned into a fiasco. He was considered an unpardonable traitor because he was believed to have double-crossed Kurosawa, a view that this author has disputed in publications in Japan.

Aoyagi's father, Nobuo Aoyagi, was a veteran director at Toho, one of Japan's most prominent and reputable movie studios. The claim the younger Aoyagi made to Williams about Kurosawa being a friend of the family was not an empty boast. His father was a workmanlike director who focused on comedies, making more than seventy movies, many of them program pictures. They were so-called 'B-movie' comedies, low-budget second features for 'double bill' shows. He was a big-hearted man of flamboyant but easy-going character who treated young directors like Kurosawa and Kon Ichikawa as protégés. There was a period when Kurosawa came and went freely at the Aoyagi home. Perhaps because his family roots were in the Tohoku region of northeastern Japan, Kurosawa didn't particularly like warm climates. His wife, Kiyo, on the other hand, disliked the cold so over the New Year's holiday she would take the children and fly to Hawaii while Kurosawa stayed with the Aoyagi family. Reflecting this family connection and because he was old enough to be Aoyagi's father, Kurosawa had a comfortable and relaxed relationship with the younger man, calling him by the affectionate nickname *Tetchan*.

After graduating from Keio University with a major in English literature, through his father's influence Aoyagi was able to go to work at Toho studios as an apprentice assistant director. He soon transferred to the foreign affairs department. Traveling to America as Toho's representative in New York, he worked on production exchanges with movie companies outside of Japan. Eventually becoming fed up with life as a white collar 'salaryman,' Aoyagi left Toho and took a job in a small, independent, movie production organization. Looking back, Aoyagi said he was poor but enjoyed the free and easygoing life he led then. He said he was mostly loafing in the early spring of 1965 when one day Kurosawa placed an international telephone call from Tokyo to Aoyagi's New York apartment.

"That phone call completely changed my life," Aoyagi said later.

"I want you to come back to Japan as soon as you can to join Kurosawa Productions and help me with my work," Kurosawa told him, saying it was a matter of some urgency and that he already had consent of Aoyagi's father, Nobuo. This came as a shock to Aoyagi but saying "No" didn't seem to be an option. Hurrying back to Japan, Aoyagi, suitcases in hand, went straight from Haneda Airport to Kurosawa's home without stopping at his own home.

Kurosawa's Decision

The story he heard from Kurosawa and Kikushima was even more of a surprise to Aoyagi. Kurosawa said: "I want to break away from Toho once and for all. So I want you to look for some organization or an individual, anywhere overseas is fine, that is interested in backing a movie by me." First, Kurosawa was already considered by Toho a risky investment because his movies cost too much. In addition, Kurosawa was contract-bound not to seek foreign investment independent of Toho's control. Kurosawa seemed to think that if the conditions of the contract with Toho remained, it would be impossible in Japan for him to make the kind of movies he wanted to make. Kurosawa explicitly stated that he would not renew his exclusive contract with Toho, which would expire on the last day of January, 1966.

In 1965, Kurosawa's film *Red Beard* opened and was lauded by many critics as reflecting the essence of Kurosawa's career. It was a moving story of a talented but arrogant intern reborn as a devoted slum doctor under the powerful influence of his tyrannical but compassionate mentor, Dr. "Red Beard," played by Toshiro Mifune. For several months after that, Kurosawa fell into a state of lethargy, tormented by a sense that a gaping hole had opened in his life. Kurosawa supporters scattered and Kurosawa Productions went deeply into debt to Toho. "The Kurosawa family finances were also close to bankruptcy, and the usual crowd was keeping its distance. The director was lonely," Aoyagi recalled later.

Kurosawa had received several offers from foreign countries in prior years. At the time, however, it was not possible for Kurosawa Productions to proceed independently with discussions that relied on foreign capital and distribution channels. Such negotiations were supposed to be carried out by Toho's international department and contracts were to be concluded via Toho.

By becoming independent and refusing to accept a Toho executive in its management, Kurosawa Productions would be able to do its own negotiating with foreign organizations. With this in mind, Kurosawa wanted to make Aoyagi the executive in charge of public relations and assign him responsibility for such foreign contacts. Kurosawa and Kikushima put pressure on Aoyagi, telling him there was no time to think things over as he had to start immediately.

In concluding these arrangements, Aoyagi's father, Nobuo, exercised strong influence. Subsequently, Nobuo quit Toho and in August 1966 established the television and movie production company C.A.L., becoming its president. Scenarist Ryuzo Kikushima, Kurosawa's bosom friend, was a board member when C.A.L. was founded.

Tetsuo Aoyagi went back to New York, disposed of his apartment, and quickly returned to Japan.

Pitfalls of Profit-sharing

For Kurosawa, the six years he had just spent both as movie maker and president of an independent production company had been a trying experience. With Toho and Kurosawa each providing half of the one million yen in capital funding, Kurosawa Productions had been established in April 1959. In those days of a fixed exchange rate of 360 yen to the US dollar, 500,000 yen was the equivalent of about 1,400 US dollars, only a nominal sum being needed to set up a corporation.

The news that Venice Film Festival Golden Lion winner and world famous director Akira Kurosawa had become a company president got considerable play in the media. In the magazine *Sunday Mainichi*, a feature article with the headline "Emperor Kurosawa Descends to Earth" cast doubt on the future prospects for Kurosawa because he would be a manager as well as an artist.

Nevertheless, Kurosawa spoke of his optimistic aspirations, saying, "I took this step because I thought it is the natural path that the movie world must take. To enable a movie director to live a comfortable life, this is the only option available. I want to act boldly."

At the start, the head of production at Toho, Sanezumi Fujimoto, became a board member of Kurosawa Productions. He said: "Akira Kurosawa has performed distinguished service for Toho, gaining worldwide honor and fame as a result. We want him to make more money." As a Toho executive, however, Fujimoto was actually using equivocation to mislead Kurosawa to think that all this would prove to his advantage. Lurking in the background of the decision by Toho top management to agree to establish Kurosawa Productions was an in-house controversy that surrounded the movie *The Hidden Fortress*, which was released in 1958. The filming of that movie was originally scheduled to take 130 days but because of bad weather and trouble on location, it took more than 200 days. Much of the photography was done on location at the base of Mount Fuji. But the weather was changeable and they had to wait for more than one hundred days for good weather. Typhoons chewed up scenery and they often had to shoot all over again. Production costs shot way over budget, reaching one hundred million yen or nearly $280,000. Moreover, the movie's box office performance fell below expectations. The controversy got to the point where the person in charge of production, Fujimoto, tendered his resignation in order to take responsibility. Some Toho executives began to call for action to put the brakes on Kurosawa's excesses and have the director shoulder more responsibility himself.

Clever Toho calculations were hidden in the complicated agreement to establish Kurosawa Productions. Media reports at the time almost all said Kurosawa and Toho would equally share any profit or loss generated by the new company's movies. This, however, was a mistake. *The Hidden Fortress* was a hit at the box office but Toho considered it a financial failure because the movie fell short of the originally planned break-even point, with its production costs exceeding total rentals.

Toho's understanding of the agreement, however, was different from that of Kurosawa Productions, as disclosed by Toho executive Fujimoto in an interview with the film magazine *Kinema Junpo*. First, a given project was to be approved through discussion and agreement between the people in charge at Toho and Kurosawa Productions. Then, after deciding the number of shooting days, production costs, and a completion date, production would start. Toho would finance the cost of production. When the movie had been completed, the total cost was to be calculated by adding print, distribution, advertising, and other costs. Producer fees and director fees were to be included. Only the cost of the screenplay was to be calculated and paid separately, with those costs to be borne by Kurosawa Productions. The number of people who would do the writing, the number of days they could seclude themselves at a hot spring resort, the amount of liquor that they drank was of no concern of Toho, and Toho would not pay a single yen to cover those costs.

Kurosawa Productions' movies were to be distributed only to Toho theaters. The Toho income earned from distribution in the three years after the movie was completed was calculated and the total cost was to be deducted from that to determine the movie's gross profit. From this figure, a specified percentage of the miscellaneous expenses incurred by Toho would be deducted. When this was done, if the movie had been completed after the originally agreed-upon deadline, an additional overhead percentage was added to the amount deducted. The profit remaining was to be divided between Toho and Kurosawa Productions using a specified formula. Roughly speaking, this was the true nature of Toho's profit-sharing.

In addition, Kurosawa's personal expenses were to be covered by an advance from Toho, with that amount (with interest added) later deducted from the final profit allocated to Kurosawa Productions. The net effect here was, simply put, that Kurosawa was like a '*salaryman*' covering his daily living expenses with salary advances and loans and then working to pay those back.

Under this profit-sharing, Kurosawa Productions would see a large inflow of funds only if it quickly and cheaply produced profitable movies. In the case of money-losing movies, it would be allocated a portion of the loss and its debt to Toho would increase. From Kurosawa's perspective, it probably seemed that the harder he worked, carefully and deliberately spending time and money following his artistic conscience to create honest movies, the more he would be exploited by Toho and lose money.

A Fresh Start for Kurosawa Productions

After dissolving its exclusive contract with Toho and becoming independent in July 1966, Kurosawa Productions opened its office in the Tokyo Prince Hotel. It was a modest room with just a desk, sofa, locker, and two telephones. To strengthen the organization's clerical processes, veteran accountant Sadahiro Kubota was hired away from Toho and appointed director of accounting for Kurosawa Productions. Back from America, Aoyagi became a Kurosawa Productions executive and, like a fish returned to water, enthusiastically set to work. Backed by the authority of the master, he promoted himself with the title of "producer," a relatively unfamiliar position in Japan at that time. Printed on his business card were two titles in Japanese and English: "Producer" and "Kurosawa Productions Managing Director."

Aoyagi was viewed harshly by movie industry people. Although he was respected for being knowledgeable about foreign matters and skilled in English, many members of the old order, including members of the old Kurosawa coterie, shunned him as being a cocky Americanized greenhorn ignorant of movie making. From Aoyagi's perspective, these were people worthy only of disdain as they could not free themselves from the antiquated conventions of a Japanese movie industry that was on a path of decline.

Kurosawa's perspective on Aoyagi was different. He was angry at Toho's relentless pressure and merciless exploitation that had continued even after the creation of Kurosawa Productions. He was well acquainted with the cockiness of this youngster he had known since Aoyagi was a child. Rather than finding it a problem, Kurosawa prized the characteristic as he had strong expectations for Aoyagi's potential to act boldly and fearlessly in spearheading an attack on the out-dated order of the Japanese movie industry, Toho included.

"I want you to look for some organization or an individual that is interested in backing a movie by me," Kurosawa had said, so for him as well as the rest of the staff the sudden Fox Pearl Harbor movie offer at the end of 1966 must truly have been considered a golden opportunity greater than anyone could have hoped for. This was a large-scale deal from what was unquestionably a major Hollywood studio. Aoyagi was determined that this project be a success. He advised Kurosawa that they should listen to Fox's proposal and begin contract negotiations as soon as possible. Ryuzo Kikushima, a Kurosawa Productions executive and old friend of Kurosawa, thought there was no need to hesitate so they should listen to what Fox had to say.

In contrast to the readiness of Aoyagi and Kikushima to jump at the Fox project, Kurosawa was initially reluctant to get on board. He was preoccupied by thoughts about another movie project, the preparation for which he had been focused on for nearly a year. The film was entitled *The Runaway Train*.

CHAPTER
2

WHEEL OF FORTUNE

The Locomotive as a Living Thing

The idea for the film called *The Runaway Train* came to Kurosawa while he was reading the February issue of *Bungei Shunju* magazine during the filming of *Red Beard* in January 1964. The article, entitled "Terror of the Runaway Locomotive," featured the line "An 80 mph thriller speeds across the plains of America." It was the translation of a *LIFE* magazine article reporting the true story of a runaway locomotive on the New York Central Railroad in 1962. Written by reporter Warren R. Young, the article appeared in the March 29, 1963, issue of *LIFE*.

The incident began at a large railroad marshaling yard on the outskirts of the city of Syracuse, New York. Four coupled diesel locomotives suddenly started moving and the engineer who tried to stop them was thrown out of the cab to the ground, leaving on board only a sheet-metal worker with no knowledge of how to operate a locomotive. Kurosawa added two brute jailbreaker convicts as juggernaut riders and changed the sheet-metal worker to a 'sand man,' the worker who checks the boxes storing sand that is thrown on the tracks so a locomotive doesn't skid when it starts or stops. The rest of the plot is basically the same as the original *LIFE* story.

Over an hour and forty minutes, the runaway locomotives reach a maximum speed of 90 mph as they speed from Syracuse to Rochester. They were almost unbelievably powerful monsters of metal. The four together were 220 feet long and weighed a million pounds. With pulling power sufficient to haul a mile-long freight train from one side of the North American continent to the other, the locomotives ran at a speed of 85 mph across rural expanses. If they could not be stopped quickly, the results would be horrendous. All the remote control attempts failed. The panic-stricken riders touched all the levers and what looked like control buttons they could find. With some luck, one of the buttons worked. It killed the engine and slowed the onslaught of the giant locomotives, which finally came to a stop as they gently crunched into ballast rocks placed on the rails by hand.

It appears that Kurosawa, without telling anyone, decided to make a movie based on this incident after finishing *Red Beard*. That kind of large-scale picture would be the first movie for the newly reborn Kurosawa Productions. When asked later about his motive for starting this movie project, Kurosawa answered, "Ever since I was a child, I have really liked locomotives." Whenever he had the time, he would go to watch them. A list of Kurosawa's favorite films included railroad-themed pictures such as the great French film-maker Abel Gance's *La Roue (The Wheel)* and John Ford's *The Iron Horse*. Trains and locomotives were an important element in Kurosawa movies such as *Sanshiro Sugata* (aka *Judoist Saga*), *High and Low*, *Dodesukaden*, and *Yume (Dreams* aka *Akira Kurosawa's Dreams)*. "Just once I wanted to make a film with a locomotive as the central subject," he said.

The Runaway Train embodied another theme that Kurosawa pursued throughout his life. Creations of man may suddenly run wild as if they had taken on lives of their own, with human beings powerless to stop them. There is terror to be found in this reversal of the power relation between man and machine. Dynamite and nuclear energy were supposed to be controlled by human beings but these creations, in the wrong hands, could threaten our existence. Huge battleships, powerful tanks, and other war machines could either threaten or defend human beings and even appear as mysterious living things driven by their own will. Human beings enthralled by their own machines could be representative paradoxes of the twenty-first century. This paradox was lodged in the back of Kurosawa's mind and the theme of a runaway juggernaut stimulated his creative imagination throughout his life. It was, of course, later an element in *Tora! Tora! Tora!*

44

In his autobiography, Kurosawa wrote, "In the course of my work as a film director, whenever my fate has hung in the balance, some kind of guardian angel has always appeared out of nowhere. I can't help being surprised by this strange destiny." A strong supporter who appeared out of nowhere in the autumn of 1965 could be considered such a guardian angel. An avowed fan of Kurosawa's movies, Hedley Donovan was the editor-in-chief of Time Inc. During a visit to Japan, he learned of Kurosawa's plan to make a movie based on the *LIFE* magazine article and went out of his way to visit the director's house and to promise his assistance.

With Donovan's influence and contacts, Kurosawa acquired valuable materials that would have been difficult to obtain through normal channels. He received from General Motors several confidential, detailed drawings of diesel locomotive designs as well as confidential technical data on traffic control. Furthermore, a producer introduced by Donovan became interested after reading an English translation of the treatment. This was Joseph E. Levine, president of Embassy Pictures, who came to be called Hollywood's *enfant terrible* as he rose to prominence after World War II. The headquarters of Embassy Pictures was in the Time-Life Building in Manhattan, and Levine and Donovan were personal friends.

Contract negotiations between Levine and a Kurosawa Productions agent began in November 1965. This agent was Creative Management Associates (CMA), which had its offices on Sunset Boulevard in Los Angeles. Toward the end of the same year, Ryuzo Kikushima and Tetsu Aoyagi went to upstate New York to gather information for the scenario. They visited the site of the episode and collected materials on the traffic control facilities of the New York Central Railroad. Through preferential arrangements made by Donovan, they were accompanied on this trip by the author of the *LIFE* article, Warren R. Young.

Carrying a mountain of materials with them in February 1966, Kurosawa, along with Ryuzo Kikushima and Hideo Oguni, his two friends who were established screen-writers, secluded themselves in Minaguchi-en, a venerable Japanese inn in the hot spa resort at Atami, about an hour by train down the coast from Tokyo. There, over a one-month period, they wrote the scenario at record-breaking speed, putting it together in half the time it would have taken ordinarily. In the scenario they crafted, and adding to the drama of the original incident, they put three people (instead of one) aboard the runaway train, two of them escaped convicts. The heightened tension included not only the movement of the out-of-control locomotives but, simultaneously, the unraveling of the conflict among the passengers riding the train.

Negotiations became earnest based on a translated version of this scenario and in June 1966, Kurosawa, Kikushima, and Aoyagi went to New York where the contract was signed by Kurosawa and Levine on June 29. The following day, Levine invited 100 movie and media people to a luncheon in a special room at the renowned Manhattan restaurant The Four Seasons. There Kurosawa announced the start of production of *The Runaway Train.* A large photograph of Kurosawa was displayed on the front wall of the room, and Kurosawa, Kikushima, and Aoyagi sat at the table in front of that photograph.

In his speech, Levine remarked that he felt honored that Kurosawa had chosen him to work with on his first movie in America. He said Kurosawa's arrival in Hollywood was the most momentous event since Alfred Hitchcock was brought from England to Hollywood by David O. Selznick a quarter of a century before.

In his own speech, Kurosawa said, "I am very grateful to Mr. Levine for giving his OK to the condition that my ideas and scenario are to be used and that the making of the movie be, on the whole, left up to me."

Kurosawa Productions's first film since becoming independent of Toho was thus decided upon speedily and without a hitch. The goddess Fortuna had spun her wheel and the momentum seemed unstoppable. It soon became apparent, however, that the person most worried by the speed with which the project moved forward was Kurosawa himself.

Arriving back in Japan, Kurosawa held a press conference in Haneda Airport's VIP room at 10 P.M. on July 4, 1966. He talked about detailed plans for the production of *The Runaway Train*. The press learned that two billion yen ($5.5 million at the exchange rate of Y360 to $1) would be spent on the movie, that it would be the first Kurosawa movie shot in 70 mm color film, and that it would be a purely American movie with the technical staff and actors all being Americans. Only producer Tetsu Aoyagi and assistant director Yoichi Matsue would be Japanese.

The shooting period was expected to be four months, starting in October 1966, and key scenes of the four connected locomotives running out of control through a snowy landscape were to be shot on location using tracks of the New York Central Railroad. An autumn 1967 theatrical release was set and it was disclosed that Kurosawa and Levine would collaborate on four more movies in America after completion of *The Runaway Train*.

Kurosawa's eyes glittered as he spoke of his grand dream and ambition: "I want to create an opening by which we can break through the stagnation afflicting Japanese movies. I want to create a path connecting Japanese movies to the world."

Waiting for Kurosawa, however, was a task that would prove more difficult than expected. Since the cast and staff were to be Americans, it was necessary to produce a screenplay in English conforming to American production procedures and to rewrite the dialogue into natural American English. To produce this shooting script in English before Kurosawa returned to Japan, Kurosawa Productions signed a contract with Sidney Carroll, who had been recommended by Levine as a reliable and skilled scenario writer. Carroll had written the screenplay for the movie *The Hustler*, which starred Paul Newman as a pool shark, and worked with Robert Rossen, who produced and directed the film that came out in 1961.

Carroll arrived in Japan in early July only a few days after Kurosawa himself. His working style was to set up workspace in a room at the Tokyo Prince Hotel where, from morning till night, he sat in front of a Remington electric typewriter, relentlessly pounding out manuscript pages with keystrokes approaching the speed of a machine gun. He planned to stay three weeks. Using a translated Japanese manuscript as a basis, Carroll was to prepare a screenplay for movie production in America, create dialogue reflecting an American way of thinking, revise the screenplay to make it consistent with American circumstances and scenes, and, in the end, prepare a final shooting script.

Carroll began by consulting directly with the writers of the Japanese screenplay—Kurosawa, Oguni, and Kikushima—to confirm the purpose of the rewrite. The general thinking was consistent. Oguni's English was good enough that he could explain his opinions in English. Kurosawa and Kikushima could understand English to some extent but they did not converse in English. With Aoyagi accepting the role of interpreter, the discussions continued.

Apparently everyone was quite optimistic. Kurosawa said, "I don't think that language will become a barrier between people working in the same world of movies." Similarly, Kikushima commented, "There are no national borders in movies. The same currency is good everywhere." Kurosawa and the other Japanese believed that, fundamentally, it was a problem of language and style, with Carroll's task being to rewrite dialogue to turn the Japanese screenplay into something usable in an English-language screenplay. As the work proceeded, however, they came to realize it would not be that easy.

Culture Shock

A reporter at the New York press conference called to announce production of *The Runaway Train* asked: "Are you worried about language differences being a problem in the creation of a movie in America?" Kurosawa answered: "With a single conductor's baton, Karajan enables the people of the world to understand his music and with a single brush, Picasso can communicate his image to the people of the world. I am confident that if you give me a camera and film, I can create a movie that will be understood by the peoples of the world." In later years, he added: "Movies communicate to the heart at a level that transcends language."

Kurosawa undoubtedly believed what he said but he was most likely thinking about the communication that occurs between the finished movie and its audience. The language issues that arose in the course of producing the movie could not be so easily glossed over.

An orchestra conductor has the musical score to serve as the common language for himself and the orchestra. A painter can face the canvas alone with only a brush in hand. Film, however, is an art form requiring people in a group that includes both cast and staff pulling in the same direction. To manage the production of a movie while reconciling differences of opinion and correcting misconceptions, a high level of verbal communication is indispensable. Even with skilled interpreters, communicating the will of the director is not easy.

Furthermore, Kurosawa relentlessly polished the script while the filming was underway and tended to be more ruthless than other directors in coaching actors on the delivery of their lines. If he trusted the discretion of the actors or entrusted the coaching to an assistant who was a native English-speaker, it would be one thing. But that was unlikely. So it was not really clear how Kurosawa intended to instruct the American actors about their English lines or how he intended to judge the success of the resulting performances. Particularly serious, Kurosawa was not aware of the pitfalls inherent in a process in which his Japanese screenplay had not been merely translated word for word but rather rewritten in a framework of the American English language in a Hollywood screenplay. Having earned a reputation as a skilled screenwriter early in his career, Kurosawa was fully aware of the importance of the screenplay. "If the screenplay is excellent, even a third-rate director can make a decent movie, but if the screenplay is no good, the situation is hopeless even for a first-rate director," he once said. Kurosawa was woefully unaware, however, of the accommodations demanded by Hollywood as standard operating procedure with respect to screenplays in English.

The ways of Japanese movie production known to Kurosawa are centered on the director. In the Japanese movie world, a director comes to be recognized as a "master," with more and more people likely to see it as natural that he be permitted to be dictatorial. In the case of Kurosawa, movie production was director-centered as he brought each project to completion by writing the screenplay—and doing the directing, shooting, and editing.

In contrast, in America the principle is that movie making is not director-centered but rather producer-centered. In many cases, it would not be far off the mark to consider the director to be a foreman who does not appear on the scene until after the preliminary arrangements have been made. From an American perspective, a Japanese movie screenplay, particularly one by Kurosawa, is inherently different from that in Hollywood. Taking Kurosawa as an extreme case, so long as he had a clear picture in mind, he would write the screenplay concisely. Even if no one else understood, he had no problem using keywords to suggest the image he desired.

In the screenplay for Kurosawa's first movie, *Sanshiro Sugata* is a scene described only as: "Quiet afternoon in the temple district." The *No Regrets for Our Youth* screenplay has a scene that says only: "Vivid young leaves." When read in Japanese, such notes might leave the reader with a vague sense of knowing the feeling Kurosawa was looking for. But a non-Japanese had no way to come up with a reliable image of the picture Kurosawa had in his head. Intimately connected to an aesthetic sensibility, these Japanese expressions are almost impossible to translate accurately into a foreign language. By nature, such scenes have no place in a Hollywood screenplay. But Kurosawa had no doubts about the propriety of instructions like "the black runaway moving along through the white snowfield at a high clip." He already had a fully developed image of the scene in his head.

This would be a problem for the American staff. It was unclear whether this was to be a live-action shot or a special effects shot. And if live action, was it to be shot from a helicopter? Was it to be shot with a telephoto lens? Was it to be shot looking at the snowfield from inside the cab of the first locomotive? Was it to be shot with a camera fixed to the side of the locomotive? Only Kurosawa knew for sure. If the American staff were to receive such a screenplay, they would have had no idea of how to prepare. It would be different from the screenplay that the producer, cinematographer, art director, and other staff in America would expect to receive as a matter of course.

From this perspective, Carroll went beyond the call of duty. Was this scene on location or in the studio? Was it morning, mid-day, evening, or late at night? How were the people to be positioned with respect to each other? What is the camera angle and what is in the frame? If Kurosawa would not decide such things, there could be no English screenplay. So Carroll repeated these questions endlessly.

In some cases, answers were immediately forthcoming but in other cases answers were like: "I have not yet thought about it at that level since we don't yet know what the situation is going to be at the site." Pushed for a reply, Kurosawa would manage to come up with a response that sometimes even he was not satisfied with.

Faced with Carroll's comment that, from an American's viewpoint, a line of translated Japanese dialogue did not make sense, Kurosawa had to change it. Changing one line, however, can affect what comes immediately before or after it. In some cases, the entire script was affected.

Carroll's three-week stay in Japan was over all too soon. He returned to America but the rewrite continued for another two weeks and the final version of the screenplay, approved by Levine, was sent back to Japan. Kurosawa, however, was not happy with that version, which had been translated back into Japanese. It was quite different from what Kurosawa had intended. Finding fault in one place after another, he sent requests for revisions to America. "Making new revisions and returning to previous versions, it seemed like we were just doing the same thing over and over," Kurosawa said.

This was Kurosawa's first encounter with culture shock. He faced a continuous series of provocative situations that made him worry that his fundamental method of movie making was falling to pieces. As getting a final version of the screenplay took more time than expected and the date to start filming approached relentlessly, Kurosawa began to doubt even his initial scenario. So he wanted to make more revisions.

With one thing left undone and another thing still unfinished, every-thing seemed to Kurosawa to be in a desperate and distressing rush. Moreover, Kurosawa became exhausted both physically and mentally.

The Mysterious Last-minute Cancellation

At his New York headquarters on November 15, 1966, Levine received a telegram from Kurosawa that left him dumbfounded. The gist of the message was that Kurosawa was due to come to America but wanted to cancel his trip. Likewise, the start of shooting *The Runaway Train* was cancelled. Kurosawa asked for all plans to be postponed for one year.

For Levine, this astonishing development was unacceptable. With only one month left until the planned start of shooting, all prepara-tions had been moving along. Sitting on Levine's desk was a detailed schedule prepared by production manager Harrison Starr for 16 weeks of shooting on location and in the studio. For 40 days of shooting along the New York Central Railroad between Syracuse and Rochester, a film crew numbering about 130 was almost completely assembled. Contracts and cast insurance covering key personnel were all in order. Levine had managed to charm Haskell Wexler into being the cameraman. Wexler was a highly sought-after cinematographer who had won the Academy Award for Best Cinematography that year for his work on *Who's Afraid of Virginia Woolf?* He was sitting waiting, having left his schedule open for *The Runaway Train*. With preparations for filming complete and the cast announcements imminent, everyone was waiting for Kurosawa's arrival in America.

In an era before personal computers and e-mail, desperate telephone calls and telegrams flew back and forth between New York and Tokyo. Questions from New York: "What is the problem? What do we need to do so that filming can start as planned?" With a single-mindedness that could not be budged, Kurosawa persisted in responses that explained nothing: "The plans are squeezed for time. There is a lack of advance preparation. It is not possible to start shooting. Please wait a year."

The American contact in Japan was producer Tetsu Aoyagi, and he seems to have been put through the wringer. Within Kurosawa Productions, there was considerable discord in discussions leading up to the decision to inform Levine that Kurosawa wanted a one-year delay. Recognizing the danger that the project could be scrapped and trying to prevent that, Aoyagi and Kikushima frantically tried to persuade Kurosawa. "I am the director and I say it is impossible," was his response. There was nothing they could do.

The Americans had two choices: Give priority to the movie and go ahead under a different director or cancel the whole thing on grounds that it would be meaningless without Kurosawa. Levine chose the latter.

Conscience about the Art of Cinema

In Japan, Kurosawa Productions sought to conceal the last-minute postponement. The media, however, began to pick up the scent when no movement could be seen even though the date for Kurosawa's trip to America (November 20, 1966) was rapidly approaching. People were surprised then when the news of a one-year postponement began to leak out. Conjecture about the reason raged. Media coverage was confusing. Among the many reports, however, a few gradually revealed the depth of anguish among the people involved.

Despite the uncertainties, Kurosawa spoke boldly and explicitly in a newspaper interview in early November, declaring there was no problem. "Unlike Japan, in America the movie production system is complex so the preparation took a lot of time, but a perfect screenplay has been produced. As long as the American staff has a detailed shooting script, the language barrier is not a worry. Skilled first-rate people have been gathered for the cast, camera operators, lighting people, and other staff."

About the significance of the movie, Kurosawa asserted. "The production cost of two billion yen is a huge amount, close to the entire annual production budget of one of Japan's movie companies. Using American capital, a Japanese director can make a movie on a grand scale impossible in the Japanese movie industry. By doing this, I want to show the world the high quality of Japanese movies."

Kurosawa was in a position like that of athletes who, blessed with talent, are put up on a pedestal when they win an Olympic gold medal. Such expectations must be a heavy burden. Serious and hard-working members of a national Japanese team can sometimes be heard proclaiming their steadfast resolve to win. Kurosawa's statement felt like the proclamations of those athletes, which to some ears could sound quite pathetic. As a representative of Japanese cinema, master director Kurosawa brought upon himself a tremendous responsibility. It must have been no easy task to hold up under that pressure.

Hideo Oguni was a long-time Kurosawa friend and co-author of *The Runaway Train* screenplay. On the evening of the day that Kurosawa made the decision to postpone the making of that film, he talked with Oguni by telephone. Oguni later recalled: "There was going to be a language barrier working with the American staff and I found it impossible to believe that the work would proceed very smoothly. Kurosawa himself seemed very apprehensive and said, 'On this movie, failure is unacceptable.' Taking his feelings into account, we made the decision to postpone the start of filming."

Kurosawa himself, after a long public silence, described the circumstances leading up to the postponement. In an interview in the January 1967 issue of the film magazine *Kinema Junpo*, Kurosawa revealed that he himself had proposed the one-year postponement. In addition, he explained that, when putting the final touches to the shooting script, significant differences had emerged with the Americans about the "root concept" of the film. As they spent time seeking to reconcile those differences, it became impossible to start shooting as scheduled. In the article headlined "My Conscience about the Art of Cinema," Kurosawa contended that the "biggest difference" arose from Levine's request that a certain "message" be incorporated into *The Runaway Train*. The article does not, however, say what that message was. In the draft of a letter Kurosawa wrote about that time, though, it appears that Levine had said something on the order of: "Every man has something that he can't run away from, even if he might want to. That is the theme of this movie." This did not seem to be a definitive deal breaker that would justify mak-

ALL THE EMPEROR'S MEN

ing a fuss, and, in fact, there were concessions from Levine later on this point.

From Kurosawa's perspective, however, *The Runaway Train* was to be an all-out action picture with the focus on the out-of-control train. Perhaps for him, Levine's request represented a grave difference in "root concept" that could not be allowed to pass unchallenged. Kurosawa noted a difference of opinion on the mounting of drama: "I believe that a movie must bring together its dramatic content in a way that is accurate from a time perspective... It is by presenting three minutes of action within a three-minute timeframe that the director is able to create thrills and suspense. If it is not done this way, my brand of cinematic expression does not work. In this area, also, there were differences in our ways of thinking."

Kurosawa's explanation recalls a famous train scene in *High and Low*. As the Tokaido Line *Kodama* express train crossed an iron bridge over the Sakawa River in just over ten seconds, Kurosawa used eight cameras to capture on film the payment of the three-million-yen ($8,400) ransom for a kidnapped child. The realistic feel of this scene makes it among the most thrilling in the history of cinema. Levine responded at an early stage that it was fine for Kurosawa to follow his own thinking on this matter. So it seems somewhat trivial to contend that the movie could not be made because of this small disagreement.

In the *Kinema Junpo* interview, Kurosawa touched upon a health issue that may have been a more serious factor than creative differences in causing him to cancel the trip to America. As the start of shooting approached, Kurosawa's anxiety intensified. "For a time, I was in a state of nervous exhaustion," he said. On the postponement, he added, "Once the decision was made, I felt a sense of relief and was able to recover some of my old energy." During that period, anxiety prevented Kurosawa from sleeping and his health deteriorated to the point where a hospital stay was advisable. Kurosawa Productions concealed this from the Americans and from the Japanese media.

Kurosawa acknowledged that the money spent prior to the planned start of shooting was enough to have made the movie *Red Beard*. While he may have been trying to justify the last-minute cancellation by brandishing a highbrow "conscience about the art of cinema," it is unlikely that Kurosawa's explanation was considered convincing by Levine, the investor who bore the brunt of the huge financial loss.

Kurosawa Productions asked that the production of *The Runaway Train* be started again in September 1967. This did not happen because Levine rejected Kurosawa's request for a postponement, cancelled the filming, and disbanded the crew. Levine and Kurosawa never made a movie together and this sorry episode was a precursor to what happened two years later with *Tora! Tora! Tora!*

Chasing Two Rabbits

Twentieth Century-Fox producer Elmo Williams said that, in November 1966, he was unaware that Kurosawa had become dissatisfied with the preparation for *The Runaway Train*. The record shows that on the day (November 15, 1966) that Kurosawa sent the last-minute cancellation telegram to Levine in New York, Williams was in Hollywood writing a letter to Kurosawa about the possibility that he would become involved in the *Tora! Tora! Tora!* project. This was certainly a mysterious, coincidental twist of fate. In any case, for Kurosawa Productions, the Pearl Harbor project proposed by Fox was certainly opportune.

Kikushima and Aoyagi worked frantically to persuade Kurosawa to accept the proposal, saying: "A deal like this may never come again. It is our big chance to break into Hollywood. We must not let this one get away. The Twentieth Century-Fox project has a budget, the organizational strength, a distribution network, and historical significance far surpassing that of *The Runaway Train*. We should give priority to the Fox project and finish the Pearl Harbor movie first. *The Runaway Train* can be shot after that."

Even with such persuasion, the four huge locomotives continued to journey on in Kurosawa's mind. "It is the perfect story for me. The image is expanding in my head so there is no room for anything else," he said. Hardly paying attention to the arguments of those around him, Kurosawa vacillated because he was fixated on *The Runaway Train*.

Negotiations on the Fox contract were handled by CMA, the U.S. agent for Kurosawa Productions and the organization that had negotiated with Levine. Encouraging information arrived from CMA. If the schedule could be coordinated, it might be possible to move forward simultaneously on both *The Runaway Train* and *Tora! Tora! Tora!*

The proposal of Kurosawa Productions on the schedule and related records of the negotiations are preserved in the Fox archives. Included are documents in which CMA notified Fox that Kurosawa wanted first to finish *The Runaway Train*, while other records show how the schedule could be adjusted to enable this to happen. In broad terms, the result was Kurosawa and Fox agreed that Kurosawa would write the screenplay for the Japan portion of *Tora! Tora! Tora!* and submit it to Fox. If Fox decided to buy the movie rights to that screenplay, Kurosawa would revise it and write a final screenplay. The date for completion of that screenplay was tentatively set for July 1, 1967. From that date until *Tora! Tora! Tora!* production began in the spring of 1968, Kurosawa would be free of contractual obligations to Fox so he could shoot *The Runaway Train*. These details were clearly stated in the contract dated March 28, 1967. The announcement of the intention to make *Tora! Tora! Tora!* took place at the Tokyo Prince Hotel on April 28, 1967. The Japanese document distributed at that event referred to *The Runaway Train*, saying that production of that film would begin in cooperation with Twentieth Century-Fox immediately following completion of *Tora! Tora! Tora!* In the English-language announcement, however, the section about *The Runaway Train* had been deleted.

Williams said later that he also had read the *LIFE* magazine article and that he was privately developing a story for a film about an out-of-control train. However, Williams said he had heard nothing about Kurosawa Productions' statement concerning *The Runaway Train*. Levine had apparently absorbed the entire cost of the abortive plan and had given up on Kurosawa. Still, no mention was found in Fox internal documents suggesting a plan for Fox to take over production of *The Runaway Train* from Levine's Embassy Pictures.

While talk of *The Runaway Train* faded away at some point, *Tora!*

Tora! Tora! also ended in a fiasco for Kurosawa two years later. This is a real-life example of a popular Japanese proverb with its origins in a Chinese classic of the seventh century: "He who chases two rabbits catches none."

A Tale of Fate

Motivated by efforts to persuade him that he could do both movies, Kurosawa began to show interest in *Tora! Tora! Tora!* He soon became immersed in the project.

In later years, Kurosawa often resorted to high-flown rhetoric emphasizing the historical significance of a movie about Pearl Harbor. He had a prior interest in the movie's subject and theme. More than that, he had an extraordinary interest in Admiral Isoroku Yamamoto, the senior naval officer who forged the strategy for attacking Pearl Harbor, and had learned much about him through his reading. Still, at the start he didn't seem to have a deep determination about the film arising from a strong regard for its historical significance or a conviction that it would revitalize the Japanese film industry. Rather than such a lofty sense of purpose, he appeared to be drawn to the project by what he saw as mysterious, fateful convergences.

Over drinks or at a party, Kurosawa often talked about the symbolic connections between age and events. When he received the Fox proposal for the Pearl Harbor movie, Kurosawa was 56 years old. The characters in Yamamoto's first name, Isoroku, can be read as the number 56 since many Japanese *kanji*, or ideographs, have at least two different readings. When Yamamoto made up his mind to execute the plan to attack Pearl Harbor, he was 56 years old. When the attack was carried out, Yamamoto was 57, and Kurosawa would be 57 when he filmed the movie. Kurosawa repeatedly said he felt that fate was at work here, that there was a connection that could not be written off as coincidence. Furthermore, from the time the decision was made, Yamamoto took less than a year to prepare and execute his strategy. So Kurosawa thought that he, too, should be able to carry out a monumental task in one year.

ALL THE EMPEROR'S MEN

Another example of fate involved Kurosawa's lifelong teacher and revered senior director, Kajiro Yamamoto. In 1942, the year after the Pearl Harbor attack, he made the movie *Hawaii-Mare-oki Kaisen* (*The War at Sea from Hawaii to Malaya*). Kurosawa appears to have been moved by the mysterious turn of fortune's wheel in which he joined hands with movie people of America, the former enemy, to make a film on the same subject that his mentor had filmed a quarter century before. *Hawaii-Mare-oki Kaisen* had the backing of the Navy Ministry and was a joint project with the Imperial General Headquarters. Toho film company staked its future on this production, which was a vehicle of state policy aimed at raising fighting morale by showing the military successes achieved by the attack on Pearl Harbor and the sinking of the British battleships *Prince of Wales* and *Repulse* off the coast of Malaya.

Despite being produced during wartime with material shortages, the brilliance of the special effects in that movie was legendary. The model of Pearl Harbor at Toho's Kinuta studio covered 6500 square yards, the pond depicting the Pacific Ocean covered almost 2000 square yards, and the U.S. airfield set ablaze by the Japanese attack covered 700 square yards. All models were built on a scale of 1/800, meaning one centimeter represented 800 centimeters, and even the size of the ocean waves was calculated to match this scale. In the studio was much talk about these sets and the sight of them was burned into the memory of the 32-year-old Kurosawa, who was able to watch the filming. Like most Japanese, Kurosawa probably heard the news of the attack on Pearl Harbor on NHK, the national radio network on the morning of Monday, December 8, Japan time.

The director of cinematography for that movie was Akira Mimura, who had trained in America and acquired the nickname "Harry." Mimura had served as cameraman on director Sadao Yamanaka's masterpiece *Ninjo Kamifusen* (*Humanity and Paper Balloons*) and was the cinematographer on Kurosawa's first movie *Sanshiro Sugata*, which was the name of the legendary judoist.

The all-star cast of *Hawaii-Mare-oki Kaisen* included Denjiro Okochi, Susumu Fujita, and Setsuko Hara, who were popular actors. The production took six months and cost 770,000 yen. (At the time, Kurosawa's monthly salary as an assistant director at Toho was 48 yen.) The cinema broke all the records and monopolized that year's film awards, taking the Minister of Education Award, Information Bureau Minister's Award, Japan Magazine Association Award, and others. (During World War II, the exchange rate for converting yen to dollars was two yen to one dollar, continuing the prewar exchange rate, artificial though it was.)

For Kurosawa personally, this movie provided unforgettable memories. Having written the screenplay for *Sanshiro Sugata,* the movie that would mark his debut as a director, Kurosawa wrapped it in a *furoshiki* cloth and carried it to Tateyama naval air station in Chiba Prefecture, east of Tokyo. Director Kajiro Yamamoto was there working on the filming of *Hawaii-Mare-oki Kaisen* in the autumn of 1942, when Kurosawa was 32 years old. Kurosawa hoped to get Yamamoto to look at the screenplay and give his advice. In his autobiography, Kurosawa said he waited for Yamamoto at the quarters where the film crew was staying. When the day's filming was over, however, Yamamoto had to go to a dinner with an admiral and other naval officers and sent word that Kurosawa should not stay up. Kurosawa found an empty bed in the quarters and fell asleep. Waking up by chance later that night, he noticed a light on in the next room, where Yamamoto was staying. Quietly peeking in, he saw that Yamamoto had returned and was sitting up on his *futon* (mattress) reading Kurosawa's *Sanshiro Sugata* screenplay.

"He was going through it very carefully page by page, sometimes turning back the pages and rereading... I will never forget that view of Yama-san's back and the sound of those pages turning," Kurosawa wrote in his autobiography, published in English as *Something Like an Autobiography.*

The Eagle-eyed Man

In addition to meeting Kurosawa, Twentieth Century-Fox producer Elmo Williams experienced one other fateful encounter with a key person during his December 1966 visit to Japan. That was Minoru Genda, who was 62 years old and a member of the House of Councilors, the upper house of Japan's national legislature, the Diet. The former Imperial Navy commander knew everything about the Pearl Harbor operation as he had participated directly in every aspect of what was code-named Operation Z, from its conception to the launching of the attack. Surviving the war, he joined the Japan Air Self-Defense Force, becoming a general and serving as chief of staff. At the age of 54, he retired from military service and, in the 1962 election, ran for the House of Councilors as a Liberal Democrat, the party then in power. Votes for Genda totaled over 730,000, the fifth highest among those elected. He went on to become an influential presence in the Liberal Democratic Party's National Defense Division.

The history professor at the University of Maryland, Gordon W. Prange, persuaded Williams that obtaining the cooperation of Genda would be critical for Fox in making the Pearl Harbor movie. Prange, widely recognized as a top authority on Pearl Harbor, indicated that he developed a personal relationship with Genda while interviewing him 70 times on the Pearl Harbor attack.

Ahead of his first meeting with Kurosawa, Williams called on Genda at the House of Councilors. When he was shown into Genda's office on December 5, 1966, Williams was surprised by the threadbare character of the room. It was cramped and messy and the only other person there was a female secretary. Years later, Williams remarked on how he had been taken aback since he was expecting a well-equipped office like those of U.S. senators.

In a dark suit fitted to a body without an ounce of excess fat, Genda's face was etched with lines and his hair was black with flecks of gray. His clear eyes seemed to look straight into the mind of his visitor. Those are truly eagle eyes, Williams thought. He had been told that the meeting would last only five minutes so after the greeting, he came quickly to the point. He said he wanted to make a Pearl Harbor movie that was faithful to historical fact. He wanted the movie to reflect accurately both the American and Japanese perspectives so a Japanese director would be engaged and the Japanese portion would be left up to him. Finally, Williams asked Genda to recognize the historical significance of this movie and to lend his support. Genda listened in silence. Williams's presentation had used up the allotted time but when he said thank you and began to stand up, Genda motioned for him to sit back down. "Have a cup of tea before you go," Genda said, speaking slowly in what seemed to Williams to be a British accent.

Genda took a small brown teapot from a nearby table, put in tea leaves from a small palm-size tea canister, and poured in steaming water from a hot-water pot. When the tea had brewed, he poured it into two tea cups and handed one to Williams—all without saying a word. Williams later recalled that he considered Genda's silence "mysterious."

Looking up suddenly, Genda asked, "How is Professor Prange?" The conversation was relaxed after that. When he left Genda's office, Williams found that he had been there for more than 30 minutes. Genda expressed interest in Williams's experience as an associate producer of *The Longest Day*, a movie he had found quite exciting. When Williams mentioned that he had lived in London, Genda said he had been naval attaché in the Japanese embassy in England a quarter century ago, in 1940, when the air raids mounted by Nazi Germany were a nightly occurrence. Before Williams left, Genda said he would consider his request.

During the four years that began with the start of production, continued through many complications, and ended with the opening of the Twentieth Century-Fox version of *Tora! Tora! Tora!*, Williams and Genda sustained a relationship marked by trust. At critical junctures along the way, Williams was repeatedly impressed by Genda's strong influence.

The Voice of Authority

At Kurosawa's request, Genda became one of five advisors who provided advice on the historical accuracy of the movie. Three others from the Imperial Japanese Navy: Commander Kameo Sonokawa, who had been

ALL THE EMPEROR'S MEN

an aviation officer in the sea battle off the coast of Malaya, advised on aviation matters; Commander Yasuji Watanabe, who had been a tactical support staff officer under Admiral Yamamoto, advised on combined fleet matters; and Lieutenant Commander Shizuo Fukui, who advised on shipbuilding. A fourth was Kazushige Hirasawa, who at the outbreak of the war had been consul general in New York and at the time of the movie production was a commentator for the Japan Broadcasting Corporation (NHK); advised on diplomacy. Genda had a hand in the selection of each of these advisors except Hirasawa.

Genda and Kurosawa, however, never developed a relaxed relationship. Coming from different worlds, they had little in common and their encounters were marked by defensiveness on both sides. From Kurosawa's perspective, Genda was six years his senior, a proud hero of the Imperial Japanese Navy who was to be approached with courtesy and reserve. On the other hand, it may be that Genda saw the world-famous Kurosawa as nothing more than a maker of moving pictures. Genda had reminded Williams of a bird of prey. But Kurosawa, at his first meeting with Genda, came away with a different impression: "Genda has a noble face and strikes a fine figure. Truly distinguished."

For Kurosawa, Genda was the guardian angel who could watch over and protect the movie project. The benefit of being under Genda's wing was brought home to Kurosawa when the Office of War History in the Defense Agency's National Defense College (now the Military History Department of the Ministry of Defense's National Institute for Defense Studies) extended complete cooperation, providing key documents without hesitation. From 1966 to 1980, the Office of War History compiled and made available records on military strategy and battles from the Sino-Japanese Conflict that began in 1937 through the Pacific War that ended in 1945. The result was the publication of a war history of unprecedented scope. More than 62,000 pages in 102 volumes, including 34 volumes related to the Imperial General Headquarters, 37 volumes on army history, 21 volumes on navy history, 9 volumes on army air service history, and a one-volume chronology were assembled. At the end of 1966, the manuscript for volume 10, *Hawaii Sakusen* (*The*

Hawaii Operation), had been nearly completed and was in the editing stage. This meant that the documentation on the Pearl Harbor attack had been completed. Therefore, almost all the materials that Kurosawa wanted could be obtained immediately.

Certainly the power of Genda's "voice of authority" was felt among defense officials and former members of the Imperial Army and Navy. Wrapped in the lost glory of the Imperial Navy, Genda had an aura that compelled obedience, thus overpowering not only defense personnel but the public. One day, Genda took Kurosawa to the Office of War History, which was in the Defense Agency facilities in Tokyo's Roppongi district. When Genda set foot in the room, the few people who noticed him first snapped to attention with military salutes. The salute then passed across the large office in a wave as every person stood to attention. Genda calmly returned the salute. From behind him, Kurosawa looked on, unsure how to act.

About this time, something was changing in the mind of Kurosawa. He began to say that making *Tora! Tora! Tora!* was his fate, his mission. The Wheel of Fortune had taken a new turn, from *The Runaway Train* to *Tora! Tora! Tora!*

CHAPTER 3

KUROSAWA'S MAGIC

Shoulder Deep in a Mountain of Documents

Once he had accepted the *Tora! Tora! Tora!* deal with Twentieth Century-Fox, Kurosawa quickly detached himself from his obsession with *The Runaway Train* and began concentrating on *Tora! Tora! Tora!* Having prepared a list of materials needed to write the screenplay, he arranged to get them. Some books on Admiral Yamamoto were already in Kurosawa's library. Nearly everything else was primary source material requested from the National Defense College Office of War History. The influence of the naval-aviator-turned-politician Minoru Genda helped Kurosawa immensely.

Simultaneously, Kurosawa coordinated schedules with his friends and skilled screenplay writers Hideo Oguni and Ryuzo Kikushima. On January 15, 1967, the three once again secluded themselves at their favorite inn, Minaguchi-en. The subsequent writing was led by Kurosawa in an even more hands-on manner than usual.

When Oguni tried in later years to convey the sheer volume of piled-up books they were dealing with, he sometimes spread his arms wide and sometimes held out one arm to indicate shoulder height. The pile of documents was over a meter high. "Just reading it would have been a hard enough task in itself," Oguni said. "But we also had to remember what we read." As a starting point, Kurosawa wanted to develop parallel timelines that related events in America and Japan to each other at key points during the several years leading up to Pearl Harbor. "For example, what was President Roosevelt doing at a certain hour and minute and what was Prime Minister Tojo doing at that same hour and minute," Oguni explained.

Thinking at a fever pitch, Kurosawa generated a cloud of images and ideas that seemed to expand endlessly. Kurosawa said his imagination kept growing day by day and it was "almost scary." Oguni recalled: "We thought his brain was going to wear out. I even said to him 'Have you gone crazy or what?' We had never worked so hard before. It really consumed every ounce of our energy."

Meantime, Elmo Williams was curious. He didn't understand how three people could work on a screenplay at the same time. In America, writing a collaborative screenplay was not unusual but the collaboration was usually in successive rewrites. It has one person pounding the typewriter with the result being passed to the next writer for revision—and then back to the first writer. But Williams couldn't get his mind around Kurosawa's method of three people eating and sleeping under the same roof and gathering around a single desk to write. So he wanted to see for himself. One day, the American arrived at the inn on short notice, bearing a bottle of premium Scotch as a gift, for a morale-boosting visit to the "troops on duty."

According to Oguni, Kurosawa explained to Williams that each of the three had a different role that he performed simultaneously with the others. For example, director and scenarist Kurosawa was quick to become obsessed with images. Hitting upon a good image, he would immediately want to write that image into the screenplay. After a succession of isolated images, however, the overall direction of the movie became muddled. Oguni, functioning as a scenario writer, would be the navigator who kept his eye on the overall picture to make sure they stayed on course. Kikushima was the skilled and speedy re-write man.

Finally the day came when they were rewarded for having spent more than one hundred days of self-torment that Kurosawa would later say was like being in prison. The initial draft screenplay was complete. The date and time of completion were written on the last page: "May 3, 1967, 8 P.M." In that inscription could be read the jubilation of the triumphant trio. In high spirits, Oguni and Kikushima said to Kurosawa: "We'll leave the rest to you." Looking serious, Kurosawa replied, "You two are lucky. There are tough times still ahead for me." Kurosawa evidently already felt the immense weight of the task ahead.

Movie Seven Hours Long

Kurosawa's first draft of the screenplay combined the Japanese and American sequences. If all had been included in the film, it would have resulted in a movie at an appalling length of more than seven hours. The script comprised 706 scenes, 361 from the Japanese point of view and 308 from the American. Twenty scenes were from both sides. Of speaking parts, 112 were Japanese and 81 were American. The handwritten manuscript ran to more than 1,000 pages, with Kurosawa calling it his "thousand-*pera* manuscript." The word *pera*, used by media, movie, and publishing people, referred to sheets on which exactly 200 characters were written in blocks. Kurosawa, Oguni, and Kikushima had painstakingly handwritten—character by character—the entire screenplay with lead pencils, fountain pens, ballpoint pens, felt-tip pens and whatever was at hand. It was indeed a handmade script by the three scenarists.

This initial script for *Tora! Tora! Tora!* was titled *junbiko* (Screenplay: First Draft) and was sent off to be printed. There were no word processors or personal computers in those days, so typists cut stencils for mimeograph machines. The printed pages were bound, with the finished work as thick as a big-city telephone directory. The text alone ran to 659 pages. In the center of its thin white cover, the film's title, *Tora! Tora! Tora!*, was written vertically in large, cursive *kanji* (Chinese ideographs), with the word *junbiko* next to it. Only about 30 copies were produced, each numbered serially on the bottom left of the cover.

Those bound copies of the first draft were distributed to Kurosawa and a limited number of staff members and were regarded as highly sensitive. One complimentary copy was sent to Elmo Williams by express airmail. For 40 years, this edition of the *Tora! Tora! Tora!* screenplay was thought to have been lost. At the beginning of 2000, at the urging of Kurosawa's daughter, Kazuko, Kurosawa Productions tried to collect materials related to *Tora! Tora! Tora!* They sent questionnaires to former members of

Kurosawa's film crew and others connected with the project and asked them to send in any materials they had. The response was apparently zero. A copy of *junbiko* was found in a library in Los Angeles in 2002.

Kurosawa's Ambition

A first reading of Kurosawa's screenplay leaves an impression of disarray and confusion. On closer examination, however, its elaborate structure becomes apparent. The script exudes Kurosawa's determination and ambition, as well as the power of the imagery that continually formed like storm clouds in his mind. Many scenes give the impression that images are being projected from its pages. To write this script, Kurosawa, before he began negotiations with Twentieth Century-Fox, put aside questions of production and budget issues. He concentrated on expanding ideas and exploring his themes. He invested every passion in his heart and soul to create a Kurosawa original.

At the press conference arranged by Williams to announce the plan to produce *Tora! Tora! Tora!*, Kurosawa said, "the Pearl Harbor attack was a record of the squandering of excellent capabilities and energy" and he wanted "to explore the question of humanity in wartime."

The protagonist of *Tora! Tora! Tora!* was to be the architect of the attack on Pearl Harbor, the Commander-in-Chief of the Imperial Japanese Navy's Combined Fleet, Admiral Isoroku Yamamoto. The admiral eventually masterminded the war plan, even though he consistently opposed the Tripartite Pact that Japan joined with Italy and Germany to form the Axis Powers, and he was equally opposed to plans to declare war on the United States. He went against his personal beliefs to orchestrate the major gambit that struck that first fierce blow in an all-or-nothing surprise attack to start the war against the U.S. On a vast oceanic battlefield, Yamamoto commanded 40,000 officers and men of the Combined Fleet and immersed himself in the war effort, achieving a victory that would go down in military history.

From a strategic standpoint, however, the damage the attack on Pearl Harbor inflicted on the United States was not as decisive as Japan's military leaders had hoped. Japan's ultimatum to the United States was to have been delivered before the assault was launched. But it was delayed that Sunday morning when Japanese diplomats in the embassy in Washington had difficulty decoding the incoming message that included the declaration of war and were slow in typing it to be delivered to Secretary of State Cordell Hull. The attack on Pearl Harbor began before that message was delivered. Consequently, Japan was accused of carrying out a sneak attack, which caused an eruption of hostility among the American people and united them as never before.

Yamamoto, having studied at Harvard between 1919 and 1921 and served as a naval attaché in the Japanese embassy in Washington between 1925 and 1928, understood that the U.S. could be a fearsome opponent and thus wanted to avoid war with America. But when he realized that he had no choice because the leaders of the Japanese government ordered the assault, he devised and executed the all-or-nothing attack on Pearl Harbor. That tactical victory, however, would ironically set Japan off on a steep path to its downfall. This was what Kurosawa viewed as "elements of classic tragedy," one that began on September 1, 1939, when Yamamoto took command of the Combined Fleet on the flagship *Nagato*. Kurosawa then assembled a chronology depicting the events during the two years and three months that culminated in the successful attack on Pearl Harbor on December 7, (December 8 Japan time) 1941.

Kurosawa Original

Williams received the English translation of the screenplay on the morning of Monday, June 12, 1967, which meant that Kurosawa's script was translated into English and delivered in only 40 days. Williams's secretary, Christa Streichert, remembers the day that Kurosawa's draft arrived. She lugged it into Elmo's office and plunked it on his desk—all four hundred pages of it. "There's enough material for three films," he remarked as he took off his jacket, loosened his tie, and attacked the script. He worked his way through it all morning, often writing comments and taking notes. "Some monumental problems lie ahead in trying to understand exactly what Kurosawa has in mind," he said.

As a producer, Williams was responsible for appraising Kurosawa's script and recommending to the president of Twentieth Century-Fox, Darryl F. Zanuck, as to whether the company should buy the film rights. This decision was effectively placed in Williams's hands. According to the contract called the "The Lending and Borrowing Agreement" signed by Twentieth Century-Fox and Kurosawa Productions on March 28, 1967, Fox was to notify Kurosawa Productions of its decision on the film rights and pay an agreed sum within four weeks of receiving the draft. For Williams, this judgment was by no means easy. Kurosawa's script was bloated, abstruse, and had too many parts that perplexed him. Having worked in Britain and mingled for many years with movie people all over Europe, Williams was flexible in trying to understand other cultures. Yet even he struggled with the sporadic incoherence of Kurosawa's worldview.

In the English translation of Kurosawa's draft in the Doheny Memorial Library at University of Southern California (USC), over 60 notes in black ballpoint pen by Williams convey his immediate thoughts. Alongside positive comments such as "usable," "OK," "good," "clever," "great," "splendid," "excellent," and "superb" are many harsh criticisms:

> Doesn't make sense.
> Incomprehensible. Ask Kurosawa to explain.
> So what?
> Speak shorter. Should be shortened and rewritten.
> Too long! Loose & repetitive.
> Impossible. Ask Kurosawa though.
> No more speech. Please!
> Too many narrations.
> Cut down on subtitles.
> Flat and dull.
> Why do we need this scene?
> Boil down & tighten up.
> Interior office scene again? I scream!

After repeatedly re-reading the script, Williams rendered his judgment: "We can use this script of Kurosawa's." Despite the shortcomings, he had grasped the appeal of the filmmaker's distinctive style and recognized the value of a Pearl Harbor story that could only have been seen through Japanese eyes. This recognition led to his decision to purchase the script's film adaptation rights. The following day, Williams put his argument in writing and sent it to Zanuck. Then he asked his secretary Christa to make a copy of Kurosawa's screenplay and to send it with a bottle of scotch to his close friend and screenwriter, Larry Forrester. His instructions to Forrester were to begin splicing the Kurosawa script, with its heavily Japanese content, with what had been prepared on the American side.

Kurosawa-esque Imagery

Williams, who considered himself to be a longtime fan of Kurosawa's films, spoke in later years of how he detected 'Kurosawa touches' in the first draft of the screenplay of *Tora! Tora! Tora!* At the same time, he says he had a premonition of how difficult it would be to combine the compelling, distinctive, cinematic expression of Kurosawa and the conventional Hollywood-style scenes in a balanced manner to tell a unified story.

One of the characteristically Kurosawa-esque qualities Elmo read in the director's first draft of the screenplay was the master-disciple theme, known in Japanese as *shitei*, that the filmmaker consistently addressed in his earlier films. Williams felt that the *Tora! Tora! Tora!* script effectively portrayed the relationship between Admiral Yamamoto and the aviator who led the attack on Pearl Harbor, Commander Mitsuo Fuchida, in the fundamental Japanese cultural construct of mentor and disciple. Yamamoto often felt he was confined to the Combined Fleet flagship *Nagato* at the Hashirajima anchorage in Yamaguchi Prefecture. He went to Tokyo frequently for meetings with navy ministry officials, held conferences with dignitaries, and visited the Imperial Palace but never left

Japanese waters and did not take part in the attack on Pearl Harbor.

Instead of the 'waterbound but immobile' protagonist Yamamoto, the story featured someone who was 'skybound and active,' an aviator who embodied the admiral's will and carried the plot forward: Commander Fuchida. The Morse code signal "Tora Tora Tora" reporting "we have achieved surprise" sent by Fuchida from the skies of Pearl Harbor to the Task Force headquarters, was also picked up aboard the *Nagato*, anchored in Japan's Seto Inland Sea. Radiomen called it a miracle.

Another aspect of Kurosawa's script that Elmo noted as being typical of the director can be traced to *Seven Samurai*. As in that film, the action in the Pearl Harbor story was founded on trust between 'profoundly compatible' individuals who had been judged by Yamamoto to be up to the job. This had parallels in the recruitment of *Seven Samurai* when Kambei Shimada (played by Takashi Shimura) brought together comrades of varying personalities and abilities, refined a strategy, and trained them for a showdown between the villagers and the threatening bandits. In both films, leading players perfected their plans in secret, overcame obstacles one by one, and moved the plan forward. Like *samurai*, Yamamoto's pilots, having been chosen specifically for their missions, staked life and limb on the Pearl Harbor operation. They joined forces to achieve a common purpose and to fulfill their mission.

With each film, however, Kurosawa caused a problem because he was careless on issues of cost and production schedules. In contrast to the down-to-earth producer Williams, Kurosawa gave free rein to his vision in writing his screenplay. Throughout the sustained tug-of-war over screenplay revisions with Twentieth Century-Fox, Kurosawa steadfastly adhered to his own basic concepts. As producer, Williams's role differed from that of Kurosawa. Williams's first priority was to see how the plot developed and how easy it was to follow, keeping in mind the need for balance between the Japanese and American accounts. At the same time, his job was to identify practical issues or limitations in the shooting of scenes, as well as the cost. This meant thinking about what scenery would be needed, props to be obtained, the source of naval vessels and aircraft, ordering miniatures for special effects, and other considerations such as extras. How might this scene be shot? What's required to shoot it and how much will it cost? Is it worth the price? And all the while, he was reading the script to discern Kurosawa's intent.

Despite the potential headaches, Williams was excited by three scenes epitomizing the 'Kurosawa magic.' In the script found at the University of Southern California (USC), Williams wrote in the margins of these scenes, "Excellent." One depicts the day the task force, destined to attack Hawaii, set sail to train. It appears in the Japanese script:

FLAGSHIP *NAGATO*'S BRIDGE—EARLY DAWN
C-in-C Yamamoto, accompanied by his staff officers, is contemplating the vast expanse of dark, empty sea. In the distance, beams of the lighthouse at Cape Sada wink through the mist. He looks at his watch and says in a low whisper.

YAMAMOTO

It's about time for the carrier *Akagi* to sail out of Saeki Bay.

He raises a hand in salute toward the lighthouse. The other officers follow suit. It is a long salute. There is a stern silence.

EXT. SAEKI BAY—EARLY DAWN
The silhouettes of the carrier *Akagi*, escorted by two destroyers, glide through darkness.

EXT. FLIGHT DECK, *AKAGI*—EARLY DAWN
FUCHIDA points in the direction of the lighthouse of Cape Sada, dimly outlined in the mist. GENDA and MURATA are beside him.

FUCHIDA

Cape Sada lighthouse.
I know the C-in-C. He'll be bidding us farewell.
They face toward the lighthouse and salute.

Williams saw this as a symbolic scene depicting the telepathic understanding and strong invisible bond between Yamamoto and Fuchida.

The second scene that Williams described as "excellent" featured the newly-built super battleship *Yamato*, the symbol of the "big ship, big gun advocacy" criticized by Yamamoto. He believed that: "From now on, it is the age of the airplane." In the script, the scene takes place during a test run of the almost fully outfitted *Yamato*, which eventually became the flagship of Yamamoto's Combined Fleet.

EXT. JAPANESE COAST—EARLY DAWN

The early dawn is shrouded with misty rain and the sea is almost entirely hidden in the mist. In a dilapidated cottage, an old white-haired fisherman peeks between the slats of the shutters. Trembling, his eyes glint with horror.

"MONSTER"—LONG SHOT—FISHERMAN'S EYE LEVEL

In the drizzling rain, a gigantic mass of steel silently glides over the dark sea. It looks vaguely like a warship but its incomplete fittings make it look all the more monstrous and ghostly—just like a horrible nightmare symbolizing disastrous war. Slowly, the "monster" steals through the dawn mists and vanishes.

INT. COTTAGE

With quivering hands, the old man closes the shutters tight. The fisherman, his face cramped with terror, crawls back into his bed, still shuddering. He pulls the covers over his head. His white hairs bristle and quiver. The bedcovers visibly keep shaking. A white-haired old woman, lying in the adjoining bed, awakens and asks.

WOMAN

Why are you trembling so?

FISHERMAN
Nothing. Just a bad dream.

His answer sounds as if he is angry with himself. He pulls the covers up further until he completely disappears.

The ominous, monster-like shape of the giant battleship could not be fully captured even on a giant 70mm screen. The sight of it terrorizing an elderly fisherman "just like a horrible nightmare symbolizing war" that "steals through the dawn mists and vanishes" thrilled Williams. It was the quintessentially powerful Kurosawa magic that could 'make visible the invisible.'

Kurosawa's third flourish that took Williams's breath away was the scene in which the entire 32-ship task force is gathered in Hitokappu Bay in the Kurile Islands. There the fleet receives its orders from Admiral Yamamoto and sets out through blizzards and high seas on the long northern route to Hawaii. The date was November 25, 1941, the day that the target of the attack, previously kept top secret, was revealed to those in the strike force.

FLAGSHIP *AKAGI*, HITOKAPPU BAY (JAPAN)—DAY
The wind-torn battle flag of the Imperial Navy flutters at the masthead amid dense fog—typical of the northern seas. Three cheers for the Emperor are heard in the distance.

A VILLAGE ON THE SHORE
The inhabitants of an island, some distance from the anchored ships, have taken to the beach. Through the mist, they see the vague outlines of the impressive assembly of warships. Chantings of *"Banzai,"* the National Anthem, the "Warship March," and the "Song of Warriors" echo from the bay. The inhabitants listen, mystified.

INHABITANT A

What day is it today?

INHABITANT B

November twenty-fifth. Nothing special.

(Several scenes are omitted)

HITOKAPPU BAY—A VILLAGE

This is an almost deserted village, consisting of a small wireless station, several fishermen's cottages, and a salmon-canning plant. On the dilapidated pier, FISHERMEN are gathered, looking out to sea through the whirling sleet. The assemblage of warships is gone...

FISHERMAN A
(awed)

Just before dawn... I think I heard the rattle of steel—like the pulling of giant chains!

FISHERMAN B
(hushed)

Yes... I, too, heard something.
It made my blood run cold ...

These three scenes that so impressed Williams were ultimately left out of the shooting completed a year and a half later. Nor are they in the Fox version of *Tora! Tora! Tora!* that exists today.

A Thorn in the Throat

Kurosawa, the youngest of eight and a sickly child, often reminisced that as a small boy he sometimes got fishbones stuck in his throat and panicked. When this happened, his mother, Shima, quite unruffled, would swiftly take a small amount of cooked rice, squeeze it firmly in her hand, and pass it to the young Akira. He would swallow it slowly without chewing and, as if by magic, the pain would disappear. His stern father, Isamu, would pretend not to notice. It was a nostalgic mealtime scene that once would have been normal in Japanese households.

Kurosawa's description of the Pearl Harbor attack as "a thorn in the throat of Japanese-US relations" may have been inspired in part by this image of himself as a young boy. A vast majority of Americans believe that Japan staged a cowardly, sneak attack on Pearl Harbor. The Japanese, on the other hand, tend to brush aside the treacherous element in the attack. A majority think only military targets were attacked at Pearl Harbor and assert that the surprise was an acceptable tactic in war. A similar pattern of conception gap between the two countries can be seen in the historic appraisal of the U.S. atomic bombing of Hiroshima and Nagasaki. Many Americans believe that since Japan drew "first blood" at Pearl Harbor the U.S. is justified in the use of nuclear might which ended the war. In the minds of many Japanese, the A-bombing of the two cities and the preceding fire-bombing of Tokyo's densely populated areas remain questionable because those attacks resulted in the deaths of too many noncombatants totalling several hundred thousand. Kurosawa was acutely aware of this vicious circle of differences that inevitably was destined never to be reconciled. He said that war is always bad and that to answer hate with hate is a human folly beyond salvation.

Even with that emotion staring him in the face, Kurosawa began preparing for *Tora! Tora! Tora!* with a strong sense of historic mission. He once said, "I want to make the kind of movies that will influence people all their lives after seeing them." Kurosawa said that a good movie is a tool for fostering compassion and better understanding between peoples. He was determined to make a movie, the definitive story of the Pearl Harbor attack, that would remain forever in people's hearts. His ultimate goal was to create a landmark in the history of mankind.

When it came to works of classical literature to which he was attracted, Kurosawa was thought to have had a respect bordering on worship and an unconditional trust in their eternal values. The director who wanted his *Tora! Tora! Tora!* to be a momentous movie that would be relevant for a hundred years looked to his beloved classics for the concept of the Pearl Harbor epic.

Kurosawa was fond of saying "the newest fact will inevitably one day become an old fact." Therefore books written long ago and still being read, works called classics that are read by people across generations, are immortal. Kurosawa said that when he wanted to liberate himself from recent memories and the information before his eyes and "reset" his own ideas, he reread the classics. As he said, "I find that if I gradually devour everything I can get my hands on: Greek tragedies, Tolstoy, Shakespeare, my favorite plays and novels, it clears my head and new ideas well up like clouds."

When writing the screenplay for *Tora! Tora! Tora!*, Kurosawa chose to look at the big picture of the Pearl Harbor attack. He wanted to develop an epic vision for the film to offer a glimpse of human history and its tragedy. He turned to one book in particular: Tolstoy's *War and Peace*. In a 1981 interview with NHK (the Japan Broadcasting Corporation) educational television, Kurosawa commented, "I've never read a book as often as I've read that one. I suspect many of its influences can be found in my work," saying he had read Tolstoy's classic "about thirty times, I suppose."

In looking at Napoleon's Russian campaign of 1812, Tolstoy attempted to depict this massive historic upheaval from a micro perspective—by telling the stories of individual people with scrupulous attention to detail—and a macro perspective, an "eye in the sky." The result was a gigantic war epic with a cast of over 500 characters. Momentous events in history, such as wars, occur when some enormous invisible force causes the ideas of large numbers of people to converge, Tolstoy thought. Moreover, individuals are not necessarily conscious of their own destiny in Tolstoy's view of war. In that, Kurosawa may have reflected the story of the Pearl Harbor attack and of Admiral Yamamoto.

On September 1, 1939, if an eye in the sky had been gazing down on Earth from the skies above the North Pole, it would have seen before dawn 62 German divisions supported by 1,300 aircraft commence the invasion of Poland. On the ground was the ominous rumbling of tanks while in the air could be heard the roar of the *Luftwaffe's Stuka* dive bombers. Thus with its *blitzkrieg* tactics, Nazi Germany sparked the Second World War in Europe.

On the same day, the summer sun streamed down from clear skies on Wakanoura (now Wakaura Bay). The newly appointed Vice-Admiral Yamamoto, welcomed aboard the flagship *Nagato* in a tightly choreographed naval ceremony known as "manning the rails," had no way of knowing the fate awaiting him, and made lighthearted comments along the line that this C-in-C lark was not bad at all. But two years and three months later, around the time Japan was buzzing with its success at Pearl Harbor, Hitler's armies, like those of Napoleon, were on the retreat from Russia, with General Winter hard on their heels. Before long Japan too would take its first steps on the road to war.

Japan has a literary classic that portrays battle with an "eye in the sky" different from that of Tolstoy: the war story told in the picture scroll *The Tale of the Heike*, known in Japanese as *Heike Monogatari*, which Kurosawa loved with the same passion he felt for *War and Peace*. To the end of his days, Kurosawa said he would like to film the Heike epic. In the NHK television interview, he said: "*The Tale of the Heike* begins with the very pious-sounding lines: 'The sound of the *Gion Shōja* bells echoes the impermanence of all things; the color of the *sāla* flowers reveals the truth that the prosperous must decline,' but it is not that sort of tale at all... psychological portraits are simple, but to my mind no work of literature better expresses people's feelings and such in their entirety, through action, or actions: in particular how the various battles are depicted."

One scene in the first draft of *Tora! Tora! Tora!* draws on an episode in *The Tale of the Heike*. Commander Mitsuo Fuchida and Lieutenant

Commander Shigeharu Murata are observing a low-flying training run for torpedoes to be launched in Pearl Harbor, which was conducted in the equally shallow Kagoshima Bay. Of the three aircraft, two are successful. Seeing this, Fuchida starts to recite the lines, "Horses have four legs, so do deer." In the screenplay, the scene continues:

MURATA

What's that?

FUCHIDA

That's the legendary surprise attack in 12th century
Japan. Samurai hero Yoshitsune was about to attack
the enemy fortress from behind, over the steep moun-
tainside path. He saw several startled wild deer fleeing
over the cliff. He wanted to be sure that his men could
ride down as well. So he sent six unmanned horses
down to make sure...

MURATA

And three of the six horses ran safely down the path.

FUCHIDA

That's fifty percent. And he won the battle. We have
two out of three—even better!

Kurosawa was fond of this scene. When Williams asserted it would be too difficult to explain, Kurosawa insisted it was "a famous story that any Japanese would know." Following further discussion, however, the nuanced sequence was indeed deemed likely to be lost in translation and in the end was excised.

Another work of literature thought to have inspired Kurosawa's concept for *Tora! Tora! Tora!* was *The Art of War* by Sun Tzu, the Chinese strategist who wrote 2500 years ago. This classic, said to have been a favorite of Yamamoto, was never far from Kurosawa's side. Kurosawa

ALL THE EMPEROR'S MEN

said he became an avid reader of *The Art of War* after he learned from Tolstoy's *War and Peace* that Napoleon was an ardent admirer of Sun Tzu, not only as a strategist but also as a philosophical thinker. The much quoted admonition that "all warfare is based on deception" succinctly captured the essence of the Pearl Harbor operation. A line in the first draft picked upsays: "The top brass have really taken the plunge with this operation: true to the adage that all warfare is based on deception."

Thus flashes of the classical literature with which Kurosawa was familiar could be found throughout the screenplay.

CHAPTER 4

EYES FROM HEAVEN

Enter Yamamoto

The Commander-in-Chief of Japan's Combined Fleet, Admiral Isoroku Yamamoto, poured everything he had into fighting for his country until he was shot down and killed while on an inspection tour of Japan's forces in the South Pacific during World War II. Despite his heroic life, it must be said that he was among those who took Japan down a road to the brink of oblivion.

It was the regrettable aspects of Yamamoto's life on which Kurosawa wanted to focus. His grand vision was an attempt to shed light on this tragic folly from the perspective of an eye in the sky. A scene on which he had long set his heart was intended to embody this symbolically. It is the only scene in the first draft of the screenplay that Kurosawa stubbornly refused to alter or cut, or let anyone tamper with in the nineteen months between the completion of the screenplay on May 3, 1967, and the start of filming on December 3, 1968.

This scene was the ceremony called "manning the rails" that was depicted in meticulous detail in the opening sequence of *Tora! Tora! Tora!* It was to have been the crystallization of Kurosawa's magic, but it did not survive his dismissal and was not included in the version of the film completed later by Fox and released in September 1970.

Admiral Yamamoto was appointed by Emperor Hirohito to the post of Commander-in-Chief of the Combined Fleet and arrived aboard the flagship *Nagato* on September 1, 1939. In the naval protocol of "manning the rails," the crew of a warship lined up on the deck along both sides of their vessel as a sign of respect and allegiance to the incoming commander. It was a tradition that originated in the British Royal Navy.

Fifty kilometers north of Nanki Shirahama in Wakayama Prefecture, Wakanoura Bay was filled with ships from the four naval stations; Kure, Sasebo, Maizuru, and Yokosuka. They comprised the Imperial Japanese Navy's Combined Fleet, then the third largest Navy in the world. On each of the eighty ships, crews assembled on deck. In the distance, Yamamoto's launch set off from its pier and began slicing through the white waves. Buglers on each ship played tattoos in honor of the commander-in-chief.

Kurosawa conceived this opening scene after reading the book entitled *Yamamoto Isoroku*, by Hiroyuki Agawa, a prominent novelist who was a veteran of the Imperial Navy. The director read it just after it was published in November 1965, while he was considering *The Runaway Train* project. After a swift reading, Kurosawa said he was inspired as he had become interested in Yamamoto and had already read several books about him. Among them was the two-volume biography *Ningen Yamamoto Isoroku* (*Isoroku Yamamoto the Man*) by Eiichi Sorimachi, who was the Admiral's lifetime personal friend, and was moved by Yamamoto's compassionate character. It became apparent, however, that Agawa's book exerted the greatest influence on Kurosawa's thinking.

Kurosawa's way of reading was like that of many people. When he found a book that interested him, he bought it, put it by his bed, and read it whenever he found the time. He was candid, however, on why he read: "I do it to look for ideas, not for self improvement, so I read carefully while translating each line into moving images." While reading Agawa's book, he mentally translated each episode into imagery that he wrote into the first draft of the screenplay of *Tora! Tora! Tora!*

Eventually, however, few of Kurosawa's scenes survived in the Twentieth Century-Fox version of *Tora! Tora! Tora!* In its opening titles, two books are listed as sources: Ladislas Farago's *The Broken Seal* and the yet-to-be published *TORA TORA TORA* manuscript by Gordon W. Prange. Perhaps unsurprisingly, Agawa's book was not credited in the 1970 Fox movie. Kurosawa had requested in contract negotiations with Twentieth Century-Fox that Agawa's book be acknowledged as a source.

Fox agreed and approved a payment to the author of $7,500, according to an internal company document at Fox. The exchange rate at the time was fixed at 360 yen to the dollar, so that amount was equivalent to 2.7 million yen. Whether this fee was ever paid, however, remains unclear. Agawa said in November 2004 that he had no recollection or record of receiving 2.7 million yen from Fox. His wife, who managed the household's finances, had no such memory either.

Manning-the-Rails Welcome

Kurosawa's draft of the screenplay began with no sound, no color, no moving things, only monochromatic still images in a cramped, empty space. Then comes a voice from a loudspeaker and a torrent of white uniforms. Even with the addition of sound and movement, the image remained a confined, monochromatic void. It was intentionally made difficult for the audience to comprehend what was happening.

SCENE 1: INT. CARRIER *AKAGI*—INLAND SEA, JAPAN—DAY
A passage amidships—empty, silent. Suddenly, loudspeakers blare throughout the ship.

LOUDSPEAKER VOICE
Attention! All officers to the flight deck!

Cabin doors on both sides burst open and OFFICERS, in dress whites and wearing decorations, flood into the passageway and head for the hatch.

The OFFICERS stand in lines, with those at the head waiting at the hatch's opening. At the head of one line, the mustached Commander MITSUO FUCHIDA speaks in a rough, arrogant tone.

SUPERIMPOSE ACROSS BOTTOM OF SCREEN:

COMMANDER MITSUO FUCHIDA
Destined to lead the attack on Pearl Harbor

FUCHIDA
This Isoroku Yamamoto guy, apparently he's strangely
fond of Great Britain and America, and a weakling
too. Bet he's a coward.

OFFICER A
But if you look at his record, he's been commander of
the flight school at Kasumigaura, commander of the
First Air Fleet, and head of Naval Air Command, so
he knows his way around an airplane. He's the kind of
leader we need.

FUCHIDA
So why has a Navy Vice Minister like him been promoted to this position? They're just high class errand
boys.

OFFICER B
Well then, if he's a vice minister, he must be really
something to suddenly become C-i-C of the Combined Fleet. Customarily, the commander of the 2nd
Fleet should be promoted to that position.

OFFICER A
There's a rumor about that. Apparently it was too dangerous for him in Tokyo.

FUCHIDA
Why?

ALL THE EMPEROR'S MEN

OFFICER A

Well, they say that the Navy hasn't approved entering into the Tripartite Pact that the Army's trying to force through. So they don't know when the Army or the right wingers will make a move on him, so here he is.

FUCHIDA

So he runs away to a battleship eh? He is a coward after all… But it's a good idea, coming here where he can't be touched, with the forty thousand sailors of the Combined Fleet to guard him.

Close-ups of faces and dialogue. A conversation begins between Commander Fuchida and two officers. This blunt beginning to the film is softened with the down-to-earth and rather rough line: "This Isoroku Yamamoto guy…" Together with the audio from the loudspeaker, it says this story began two years before the attack on Pearl Harbor with the ceremony honoring the arrival of the new Commander-in-Chief of the Combined Fleet.

From a dramatic perspective, the officers in white uniforms with medals resembled a Greek chorus in a tragedy. Fuchida and the other officers represent a shared destiny as chosen members of the Imperial Navy and are intermediaries between the protagonist and the audience. A devotee of Greek theater, Kurosawa opened with what looked like a Greek chorus, the rule for which calls for twelve members in tragedies, and 24 in comedies. Kurosawa might have opted to use a lineup of 12 officers in this opening scene.

FUCHIDA pokes his head out of a hatch and looks around.

SCENE 2: EXT. CARRIER *AKAGI*, FLIGHT DECK
The camera pans across the flight deck, taking in the majesty of the 80 warships of the Combined Fleet crowding Wakanoura Bay.

In the script, Fuchida surveys the surrounding scenery at deck height and the camera shows his perspective. In an instant, the confined space suddenly explodes and a vast space opens up. The camera's point of view overlaps Fuchida's gaze. As he scans from the left to the rear to the right, the perspective shifting 70 degrees in each direction, the screen is filled with an expanse of warships, the sea, and the sky. A sense of freedom was intended to thrill the audience and the visual rhythm was typical of Kurosawa. To evoke that sense of freedom, the most up-to-date audio-visual system available in the 1970s—Panavision, DeLuxe Color, and surround sound—would have made an outstanding impression.

Additionally, what Kurosawa strove for was "something that does not fit on the screen." The audience would see only the view from starboard, aft, and port of the *Akagi*'s flight deck and a limited portion of the Combined Fleet. Off screen, from starboard forward to aft and directly to port would be the vast sea and sky and rows and rows of the Combined Fleet. The audience would sense an unseen presence all around and far into the distance of the darkness behind them.

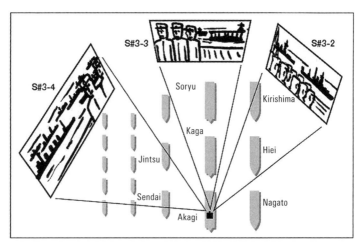

Three different camera angles. S#3-2: A view from the carrier Akagi, *panning from center deck to port aft. S#3-3: A view from the center of the deck of the* Akagi *to the stern. S#3-4: A view from the center of the* Akagi's *deck to the starboard.*

ALL THE EMPEROR'S MEN

S#3–2 *A view from the carrier* Akagi, *panning from center deck to port aft. The crew on deck is facing the ship's bow and as the camera captures their faces from the right, with the battleships* Kirishima *and* Hiei *seen over their heads.*

S#3–3 *A view from the center of the deck of the* Akagi *to the stern. The faces of the crew on deck are shot from the front. The carriers* Kaga *and* Soryu *are visible behind them.*

S#3–4 *A view from the center of the* Akagi's *deck to the starboard. The crew on deck faces the ship's bow, beyond which the light cruisers* Sendai *and* Jintsu *and other destroyers are lined up.*
The camera moves along the heads of the crew on the deck of the Akagi, *showing the immense Combined Fleet. (Sketches on page 93 are based on Kurosawa's rough drawings from the author's collection.)*

93

The situation around Yamamoto was complicated. Journalists often dubbed him one of "the Navy anti-treaty trio" who stubbornly resisted the conclusion of the Tripartite Pact among Japan, Germany, and Italy that was promoted by the Army. The other two were the Navy Minister, Admiral Mitsumasa Yonai, and his confidant, Rear Admiral Shigeyoshi Inoue, who was the head of the ministry's Naval Affairs Bureau. The Army and right-wingers believed that Yamamoto, who had declared that "the Japanese Navy is no match for that of the U.S. and Great Britain," was the instigator of opposition to having Japan join the Tripartite alliance. Anonymous documents were circulated in an attempt to exclude him from influencing political decisions. There was even a credible plot to have him assassinated.

The cabinet of Prime Minister Kiichiro Hiranuma, under which Yamamoto served as Navy Vice Minister, resigned in August 1939, after Germany, with which Japan had been negotiating an alliance, suddenly agreed to a non-aggression pact with the Soviet Union, Japan's enemy. Many Japanese saw that as a betrayal. Moreover, the Japanese Army had recently suffered a massive defeat in Mongolia at the hands of the Soviets. The Hiranuma Cabinet resigned en masse to take responsibility and Yonai and Yamamoto were obliged to leave the naval ministry for which they had worked for two years and six months. Thanks to Yonai's good offices, however, Yamamoto could take refuge at sea with his appointment as Commander-in-Chief of the Combined Fleet. The opening scene of Kurosawa's *Tora! Tora! Tora!* screenplay was a poignant reference to Yamamoto's plight.

Standing in the gangway of the *Akagi*, the OFFICER of the DECK peers through binoculars and calls out.

OFFICER of the DECK
C-in-C has boarded his launch!

The OFFICER OF THE DECK issues an order.

ALL THE EMPEROR'S MEN

His voice rings out from the ship's loudspeakers.

OFFICER OF THE DECK
All hands on deck!

The crew pours from various hatches. Mixed with the sound of their footsteps thudding on the deck, the same order can be heard across the water from the loudspeakers of the anchored vessels.

Beyond the crews who face toward the bow of their ships in unison, a launch bearing a vice admiral's flag on its bow and a naval ensign on its stern sets off from its pier in Wakanoura and stirs up white waves as it begins to move forward.

With confirmation that the new commander-in-chief's launch had left shore, "All hands on deck!" is ordered to the crew standing by in the corridors of the carrier *Akagi*. Mixed with the rhythmical thudding of footsteps running across the deck, orders from each ship of "All hands on deck!," "All hands on deck!," "All hands on deck!" echo near and far across the water. Hearing those sounds, the audience imagines the crews of all the ships running to line up even if they are not depicted on screen. The sound of footsteps was a theatrical device akin to a drum roll for a major event that was about to take place.

In the Fox version of *Tora! Tora! Tora!*, the camera slowly and repeatedly cuts back to show the ranks of crew members on deck. Then the faces of three officers are shown in a close-up. One is Fuchida. Capturing his face diagonally from the front, Fuchida's conversation begins with "This new Commander-in-Chief..." There is no scene where Yamamoto arrives on board a launch and neither do we see or hear the crew rushing to the deck to line up in unison.

In Agawa's book, "manning the rails" took place on "a warm, fine day." Yamamoto arrived at the pier around noon, boarded a launch, and entered its cabin. The fleet, floating in the calm waters of the bay, watched as Yamamoto's approaching launch was faintly visible, in a concept developed by Kurosawa that had its origins in Agawa's book.

A 15-cannon salute rings out.
Next, an order of "Salute!" is issued every time the commander-in-chief's launch comes to a 45-degree angle with each ship. Bugles play resounding tattoos that ripple out from each ship in succession and drifts over the surface of the sea.

Boom! Boom! Boom! *Nagato's* guns blast out a 15-gun salute that resounds across the sea and sky. This is followed by bugle calls, reverberating from each vessel to form a receding echo like a fugue or trumpets resounding from the heavens that greeted Yamamoto. They proclaim the opening of a tragedy in which an array of characters becomes tangled up in a complex web. In the western classical music tradition, the bugle or trumpet often invokes a rousing celebration or the threat of battle. In Christianity, the trumpet sounds to mark the end of the world. At the Final Judgment, the archangel Michael sounds his horn. The dead come back to life and humanity is powerless to resist the fate bestowed upon it.

A colossal and ominous feeling of inescapable oppression cannot be adequately expressed in images. So the audience must imagine the terrible presence that is not shown on the screen. Kurosawa once said: "It's probably impossible to shoot something better than what can be imagined." This expressed the director's confidence that the images he shot were striking but to create something that surpassed them, he would induce his audiences to create them for themselves.

The bugle tattoo that greeted Yamamoto was the eight-bar signal called *Umi Yukaba (Song of Warriors)*, which was 10 seconds long. It was played each time his launch passed by one of the warships, with the overlapping sound coming to resemble another fugue. In the Fox version of *Tora! Tora! Tora!*, the cannon salutes boom slowly at low volume like background music. The hands of a bugler on the *Nagato* appear in a close-up as he plays a single greeting for the admiral. Next, the camera pulls back to show two buglers who play the same refrain once more.

The next scene evokes the unseen through more realistic, technical sound direction.

SCENE 3: EXT. BATTLESHIP—FLAGSHIP *NAGATO*

The crew stands in a rank on one side of the deck. Near the gangway, officers and sailors line up to greet the commander-in-chief.

Seen by the crew near the gangway, YAMAMOTO's launch cuts through whitecaps as it approaches, the ranks of the crew are clearly visible. With the sounding of a ship's bell signaling that the launch is slowing, it disappears out of sight and the voice of a LIEUTENANT breaks the silence.

LIEUTENANT

Eyes front!

A sense of the approaching launch, the sound of a grab rope being thrown, the sound of a boat hook. The CHIEF BOATSWAIN sounds his whistle.

"Pi-yo!"

The sound of footsteps running up the gangway ladder at a rapid pace.

The GANGWAY GUARD presents arms.

Commander-in-Chief YAMAMOTO, who has run up the gangway, returns the salute of the GANGWAY GUARD.

The CHIEF BOATSWAIN blows his whistle once more.

"Pi-yo!"

YAMAMOTO turns 90 degrees to the left and proceeds onto the deck.

The CAPTAIN of the *Nagato* salutes him.

YAMAMOTO returns the salute.

Now he turns 40 degrees left.

The ship's BANDMASTER, who has drawn his sword, salutes him with a downbeat.

With this signal, the ship's band begins to play a ceremonial tune.

In honor of the Commander-in-Chief, the waiting officers and men salute in unison, and both the outgoing Commander-in-Chief, Vice Admiral ZENGO YOSHIDA, and new C-in-C YAMAMOTO take a step forward toward each other.

The two exchange salutes.

The Commander-in-Chief's flag is swiftly raised on the *Nagato*'s mast.

After a salute, YOSHIDA makes a turn and solemnly leads YAMAMOTO toward the C-in-C's hatch.

YAMAMOTO briskly follows after the former Commander-in-Chief YOSHIDA, returning the salutes of the officers and men lined up on his left and right. The two climb down the hatch.

Thus Yamamoto makes his entrance. His stage is the deck of the *Nagato*. That Kurosawa went to the trouble of including diagrams in his script showing the arrangement of the crew on deck shows his obsession with meticulous stage design. In addition, he gives the positions and ranks of the crew of Yamamoto's launch. The officers lined up on the deck of the *Akagi* can only see a little of the commander-in-chief's launch. This is also the audience's perspective. The boat approaches the *Nagato* and the moment we think we can see it, it slips out of sight beside the hull of the ship. The viewer is forced to become aware of what has happened to the launch. The only assistance, as they brace their minds and watch the screen closely, is a tapestry of sound.

The launch rocks with the waves as it draws near the huge battleship. Between the ships the waves crash and burble as the launch and warship bump with the sound of their fenders rubbing against each other, grating and grinding. Then the launch becomes stabilized and secure alongside the ship, as the grab rope is thrown with the sound of it falling, and a boat hook is extended from the *Nagato* and thuds on the launch's deck, after which they pull it in. Next is heard the boatswain's high-pitched whistle, "pi-yo-," and the light rat-a-tat of Yamamoto's footsteps as he runs up the gangway.

During this sequence, the admiral is not shown on screen. The sound is intended to establish a clear picture in the minds of the audience. This was Kurosawa's way of 'seeing with sound.' In contrast to the viewer's expectation that the dramatic story is about to begin, the protagonist appears only briefly. "Yamamoto briskly follows former Commander-in-Chief Yoshida, returning the salutes of the officers and men lined up on his left and right in a casual fashion," the script said. His brisk gait, with its light and quick movements, hints at his easy-going manner.

The Fox version of *Tora! Tora! Tora!* has no scene showing the approach of Yamamoto's launch, nor of him running up the gangway. Instead the shot begins with him appearing suddenly in the gangway. The actor So Yamamura, in the role of Yamamoto, walks ahead confidently in time with the music, salutes once again to the right and left. This serious and dignified, stoic image of the man could not be more different from the one depicted in Kurosawa's script.

In Agawa's book, the launch carrying Yamamoto docks alongside the flagship *Nagato*. "Yamamoto jumped nimbly onto the gangway... Yamamoto carried himself lightly and seemed to be impatient." The lightness of his movements was emphasized. Furthermore, "the moment Yamamoto's feet hit the gangway... the admiral's flag was hoisted up the *Nagato's* mast... and the ship's band began to play traditional ceremonial music for welcoming the Commander-in-Chief. Leaving the gangway, Yamamoto returned a salute to the welcoming officers and entered the Commander-in-Chief's office at the rear of the ship through the command hatch." This scene was used virtually unchanged in Kurosawa's script. Most of the depictions of Yamamoto's entrance, his easy appearance and bearing were taken from Agawa's book.

At Kurosawa's request, the musical score for *Tora! Tora! Tora!* was originally to be composed by Toru Takemitsu, an up-and-coming self-taught genius, later internationally renowned for his unique skill in the subtle manipulation of instrumental and orchestral timbre drawn from

Japanese music and other wide range of other influences. When inviting Takemitsu to accept the commission, Kurosawa sent him a copy of his screenplay. Takemitsu spoke of his thoughts about its opening scene: "I was deeply impressed by the initial script... From my standpoint, only a little was written about the sound plan and such matters, but it had been written with such confidence. The sound plan for *Tora! Tora! Tora!* was particularly excellent... First of all, there is a scene where Isoroku Yamamoto boards a launch or some other vessel, heads off to be appointed as Commander-in-Chief, and transfers to a battleship... and the details of those actions are mostly written with regard to sound only. The sound of the launch rubbing up against the battleship, the sound of ropes colliding, that sort of thing. Plus the treatment of the performance of *Over the Waves* tune and other sound is very well done. Basically, it's written in a very spatial manner, and its treatment of directional sound and other things is truly ingenious."

Takemitsu was 37 years old when he received Kurosawa's commission in 1967. That same year, he completed his highly acclaimed musical composition *November Steps*, for which he had been commissioned by the New York Philharmonic to commemorate the orchestra's 125th anniversary. Takemitsu incorporated traditional Japanese instruments, such as the *biwa* and *shakuhachi*. into that score. It premiered in Japan the following year.

The excerpted second half of *Over the Waves*, mentioned by Takemitsu, is heard from scenes 179 to 181 of Kurosawa's script. The scenes are set for October 1941, less than two months before the planned attack on Pearl Harbor, when preparations by the Combined Fleet were nearly complete but the Imperial Navy headquarters was still reluctant to give formal approval to the operation. Time was running out, Yamamoto thought, and there was no going back. He decided to throw in his last bargaining chip and sent a confidant and senior staff officer, Captain Kameto Kuroshima, as his personal emissary—armed with a secret weapon. If the Imperial Navy's answer was no, Kuroshima was authorized to say that Yamamoto would resign because he could no longer be held responsible for the security of the Empire.

Exasperated, Yamamoto says: "All right, go for it, Gandhi (Kuroshima's nickname)! The General Staff will be the first target of a surprise attack before Pearl Harbor!" Then he invites chief of staff Rear Admiral Sonosuke Kusaka to share a glass of wine in the officer's mess and requests the ship's band to play *Over the Waves*. The northern route to Hawaii promised turbulent seas, an apt echo of his political bargaining with the top brass. The use of this lilting music in the screenplay, which surprised even a master of modern music like Takemitsu, was an example of Kurosawa's cinematic counterpoint, intended to provide contrast, in this case, to Yamamoto's hidden anxiety.

On the use of other popular music in the screenplay, Takemitsu was deeply impressed, saying: "It is well thought-out right from the beginning and is exquisitely well done." The composer, who sensed limitless music in the natural sounds of the world, was without inhibition in making music spanning that of the Orient and the Occident. He shared that trait with Kurosawa, who drew images and sound out from his freewheeling imagination. In Takemitsu's book *Sound: Confronting the Science*, published in 1971, he says: "In film, music absolutely requires direction. Not only in simple terms of its role in enhancing a film's ambience but in possessing characteristics of its theme to make it more tangible... I want the task of turning a lie into the truth through music. Dialogue is clearly conceptual, while music adds a physical dimension to it, and this must be done directly... Of course, film is obviously a visual art, but I believe that music, as with dialogue, takes on a greater role in certain situations."

Kurosawa always strove for sound that emphasized his images and music that told his story effectively. Takemitsu was aware that sound and music can have a greater effect than the words of actors and that sound itself required direction. Unfortunately, their collaboration on *Tora! Tora! Tora!* ultimately went unrealized.

SCENE 4: INT. COMMANDER-IN-CHIEF'S OFFICIAL CABIN—*NAGATO*

YOSHIDA takes off his cap as he enters. He stands with his

cap neatly placed on the front right side of the table. YAMAMOTO follows, tosses his cap onto the hat rack, walks acround the oblong table, facing the waiting The CHIEF OF STAFF enters and stands waiting. YOSHIDA and YAMAMOTO walk around the table, exchanging their positions.

> YOSHIDA
> Here is the official order transferring the fleet to your command. The present strength of the Combined Fleet consists of the Battleship *Nagato* and the...

> YAMAMOTO
> (smiling)
> Save your time, Yoshida. All that detail is in those documents, I suppose?

He points to heaps of documents stacked in front of the CHIEF OF STAFF.

> YOSHIDA
> (returning the smile)
> You haven't changed.

> YAMAMOTO
> By the way, you've picked a terrible time to become naval minister, but I'm counting on you..

> YOSHIDA
> You've had a tough time of it yourself these last few years.

> YAMAMOTO
> Yes.

YOSHIDA, his face darkly tanned by the sun and sea wind,

ALL THE EMPEROR'S MEN

and YAMAMOTO, slightly pallid after his long term ashore as a naval official, stare silently at each other. YAMAMOTO suddenly has a mischievous look in his eyes.

YAMAMOTO
But you know, it feels good to be Commander in Chief, doesn't it? I feel quite popular.

Saying that, he drops down into a chair.

Yoshida and Yamamoto enter the Commander-in-Chief's office on the *Nagato*. The two stand on opposite sides of a table. The ship's band on deck plays *Umi Yukaba (Song of Warriors)*, followed by *Matsubara Toku (Ode to the Ocean)*, in the background. The two men walk around the table and face each other, exchanging positions. The moment that they finish swapping positions, the change between the past and present commanders-in-chief is complete, according to naval convention. This action fits with the approximately 15-second-long opening phrase of *Matsubara Toku*. This synchronization of sound and images is another striking example of the Kurosawa style. On Christmas Eve 1967, Kurosawa threw a party for his crew at his Matsubara residence in Tokyo. At the height of the revelry, Takao Saito, the chief cameraman, picked up an imaginary camera and pretended to shoot while assistant Yutaka Osawa, the principal assistant director, played the role of Yoshida and Kurosawa slipped into the character of Yamamoto. As the trio sang along the opening phrase from *Matsubara Toku*, Kurosawa comically orchestrated the change of command to the delight of his guests.

Kurosawa felt a great affinity for Yamamoto as a cheerful and mischievous, jocular and lovable, passionate man. This character was described with zest in the opening sequence of the script. But in the Fox version of *Tora! Tora! Tora!*, Yamamoto walks with a leisurely gait in time with the tune of *Umi Yukaba* and returns the salutes of the officers and men in a dignified manner. He does not throw his cap after he enters the Commander-in-Chief's cabin but solemnly takes a seat

EYES FROM HEAVEN

and exchanges grave words with Yoshida expressing concern for Japan's future. The Yamamoto played by Yamamura is dignified, serious, trustworthy, calm, and composed. In other words, he is overly respectable and bland, too much of the good guy. Yamamura's interpretation is out of place, because it does not agree with the image of a man who could conceive of an unexpected and daring all-or-nothing gambit, one that his colleagues would never come up with, or that his enemies could anticipate.

In Agawa's book, after Yamamoto has met with the staff and commanding officers in the Commander-in-Chief's cabin, his relief is evident in his quip that he feels "quite popular." In the screenplay, he continues by telling an adjutant: "You might be Navy Minister but you're just a high class errand boy." As a Navy Vice-Minister, Yamamoto had been regarded as the instigator of the Navy's opposition to the Tripartite Pact, putting him in mortal danger when he was shadowed by right-wingers. "Heading out to sea for the first time in six years, Yamamoto was undoubtedly quite relieved," Agawa wrote. Kurosawa relied on Agawa's book to interpret Yamamoto's situation and emotional state, which is why he makes him "toss his cap," "drop down into a chair," and relax.

Sad Fool

Admiral Yonai saw Yamamoto as a "mischievous devil." Yonai had been close to Yamamoto for over a quarter century and liked him a lot. So much so that when a state funeral was to be held for Yamamoto after he had been shot down, Yonai volunteered to chair the funeral committee. Yamamoto's remains were recovered and cremated in the Solomon Islands and returned to Japan. After the funeral, with full military honors, he was buried in a public cemetery in a suburb of Tokyo.

Agawa described Yamamoto as not being a drinker but someone who loved frolicking with *geisha* girls. He loved lively occasions and enjoyed entertaining others. When he really got going, he would display his talent for plate spinning, allow himself to get carried away by flattery, and proudly perform his specialty of acrobatic handstands. He was compas-

ALL THE EMPEROR'S MEN

sionate and frank and was clear about whom he liked and disliked. He was easygoing and little bothered by trivial things. A dyed-in-the-wool gambler, he would start with *Shogi* chess, then move on to *Mah Jong*, poker and bridge card games, which he was said to have played well with Americans. At times, he would spend the whole night playing poker. He was a dedicated letter writer and even replied to fan letters from elementary school students. Yonai's description of him as a "mischievous devil" pointed to his attractive and likeable nature.

Kurosawa was intrigued by Yamamoto and wanted to know everything about him. Before writing his first draft, Kurosawa visited the Nyo-ze Zo Museum in Nagaoka City, Yamamoto's home town in northwestern Japan, and looked at Yamamoto's numerous writings and personal effects. That included his artificial finger replacing one blown off during the Russo-Japanese war of 1904-5. It had been a gift from the Emperor Meiji. Kurosawa met several times with Yamamoto's eldest son, Yoshimasa, and painstakingly researched his father's hobbies and tastes, from the way he wielded chopsticks to the smallest gestures, habits, and manner of speech.

Aside from the opening sequence, the *Tora! Tora! Tora!* screenplay contains an abundance of episodes evoking Yamamoto's down-to-earth character. All were omitted from the Fox version of the film. For example, one scene was obviously an adaptation from Agawa's *Yamamoto Isoroku*. In that book, the scene takes place when the Combined Fleet was in Sasebo in February of 1941. In Kurosawa's version, the scene was set when the battleships entered the port in Kure in September of 1940. A newspaper displays the headline "Navy to accept Tripartite Pact." The pact was signed by Japan, Germany and Italy on September 27th, 1940, so this episode takes place directly beforehand.

EXT. KURE RAILWAY STATION
Waves of people flood out of the station.
Among the crowd, YAMAMOTO in civilian clothes appears, accompanied by his ADJUTANT.
Streets are crowded with petty officers and sailors. From an

EYES FROM HEAVEN

inn near the station, a song is heard, sung loudly by hoarse, gruff voices.

SONG
Holding me firmly by the sabre,
Take me wherever you go, she says.
Seems so easy to take you, darling,
But, alas, no girl's allowed
On board a torpedo bomber.

YAMAMOTO
There they go.

ADJUTANT
It's half watch ashore tonight, sir.
I've reserved your room at an inn nearby.

YAMAMOTO
OK, let's walk.

ADJUTANT
I've read in the newspapers about the Tripartite Alliance. The Navy has finally…

YAMAMOTO
This is me!

So saying, YAMAMOTO suddenly begins trotting along with toes turned out, comically imitating Charlie Chaplin's baggy pants walk. The ADJUTANT halts and looks on in blank amazement. Two WARRANT OFFICERS walk by.

WARRANT OFFICER A
Hey, that's our admiral, isn't it?

ALL THE EMPEROR'S MEN

WARRANT OFFICER B
Idiot! No admiral walks in public like that.

Another tragi-comic episode that Kurosawa tried to write but eventually gave up was about Yamamoto's girlfriend. On the afternoon of September 1, 1939, following the "manning the rails" ceremony, Yamamoto dines with former C-in-C and Vice Admiral Yoshida and staff officers, completes an inspection of the ship's interior, then quietly leaves the flagship and heads back to land. Next he boards a Nankai line train bound for Shirahama and checks into a hotel. On NHK radio that night, he hears the news that Nazi German troops have invaded Poland. With Yamamoto was his mistress, a woman named Chiyoko Kawai, a former *geisha* based in the Shinbashi section of Tokyo, and they were deeply in love.

"Another day spent kissing your portrait,
and calling your name so many times…"

This love poem was sent to Kawai by Yamamoto from Kure Naval Port on May 26, 1941, two years before he was killed in action. As a dedicated letter writer, Yamamoto wrote frequently to Kawai. After his death, Kawai had a wicker trunk full of letters from Yamamoto. The Navy confiscated all the letters from her in an attempt to keep a lid on a scandal that might have erupted had the war hero's love affair become widely known. He was married and the father of two sons and two daughters.

In the first draft of the *Tora! Tora! Tora!* screenplay Yamamoto's complicated, extraordinary human qualities, and appealing personality are richly described. In doing so, it seems that Kurosawa wanted the audience to feel all the more the tragic cruelty of the warrior's fate even as Yamamoto embraced it.

Exit Yamamoto

Yamamoto's last scene in Kurosawa's screenplay takes place inside the operations center of the flagship *Nagato* while anchored at Hashirajima. The Combined Fleet's key staff officers are gathered around a large table, listening to a radio broadcast. An NHK radio announcer reads a statement from the naval division of the Imperial General Headquarters at 1 P.M. on December 8, enumerating the military gains made by the Pearl Harbor attack.

SUPERIMPOSE TITLE:
SETO INLAND SEA—JAPAN

INT. *NAGATO*'S OPERATIONS CENTER

RADIO
'Before daybreak today, the Imperial
Navy successfully launched a bold,
large-scale air raid against American fleet and air
power in Hawaii.' May I remind you that the Commander In Chief of our Combined Fleet is Admiral
Isoroku Yamamoto…

The announcement is followed by a stirring Warship March.

YAMAMOTO slowly stands and, without saying a word, walks from the cabin. A somber, disheartened mood settles over his back—a sharp contrast to the lively music.

EXT. PEARL HARBOR
Flames and smoke are scorching the night sky.
SLOW FADE OUT. (*THE END*)

In this scene, there is no applause, no cheers, and no speechmaking.

The all-or-nothing Pearl Harbor operation ends in triumph. The difficult part lies ahead. As if unable to bear the rising tempo of the heroic Warship March, Yamamoto leaves the operations center. He is last seen from the back, in a "somber, disheartened mood" leaving behind only an uncomfortable silence and dark premonitions. The warship march plays on over the images as a striking counterpoint and the film ends with a vision of hell as flames and black smoke sear the skies above Pearl Harbor.

A superb drama had been skillfully woven into the *Tora! Tora! Tora!* screenplay. First is the Greek chorus at the story's opening. Then the newly appointed Commander-in-Chief Yamamoto strides up the gangway to appear on the deck of the battleship *Nagato* as if summoned by trumpets resounding from the heavens. After this man has rampaged and bellowed around this narrow stage and completed his role in this tragedy spanning two years and three months, he falls silent, sorrowfully departs, and fades out of sight.

In some ways, the tale of Isoroku Yamamoto and Pearl Harbor was a fleeting drama. From a macroscopic perspective, it may well be nothing more than the story of a solitary figure that disappeared right after he appeared. The red flames and black smoke jutting into the sky over Pearl Harbor in the last scene can be juxtaposed with the air raids raining firebombs from an armada of B-29 bombers that transformed Tokyo and other cities in Japan into scorched wastelands. It provided a striking image of the war and destruction that humans have waged time and time again and may be destined to repeat in the future.

The final sequence of the first draft concludes with this basso theme that runs through Kurosawa's filmography, lingering in our ears like the wailing of restless souls in the netherworld. It would seem that this harks back to Kurosawa's favorite quote from Shakespeare's *Macbeth*, Act V Scene v:

> Life's but a walking shadow, a poor player
> That struts and frets his hour upon the stage
> And then is heard no more ...

EYES FROM HEAVEN

CHAPTER
5

INTO THE DEN
OF TIGERS

Three Tigers

Kurosawa liked to play word games with the title *Tora! Tora! Tora!* ("Tiger! Tiger! Tiger!") and frequently elicited a laugh with remarks such as: "This is no easy task. I am working with three ferocious tigers. If I make them mad, I'm finished."

On New Year's Day 1968, Kurosawa sent a tongue-in-cheek letter to one of his trusted assistants, Teruyo Nogami of Kurosawa Productions. It referred to the Oriental Zodiac calendar of 12-year cycles:

Happy New Year! This may be the Year of the Monkey but for me the Year of the Tiger will continue for some time. I am reading through mountains of reference materials and writing an unending stream of pages of manuscript. This is one tough job. The American producer is a real goof-up but, unlike certain people we know in Japan, he is not the kind who just sits back and does nothing. His zeal and tenacity are something to behold. Big boss Zanuck has a great love of movies and I can really appreciate the things he says, so there is a genuine sense of purpose in the work. I wish certain executives would take at least a small lesson from him. Japanese movies have hit rock bottom. I am doing my best to somehow turn things around. I have been out of touch for awhile but I have not forgotten the people I have worked with. Please give everyone my regards. After New Year's, I will once again go into battle against the tigers!

The zealous producer Elmo Williams also saw himself battling with tigers. He commented later on the days *Tora! Tora! Tora!* was in production:

'TORA' is the Japanese word for tiger. Put three tigers together in Japan and you have *"TORA! TORA! TORA!"* I can tell you that it is one hell of an experience to tangle with three tigers. After four trying years, I now consider myself an expert on the Pearl Harbor incident and I know something about going to the mat with tigers. If any of you decide to do anything as foolish as that, let me give you a few pointers. Pull a tiger's tail too hard and you make him mad. If you're too gentle with him he takes advantage of your timidity and takes a swipe at you when you aren't looking. And when you match wits with three tigers, there is no use trying to anticipate the next move by looking into their eyes because they've got six of them. Finally, if you insist on doing battle with tigers, don't pick on the Japanese variety. (Excerpt from an article by Elmo Williams in "The CINEMAEDITOR" in the summer of 1970)

The tiger is, of course, a wild animal indigenous to East and South Asia. In Japan it is seen as a mysterious beast even though recorded history contains no evidence of tigers living in the country. Outside of Asia, tigers have long been considered exotic. In the culture of the English-speaking world, the tiger has been a symbol of oriental mystique as well as a beautiful creature associated with cunning and savagery.

Kurosawa was famous for being an animal lover. The wild animals in which he had a particular interest were gorillas and tigers. Among the books in his bedside reading was one on raising gorillas. He once said that, while in New York, he left the hotel early in the morning almost every day to go to the Central Park Zoo, where he spent an enjoyable hour trying to outstare the gorillas. With tigers, he appears to have been fascinated by the ferocity beneath their mystical beauty and by the tough suppleness of felines in general. Kurosawa tiger trivia included the title

ALL THE EMPEROR'S MEN

of the movie he was directing when Japan lost the war in 1945. *The Men Who Tread on the Tiger's Tail* was based on the *Kabuki* play *Kanjincho* (*An Appeal for Charity*) and the *Noh* play *Ataka*, which was the name of a fort. Thirty years later, Kurosawa directed the Russian film *Dersu Uzala*, which depicts a phantom Siberian tiger as a symbol of the deep reverence that the solitary hunter Dersu carries in his heart.

A Love-Hate Relationship

The Twentieth Century-Fox executive with the highest level of responsibility for *Tora! Tora! Tora!* production was vice president and head of production, Richard Zanuck. Lurking above his head was his father, Darryl F. Zanuck, the person who had risked the company's future on this movie and who was determined to see it through under his own personal guidance. Zanuck Senior was Fox's president and CEO. According to Williams, Darryl and Richard were eternal rivals. Richard's full name was Richard D. Zanuck, with the D standing for Darryl. Born in 1934, he was the same age as Tetsu Aoyagi and twenty-four years younger than Kurosawa. While still a student at Stanford University, Richard earned money for his tuition by writing movie scenarios. After graduation, he became vice president of the production company his father had started. When Darryl became president and CEO of Fox, he made Richard a vice president.

Richard was always critical of Darryl as a father. When Richard was twenty-two, Darryl had separated from his wife, Virginia. Richard could not forgive his father for deserting his mother as well as Richard himself and his two sisters, then going on to indulge himself with a series of young lovers. On the positive side, Richard respected his father as a great moviemaker and, so long as he worked in an organization run by Darryl, he had to accept a subservient role. Those mixed emotions toward his father caused Richard considerable pain and frustration.

A highly capable producer deeply trusted by Darryl, Elmo Williams was a difficult presence for Richard to deal with, as Williams recalls. "One day in 1966, Zanuck asked me to go to Hollywood to help his son

Richard with the *Tora! Tora! Tora!* project." Richard was then the head of production at the Fox studio. "When I got to Hollywood," he said, "I was not very welcome because I had had a very good long-standing relationship with Darryl Zanuck. His son was jealous of that relationship. So I was never made to feel very comfortable at the studio. And that certain sort of discomfort persisted throughout the *Tora! Tora! Tora!* production."

Williams was supposed to go to Richard for executive decisions but Darryl would sometimes tell Williams to report directly to him rather than informing his son. Drawing on his considerable experience in weathering life's difficulties, the resourceful Williams tried to get the work done properly while making both father and son look good. It could be said that he had one tiger at the front door and another at the back.

Guidelines

Ahead of a meeting with Kurosawa in June 1967, Williams organized into six points the guidelines approved by Fox as conditions applying to the completion of the movie scenario. He gave these guidelines to Kurosawa Productions:

1. We aim for a three-hour film. The theater version presupposes an intermission that would last for 15 or 20 minutes.
2. The film would be broken down into three time segments. The story prior to the attack is to last for two hours, with the Japanese and American sequences each lasting approximately one hour. The dramatic attack upon Pearl Harbor and the summation is to last another hour.
3. The film aims at a gripping story, making an authentic account of political, diplomatic, military events which led to the Pearl Harbor incident, balanced with human interest touches based on factual records.
4. With those guidelines in mind, Japanese and American

writers will submit stories based on their own perspectives. Those materials will then be integrated into one coherent final screenplay.

5. The coordination and integration of Japanese and American sequences will be done under the jurisdiction of Producer Elmo Williams. The completion of the final shooting screenplay is subject to the approval of Richard D. Zanuck and Darryl F. Zanuck.

6. The final screenplay should be good enough to be submitted to the governments of Japan and the United States (the Defense Agency and Foreign Ministry of Japan; the Department of Defense and the State Department of U.S.) for their scrutiny of factual accuracy and fairness of description, which is essential for the official blessing of and cooperation with the *TORA! TORA! TORA!* production.

For Williams, the final point was particularly significant. If the producers could not obtain the cooperation of the U.S. Department of Defense, it would be impossible to use the facilities of Pearl Harbor, the base of the U.S. Pacific Fleet, and more difficult to obtain and use military ships and planes.

Today, computer graphics make it possible to create imaginary worlds on screen. In that era, however, the 70 mm Panavision that relied on miniatures would have weakened the big-screen impact of a film. Consequently, it was Fox's basic policy, wherever possible, to shoot live action using actual warships and warplanes. To obtain the critical approval and proceed with the production, a screenplay had to be submitted to US government authorities no later than July, 1967.

Miscalculation

The ordeal that began in Tokyo in mid-June 1967 was a new experience for both Kurosawa and Williams.

Twentieth Century-Fox had already announced the timing of the movie's release as January 1969. Therefore production needed to start no later than one year earlier so the film could be completed by the end of 1968. This meant that preproduction tasks had to be completed by the end of 1967. In short, as of June 1967, only six months were left—and it was still necessary to complete the screenplay before preproduction work could begin.

Initially Williams had been optimistic that the screenplay would be completed on time. Two separate movie screenplays were being written by American and Japanese writers and the two scripts had to be combined into one. This task, which sounded simple in theory, turned out to be nothing close to it in reality. The longer the work continued, the more difficult the problems became. They escalated into a battle between Williams and Kurosawa, with the conflicts ending in impasses rather than solutions. Consequently Williams was in a state of high anxiety.

In Kurosawa's head, the movie was taking on the character of a grand epic. His basic images of the scenes had become increasingly elaborate following the completion of his first draft in May, 1967, and it appears that by this point those mental images were well defined. On the other side, Williams had turned to planning the film nearly six months before Kurosawa, and he had been refining his ideas for about a year. Williams had received the second script written by Fox screenwriter Larry Forrester months before Kurosawa finished the draft of his screenplay. Williams had worked out a provisional production plan on the basis of Forrester's script. He had in his head the basic concepts down to the level of concrete details. Kurosawa knew nothing about this.

At this stage, Kurosawa paid little or no attention to production-related problems and costs. In considering the screenplay, his artistic ambitions expanded, centering on the theme of "the tragedy of Admiral Isoroku Yamamoto." Doggedly adhering to his own concepts, he tried to develop the story within that framework. Williams was willing to incorporate good ideas from Kurosawa's screenplay but he tried to strike a balance between the Japanese and U.S. sequences while bringing things together in a way that gave priority to the flow of the plot and the audience's understanding of the story.

At the same time, Williams was examining the emerging screenplay with an eye to identifying the practical production problems and constraints for shooting each scene. Of course, he thought a lot about costs: the stage sets and props, warships and warplanes to be obtained, miniatures for special effects, and extras. Unconcerned with such issues, Kurosawa showed no inclination to listen to Williams's concerns and every time things did not go his way, he exploded in a fit of rage.

"Why won't they let me do it the way I asked?" he complained. When questions and doubts were brought up by the Americans, Kurosawa would be annoyed: "Why do they have to be so cheap about this? They have no understanding of the aspects I see as most important!"

Williams felt that Kurosawa had not accepted the reality that Fox was in charge, and he was shocked that Kurosawa—as president of Kurosawa Productions—could be so indifferent to production constraints and costs. To Williams's eyes, Kurosawa appeared to be high-handed and self-righteous, one who held obstinately to his own opinions and would not listen to the views of others. He was occasionally driven to despair at the way that Kurosawa, without permission or warning, added a new scene, deleted or rewrote a scene on which they had already spent a vast amount of time discussing.

In a letter to a friend, Williams spoke of his inability to understand the Oriental thought processes and of the frustration he was experiencing. Still, Williams patiently controlled his anger and dealt with the situation coolly. Ironically, this calm composure sometimes made Kurosawa ill at ease and irritated.

After he had spent more than one hundred days secluded at Minaguchi-en hotel, Kurosawa was back in Tokyo, where he did much of the revision of the screenplay at home. In the early stages, Kikushima was involved in the revisions but before long Kurosawa continued to work alone. Oguni's involvement had ended at the completion of the draft.

During the second half of June 1967, Williams stayed at the Tokyo Prince Hotel, home to the Kurosawa Productions office. He had come to Japan intending to get a firm grip on the integration of the American and Japanese screenplays but was at his wit's end dealing with myriad unexpected difficulties. Often late at night, he stood in his pajamas, a glass of Scotch in hand, staring deep in thought at the screenplay pages spread out across the room.

Never the Twain Shall Meet

Sensing that disaster loomed, Williams returned to Hollywood at the end of June. He was determined to combine the two screenplays into one by late July. As soon as the screenplays had been combined, without waiting to discuss it again with Kurosawa, Williams intended to submit it to Twentieth Century-Fox executives to seek their agreement and then to send it to the Departments of Defense and State for their approval. He planned thereafter to meet with Kurosawa in Hawaii in the last week of July to firm up the final screenplay and to begin practical discussions aimed at starting production. This was a last-ditch effort that Williams decided to make.

At the end of an interim report to Darryl and Richard Zanuck on the status of the screenplay, Williams revealed a certain amount of chagrin over how difficult the meetings with Kurosawa were proving to be.

Working with Orientals is a new experience for me. So far, I have managed to get along. And so far, my education in this direction has reached stage one. This means that I now understand why there is *NO* understanding between the Occident and the Orient. But it is this lack of understanding between two peoples that is an integral part of our story. Therefore, it will be worthwhile going on with the Japanese because the difference in points of view when it reaches the screen will be a plus factor for this film.

Sequestered in an office at the Fox studio in Beverly Hills, Williams and his close friend, screenwriter Larry Forrester, worked night and day pounding the keys of electric typewriters. They produced the second revised screenplay of *Tora! Tora! Tora!* dated July 21, 1967. The credits list only Forrester but it is clear that the content was a collaboration between Forrester and Williams. Many sequences from the Kurosawa draft were retained but none of the Japanese writers were credited.

The collection of the Academy of Motion Picture Arts and Sciences (AMPAS) in the Margaret Herrick Library in Los Angeles contains a single copy of this screenplay. Altogether there are 363 pages and 1,229 scenes. In hand it feels quite heavy, perhaps three and a half pounds. Longer than the Kurosawa draft, if filmed it would exceed seven hours of screen time, more than double the three-hour length defined by Fox as the maximum. Williams knew it was too long and promised Fox executives that he would polish it and reduce its length by more than half.

The meetings in Tokyo in June had impressed upon Williams the great obstinacy with which Kurosawa would insist upon proceeding as he envisioned. Williams felt, however, that if Kurosawa's demands were accepted, the film could become the personal story of Admiral Yamamoto. That would undermine the original purpose of the project, which was to show the path of tragic mistakes that Japan and the U.S. had made on the way to the Pearl Harbor attack and to do so in a way that was historically accurate, fair, balanced, and, of course, dramatic.

In Williams's report to the Zanucks, he said:

> Kurosawa will, undoubtedly, scream when he sees that I have thrown out all of the scenes of the political maneuvering between Japan and America during the years 1939 and 1940. This is interesting stuff to read but it is dull material for a motion picture. But I am convinced that the "director" in him will be the deciding factor when he considers this new approach to the Pearl Harbor story, in motion picture terms.

Williams's idea was to write a "raw material" screenplay encompassing those scenes that the Japanese and Americans each absolutely wanted to

121

keep. Then, at a conference to be held in Hawaii at the end of July, both would use their ingenuity to agree upon where to make cuts to produce a movie half the length of the current screenplay. However, Williams had not anticipated a serious pitfall.

The Two Richards

When the *Tora! Tora! Tora!* project was announced in Tokyo in April, 1967, the director of the American sequences had not been named. By that time, however, an internal decision had been made at Fox. Vice president Richard Zanuck had strongly pushed for Richard Fleischer. Six years younger than Kurosawa, Fleischer was born in New York in 1916, the son of a famous feature-length animation pioneer, Max Fleischer, who had produced *Gulliver's Travels* in 1939. Richard Fleischer first studied medicine at Brown University but transferred to Yale University, majoring in drama and continuing to graduate school. After working in theater, in 1942 he joined RKO, where he gained experience as a director, editor, and producer of newsreels. Richard Zanuck and Richard Fleischer met when Fleischer directed the Twentieth Century-Fox 1959 crime suspense movie *Compulsion,* which portrayed a "motiveless murder" in Chicago in 1924. At the 1959 Cannes Film Festival the movie's three leading actors—Dean Stockwell, Bradford Dillman, and Orson Welles—won best actor awards. The movie itself was nominated for the best picture award in the British Academy of Film and Television Arts awards of 1960 and was a milestone in the career of Richard Zanuck. At the age of thirty-eight in 1954, Fleischer established himself in Hollywood after directing Walt Disney's *20,000 Leagues Under the Sea.*

Sharing the torments that can come from having illustrious fathers, the two Richards hit it off well, which led Richard Zanuck to urge that Richard Fleischer be named director on *Tora! Tora! Tora!* But Williams had several strong candidates in mind for the American director and opposed the selection of Fleischer. From his perspective, even though Fleischer was a skilled director, he lacked the stature to stand up to Kurosawa. Darryl Zanuck, however, did not seem interested in the selection of the American director. According to Williams, he said that if his son, Richard, was set on Fleischer, they should go with him.

Mismatch

"Personally, I didn't think Fleischer was a good choice," Williams recalled later. "But Kurosawa's outright rejection of Fleischer as a 'second-rate director' was totally unexpected and extremely annoying. It caused a lot of trouble all the way through."

Kurosawa learned of Fleischer's selection when he received notification from Williams of the meeting to be held in Hawaii from July 14 to July 31, 1967. The American participants were to be Williams and Richard Fleischer. Williams planned to bring to the meeting his combined "raw material" screenplay. There would be intensive discussions with the result being a final version of the screenplay. Williams explained this in a letter to Kurosawa.

Kurosawa was not happy with any of it. Perhaps because his family roots are in the north in the Tohoku region, Kurosawa didn't like summer, much less warm Hawaii. He took a dim view of the screenplay discussions, apparently believing that it would not be easy to resolve the issues. On top of that, they had selected Richard Fleischer to be the American director. Kurosawa was displeased. He did not like the choice and, even more, he was angry because they had made it without consulting him.

Rumors circulated in Hollywood about the selection of the American director. One held that Kurosawa wanted Fred Zinnemann, who had a reputation as a first-class director comparable to Kurosawa in stature, and Fox had agreed. A search of Fox company records, plus a query to Williams, led to the conclusion that the rumor had no basis in fact.

The reason for Kurosawa's aversion to Fleischer was clear. In 1966, Kurosawa had seen Fleischer's movie *Fantastic Voyage* and found it irritating. It is a science fiction adventure in which, to save an important person in danger of dying because of a blood clot in his brain, a group of selected scientists board a nuclear-powered submarine and are shrunk

INTO THE DEN OF TIGERS

to microscopic size to be injected into the patient. Kurosawa said that while watching it his body became itchy and he began to feel sick. This was the only Fleischer film that Kurosawa had seen but the unpleasant memory had caused a visceral rejection of Fleischer, whom Kurosawa had never met. The aversion persisted with Kurosawa referring to Fleischer for many years as "the micro guy."

Kurosawa was known for having strong likes and dislikes with respect to people. "Once he developed a dislike for someone, that person was no good forever," Shiro Moritani said. "He would not revise his opinion. In that sense he had a paranoid bent. So there was a danger that if he wasn't careful he would end up surrounded by flatterers." Moritani was Kurosawa's chief assistant director for five pictures, from *The Bad Sleep Well* in 1960 to *Red Beard* in 1965. Richard Fleischer seems to have been a victim of Kurosawa's tendency to dislike certain people out of hand.

Disaster in Hawaii

On July 24, 1967, Kurosawa departed a sweltering Haneda Airport, arriving the same day in a warm and humid Hawaii, where he checked into the Ilikai Hotel on Waikiki Beach. With the director were producer Tetsu Aoyagi and chief assistant director Yutaka Osawa.

Once settled in their hotel, Kurosawa found waiting for him the second revised screenplay fashioned through the hard work of Williams and Larry Forrester. Learning that discussions based on this tome would begin the following day put Kurosawa in a bad mood. Having this fat screenplay thrust in his face and being told it would be the starting point from which the work would proceed would no doubt have been difficult for Kurosawa to deal with. Moreover, everything was in English so he was unable to read it without help.

From Williams's perspective, this was the screenplay he had labored day and night to complete barely in time and he was confident it reflected the results of earlier discussions in Tokyo. Even so, reading and checking the content of this screenplay would be no easy task. Williams summarized the work objectives of the Hawaii conference into a number of points that were communicated to Kurosawa in advance. They were to discuss the overall style of the film. They were to discuss the integration of the Japanese and American sequences, including cuts and transitions. They were to discuss the division of work between the Americans and the Japanese, the use of color, miniatures, the work to be done by the second unit director, and the shooting schedule. They were to discuss music, scoring, dubbing, and all other phases of the post-production phase. And to gather impressions for discussion of the attack scenes, they were to be flown by helicopter or private plane along the routes traveled by the various attacking units of the Japanese planes when they struck the Pearl Harbor naval station, plus Hickam and Wheeler airfields on the island of Oahu.

Forced to rely on Aoyagi's explanations, Kurosawa had his hands full just trying to identify problems in the screenplay. Thus occupied, he hardly set foot outside his hotel room. Kurosawa held tenaciously to the position: "The screenplay comes first. Without a finished script, it is a waste of time to even talk about production." He refused to meet with Williams or Fleischer. His anger had exploded the moment he learned that his cherished opening sequence depicting the ceremony of manning the rails had been deleted and replaced by a different scene written by Forrester and Williams. After that, he was in no mood to consider Williams's proposed revisions but rejected them one after another as being stupid, pointless, irrelevant, or outrageous.

Aoyagi was forced into being a messenger, shuttling endlessly between the rooms of Kurosawa and Williams. There was hardly any point in them being in the same hotel, except that it made Aoyagi's shuttles shorter. In addition to the production discussions, Aoyagi intended to talk to Williams about contractual issues, but that never happened.

Kurosawa's dissatisfaction with Fleischer surfaced. In his autobiography, Williams says: "Later in the day, Tetsu [Aoyagi] wanted to tell me something confidentially. It seems that Kurosawa considered Dick Fleischer a second-rate director and, therefore, he hesitated about meeting him. Kurosawa wanted me to find someone with more prestige. I had to send a strong message back to '*Tenno*' ['Emperor'] to get him to at least show Dick some courtesy." Perhaps because of harsh words from Williams, Kurosawa did show up at a dinner in the hotel's restaurant. Williams and Aoyagi did practically all the talking, however, with Kurosawa and Fleischer hardly saying a word. The discussion never made it to a substantive level.

During this dinner Kurosawa paid little heed to the talk but one thing managed to catch his attention: He was amazed by the way Fleischer, without tasting his food, poured ketchup over each of the many dishes set before him. From then on, Kurosawa had a second nickname for Fleischer; in addition to being "the micro guy," he was "the ketchup guy."

Mercifully, the Hawaii conference came to an end, albeit with misunderstandings and distrust remaining on both sides. It must have been a humiliating week for Fleischer but he did not seem particularly put out. He relaxed, spending much time at the hotel poolside, enjoying the Hawaiian holiday. Immediately upon returning from Hawaii, Fleischer had waiting for him the start of shooting on a major fantasy adventure musical on which Twentieth Century-Fox had staked its future. This was *Doctor Dolittle*, starring Rex Harrison.

The cost of the conference in Hawaii was borne by Fox. For Williams, reporting the truth of the debacle to the company was an unappealing option. So he swore Fleischer and Aoyagi to secrecy and kept the story of the conference under wraps for many years. At the time, he wrote in his report to Fox:

> At the Honolulu meeting, we agreed on our main objectives in the rewriting of the final screenplay for *Tora! Tora! Tora!*
>
> 1. To cut a minimum of 120 pages from the screenplay dated July 21, 1967.
> 2. To rewrite the first 105 pages following the new continuity that was agreed upon.
> 3. For the balance of the screenplay, we agreed to send each other our suggestions for the scenes that could be eliminated.

ALL THE EMPEROR'S MEN

For both Kurosawa and Williams, the road to Pearl Harbor still stretched far into the distance.

Impatience and Annoyance

Returning to Hollywood, Williams had no time to contemplate the mistakes. His more serious headache was the slow progress on making arrangements necessary for movie production. A further blow to Williams came in mid-August, 1967, when the Departments of Defense and State sent some severe comments on the 363-page revised screenplay.

The comments focused on the American sequences, with nothing being said about the Japanese scenes. The departments had a serious objection to what they saw as the overall impression given by the film. They said that the screenplay would suggest to movie goers the idea that U.S. noncommissioned officers were all capable and acted appropriately during the Pearl Harbor attack but that their superior officers were all incompetent and therefore made the damage worse. This, they contended, could cause Americans to lose confidence in the U.S. armed forces and such an impression could have an adverse effect on recruitment. Consequently, both departments said they could not promise to cooperate with the production if the screenplay remained in its current form.

Williams discussed this problem with Darryl and Richard Zanuck and immediately set to work on revising the screenplay. Considering the many doubts and dissatisfactions that continued to arrive intermittently from Kurosawa, Williams wanted to complete the final version of the screenplay by late September. Without screenplay approval from both Fox executives and Washington, it would be impossible to proceed with pre-production work. Further delays would play havoc with the schedule that called for shooting to start in January, 1968, and the release of the movie in theaters in January, 1969.

Williams and Forrester began another day-and-night marathon of scriptwriting and finished the final screenplay on September 20, 1967. At 222 pages, it was 141 pages shorter than the July 21 edition and included 1,133 scenes. Although that would make the movie more than three hours long, it was at least a finished product with all the necessary elements in place. This screenplay in English was the first of *Tora! Tora! Tora!* to include the names Akira Kurosawa, Hideo Oguni, and Ryuzo Kikushima in addition to Larry Forrester's name on the title page. Below the names, it says: "The Japanese scenes are to be translated into the Japanese language, as those scenes will be filmed in Japanese. Subtitles will explain these scenes when the picture is exhibited." This statement implies that Fox expected this screenplay to be the definitive script for the directors, production staff and cast in both the U.S. and Japan.

On the same date, this screenplay was sent to Fox executives and the Departments of Defense and State. The next day two copies were sent to Kurosawa Productions by international mail. Williams knew he would have to fight with three "tigers" to get this screenplay approved, the tigers being the Fox board of directors, Washington, and Akira Kurosawa.

First, he wanted to firm up prospects for obtaining budget approval at Fox by the end of October. For this to happen, he needed to calculate production costs for each scene, then aggregate those figures into an estimate of the total cost of production that would go to the board to be approved. It would be necessary to present the board with a convincing and executable plan. Darryl Zanuck had a strong emotional investment in the project but a majority vote of the board was necessary. Approval could not be taken for granted.

For the review of the project by Washington, there was no choice but to wait for the relevant authorities to come to a conclusion. Based on the previous review of the second-revision manuscript, Williams figured it would take three to four weeks for the government to announce its findings. Considering the severe response last time, the fear was that here too things may not be so easy.

And then there was Williams's third foe: the ferocious "Japanese tiger," Akira Kurosawa. Based on experience, Williams figured that Kurosawa would strongly reject the final screenplay. Expecting this opposition, Williams had included in the Japanese sequences those scenes that Kurosawa had obstinately demanded not be cut.

Unsettled Waves and Winds

The final screenplay was mailed to Tokyo on September 20, 1967. Twenty-four hours later, Williams sent a letter to Kurosawa. In the period of 1966 to 1970, Williams wrote several hundred reports, letters, telegrams, memos, and other documents about the production of *Tora! Tora! Tora!* This letter was one of only three that he addressed directly to Kurosawa. The other two were the initial contact letter of November 15, 1966, and the dismissal letter of December 25, 1968. All other communications from Williams to Kurosawa Productions were addressed to Tetsu Aoyagi.

This letter, about a thousand words long, was polite, respectful, even solicitous. Williams asked for Kurosawa's understanding, explaining that while circumstances had made it necessary to put together a final screenplay quickly, they had done their best to balance the U.S. and Japan sequences and to create a clear plot that would bring drama to the movie. He said that they had taken full account of Kurosawa's opinions as well as those of specialists. Williams asked Kurosawa to make his part of the movie from this final screenplay:

> I know how hard you have worked, how conscientiously you have researched your material and personally prepared your script. Without your outstanding talent and dedication, we never would have attained the excellence of the Japanese sequences now in the final screenplay.
>
> I know that for a sensitive artist, after all the months of loving labor, the cuts that have been made in this final version must at times be painful. But I appeal to you, as one who has admired your work for many years, to endure the initial pangs and, after the first shock, to examine the results objectively. I feel in my heart you will agree that this picture

129

is a unique project, with unique problems, and it cannot be prepared by the normal processes.

We have reached this stage only by making concessions to each other, by working doggedly and exercising patience. It has been a great act of faith between us that has paid off... Looking back over the months of our cooperation on this project, I realize just how many barriers we have broken down, how many formidable problems we have solved together. We have battled through the frustrations of the language and translation difficulties. We have bridged the gulf between our cultures, and our vastly different methods of film-making.

Time and time again we have subdued our emotions, our egos, and even our professional instincts in the interest of making a motion picture of almost unprecedented and international importance. I do not believe such a task has ever been attempted before. And I feel sure, with this final script, we can continue working together to make a great motion picture.

I am confident the American sequences of this final script now are pin-point accurate, and that we will get Washington's approval and cooperation without difficulty. The ending—as Dr. Prange mentions in one of his comments—avoids any note of vengeance, and presents war as the ultimate human tragedy, with neither side as victor. For today's audiences, I feel sure you will agree that this is the correct psychological approach, and the right spirit in which to close a picture which has been produced in close and friendly cooperation by representatives of the two nations involved in conflict a quarter-of-a-century ago.

The ending was the joint work of Williams and Forrester. The idea was praised by University of Maryland history professor Gordon W. Prange, author of the book that was one of the key sources for the movie.

ALL THE EMPEROR'S MEN

The ending was like this. Following Admiral Yamamoto's last speech, the USS *Enterprise* is seen returning to Pearl Harbor. Admiral William F. Halsey surveys the devastation of Pearl Harbor with blazing eyes. Sunk by a torpedo attack, only the superstructure of the battleship USS *California* is visible above the water. There, a shot-up 'Old Glory' is still flying. An instrumental arrangement of the military march "Praise the Lord and Pass the Ammunition" slowly plays, growing gradually louder. The camera returns to Admiral Halsey, who says, "We're going to scour every square mile of the Pacific. However long it takes, we'll keep hunting until we find 'em—if we have to sail all the way to Tokyo Bay."

Moments later this scene begins:

AERIAL SHOT—KOLEKOLE PASS

As we glide Northward through Kolekole Pass, we see again the vast, tranquil Pacific Ocean. The engine ROAR FADES—until only the SOUND of the sea remains. A brief pause, then we hear once more the poem the Japanese Emperor read to his Staff—

NARRATION
(O.S.)
'I think all the people of the world are brethren.
Then why are the waves and the winds so unsettled?'

Once again we SUPERIMPOSE, over the sea, the title "TORA, TORA, TORA," in Japanese characters. This TITLE FADES OUT, then as we FADE INTO the END CREDITS, we hear a reprise of the MUSIC we heard over Halsey's last speech.

The original 31-syllable Japanese poem is a well-known *waka* written by the Emperor Meiji. On September 6, 1941, a meeting took place in the presence of Emperor Hirohito to debate the issue of whether to embark on war with the United States and Britain. During the deliberations, the Emperor (known now by his posthumous name, Showa) pulled a piece of paper from his pocket and recited the Emperor Meiji's *waka* as an expression of his personal desire for peace. In the movie, the same poem appears in the scene where Prime Minister Fumimaro Konoe asks Admiral Yamamoto about Japan's chances of winning if Tokyo goes to war with the U.S. and Britain. Yamamoto answers that if he is told to fight he could raise havoc for a year or so but that he could guarantee nothing after that.

After reading this ending, Kurosawa dismissed it: "No good."

Horns of a Dilemma

Five days after writing to Kurosawa, Williams wrote to producer Tetsu Aoyagi to explain his intentions and to push for more action. Dated September 26, 1967, this letter indicated that the final screenplay had been well received by Richard Zanuck and other executives at the Fox studio in Beverly Hills.

Although the reactions of Darryl Zanuck and other executives at the New York headquarters were not yet known, Williams thought that the project would be approved by the Fox board and the Department of Defense, and thus he felt it right to get started with preproduction work. Without progress at this stage, Williams would not be able to calculate the cost of each part of the production. This, in turn, would preclude him from presenting an overall budget proposal to the Fox board. He needed information on the eight Japanese scenes he felt would present particular difficulties. He asked Aoyagi to check with Kurosawa about how he planned to stage those scenes and then to write back with the details. In a memo, Williams said:

It would help me a great deal, if you and Mr. Kurosawa could put on paper for me Mr. Kurosawa's thoughts on how he intends to direct some of the more difficult scenes, such as:

1. The sequence when Yamamoto takes over as Commander-in-Chief of the Japanese Fleet.
2. The torpedo bomber training scene at night.
3. The torpedo planes and the dive-bombers practicing hitting their shallow-water targets.
4. The assembly and the sailing of the Fleet from Hitokappu Bay.
5. The refueling sequence at sea while the Japanese Fleet is en route from Japan to Hawaii.
6. The arrival of the Japanese Fleet in Hawaiian waters.
7. The take-off of Japanese aircraft from the various carriers.
8. The various scenes of Japanese pilots during the attack sequences.

Miniatures would have to be fashioned for these eight scenes, so Williams asked Aoyagi to send storyboards showing Kurosawa's concept for each. It was Hollywood convention that storyboards were drawn by professional sketch artists. Williams never imagined that Kurosawa would himself draw all the storyboards for the Japan sequences.

The Williams letter was written to give the impression that screenplay problems had been solved and the project had moved on to the pre-production stage. But the Fox decision necessary to start full-scale preproduction had not yet been received. Nor had the screenplay review by Washington been received. If Williams had waited for those decisions, however, there was a risk that shooting would not be able to start by the date scheduled.

War Games

Although Williams included most of Kurosawa's favorite scenes in the final screenplay, he still had one major worry. He was most concerned that he had deleted a long sequence of Japanese war games to assess the feasibility of the Pearl Harbor operation. Kurosawa had been stubborn about including it.

Historical records showed that these war games were held secretly at the Naval Staff College in Tokyo over a ten-day period from September 11 to 20 in 1941, less than three months prior to the Pearl Harbor attack. Full-scale war is usually a life-and-death collision of powers that decides the fate of nations. The totality of a country's military might and national resources are put into action along with the knowledge, judgment, experience, and wisdom of its leaders. In a battle, however, there are always uncertainties so victory can never be known for sure beforehand. Simulations often evaluate the feasibility of a planned operation as objectively as possible, using top-secret intelligence but without wasting resources.

Kurosawa had painstakingly investigated the war games at the Naval Staff College and dramatized them in forty pages of his draft screenplay. Evidently, he had the cooperation of the Defense Agency's Office of War History in this endeavor. The scene in Kurosawa's script opens:

The Japanese naval ensign, with the vermillion emblem of rising sunbeams, flutters in the blue skies of September. Just below the flag, on the fourth floor of the Naval Staff College, there is a hall with a veranda. All the glass windows of the hall are tightly closed and curtained. So are the windows of the adjoining rooms on both sides—despite the extreme, full-day heat.

Kurosawa's screenplay included a diagram of the room in the Naval Staff College, and it portrays the games being played out the "Red Forces" of America and "Blue Forces" of Japan fought with all their skill. Packed into the room of the Blue Forces were the commanders in chief, chiefs of staff, and top naval and air staff officers of the Combined Fleet and the First Air Fleet. The leader of the opposing Red Forces was Captain Kanji Ogawa of the Intelligence Bureau of the Imperial Japanese Navy General Staff. He had spent considerable time in America and was viewed as one of the Navy's top experts on US military affairs.

The war games were based on the premise that war with the U.S. would start two months later, on November 16, 1941, so it was a realistic scenario. The judges evaluated the strategic actions at each stage, taking into account the probable weather and enemy response to decide on the success or failure of each move. At the end an evaluation was given. Historical evidence shows that the assessment of the attack plan was critical. The evaluation held that great risk was involved and it might be difficult to succeed, the key issue being whether the enemy could be caught off guard.

After the games, even among top officers under the command of Admiral Yamamoto, there was outspoken criticism and pessimism that the Pearl Harbor attack plan was too dangerous. The authority to make the final decision rested with the Navy General Staff, which had been less than enthusiastic about the strategy from the beginning. Admiral Yamamoto pushed the plan, steamrollering all opposition. Even though he had been vigorously opposed to starting a war with the United States, Yamamoto now dedicated himself to this war, seeking to open hostilities with a major and decisive attack.

Historically, the Pearl Harbor attack was a brief moment of glory for Admiral Yamamoto, but he would soon walk a path that led to an inevitable fall and a violent death. Considering that history, Kurosawa felt the war games represented a critical juncture in the tragedy of Admiral Yamamoto. Moreover, Kurosawa may have had another motive for including the war games sequence, which was to deepen the audience's understanding of the Pearl Harbor operation. Its inherent risks foreshadowed events to come, getting the audience emotionally involved and thereby heighten the coming thrills.

Despite everything, Williams experienced a rare pleasant surprise when he visited Tokyo in October 1967 to discuss the revision of the final screenplay. After listening to the explanation by Williams, Kurosawa accepted the deletion of the war games sequence. Williams was even more surprised when Kurosawa showed up on the following day with a concisely written replacement for the war games. He shifted the scene to another meeting that took place on the quarterdeck of the flagship *Nagato*. Williams was once more impressed by Kurosawa's remarkable talent and his ability to shift gears brilliantly when he willed it.

Kurosawa agreed with the structure of the American sequences, particularly showing how, despite the decoding of secret Japanese diplomatic telegrams and the distribution of crucial information in Washington, the vital intelligence was not relayed to the officers responsible for the defense of Pearl Harbor because of errors of judgment.

Deep Divide

Even at this stage, there appeared to be no way out of the impasse over the opening scene. Kurosawa would not budge in his insistence on the sequence he had written: the traditional "manning the rails" ceremony. Repeatedly Kurosawa rejected suggestions from Williams for alternatives.

Knowing Kurosawa's directing style, Williams felt he understood why the director was so obsessed with his opening scene. Williams was under the impression that it would result in stunningly beautiful imagery on the 70mm Panavision screen. But time, effort, and cost needed to be considered. Even Kurosawa did not have a clear idea of how many people would be required for the shoot. As producer, Williams could not accept such a grandiose opening scene without having a detailed plan and an estimated cost.

The opening scene brought with it other problems. The ceremony took place on September 1, 1939, which meant the Pearl Harbor attack would start more than two years later. The story would be too complicated if the road to Pearl Harbor was portrayed over a two-year period in which Japan's war in China, Nazi German aggression in Europe, and the political, diplomatic, and military maneuvering between Japan and the United States had to be explained. For this reason, Fox wanted to start the story no earlier than the beginning of 1941, when Yamamoto resolved to attack Pearl Harbor.

Williams felt that the most natural approach would be to start in Hawaii. The opening scene in his screenplay begins thirty seconds before the attack:

ALL THE EMPEROR'S MEN

BLANK SCREEN
Very gradually, introduce the steady TICKING of three clocks. After several beats—

SLOW FADE IN

THREE CLOCK FACES

They materialize in line across the blank screen. The second hands jerk round in perfect unison, but the minute and hour hands indicate different times. The clock on the right of screen registers precisely 24 minutes and 30 seconds after one. The center clock: 5 minutes and 30 seconds before eight. The clock on the left: 24 minutes and 30 seconds after three. The concerted TICKING continues to grow louder... louder...

Now a date appears, in both Japanese and English characters, simultaneously, straddling all three clocks—

DECEMBER 7, 1941

Next, beneath each clock, again, in both languages, a place-name comes up.

First, on right of screen—WASHINGTON, D.C.

Then on the left—TOKYO

Finally at the center—HAWAII

CAMERA starts to MOVE IN on the middle ("Hawaii") clock, losing the other two. And now, mingling with the TICKING, we hear the mysterious sound of a huge

INTO THE DEN OF TIGERS

GONG, low and distant... vibrating... slowly fading...
Then a second beat, slightly louder. A third beat follows, louder still.

The fourth gong beat—the loudest yet—comes at the precise instant when the face of the center clock fills the depth of the screen and the hands register exactly 7:55.

Then a vast expanse of calm, empty sea is shown behind the movie's title, which is written in bright red *kanji* (Japanese characters). Next, the English opening credits begin. At the same time, the drone of aircraft engines grows gradually louder until it reaches an almost deafening roar. The aircraft themselves are as yet unseen.

Positioned as the eyes of a Japanese pilot, the camera looks out from the cockpit and down on the island of Oahu. From the roar of the engines, it is clear the aircraft is one of a large formation. The pilot and aircraft still cannot be seen. The camera's eye passes Opana Point and Kolekole Pass, and after flying low between rocky peaks, visible directly in front is the horseshoe-shaped Pearl Harbor and a column of warships at anchor. At this point the credits end.

The roar of the large squadron continues. The coded "surprise attack achieved" message of attack force commander Mitsuo Fuchida cuts through the engine roar: "Tora! Tora! Tora!" Fuchida repeats his triumphant war cry, and in sync with his shout, the bright red English title bursts onto the screen one word at a time.

After a fade-out and fade-in, Admiral Yamamoto is shown taking the post of Commander-in-Chief of the Combined Fleet on September 1, 1939, while Admiral Husband Kimmel is shown taking the post of Commander-in-Chief of the U.S. Pacific Fleet on February 1, 1941, and then the story proper begins.

Upon reading this opening in the translated version of Williams's screenplay, Kurosawa's reaction was succinct: "This is totally unusable."

The most serious problem, however, was not the opening itself, but rather a fundamental issue: a difference of opinion over what the movie was supposed to portray. That Kurosawa and Williams were in basic conflict on this point is clear. Williams and Kurosawa each had his own convictions and neither showed the slightest sign of compromising. Furthermore, Kurosawa feared being forced to start production before completing an acceptable level of preparation.

From the drafting of his screenplay onward, Kurosawa's thinking remained consistent: This movie was neither documentary nor spectacle, it was an epic tragedy. Kurosawa wanted to bring to the screen the tragedy of a noble warrior—Admiral Yamamoto—who lived and died at the mercy of fate. He wanted to articulate the Pearl Harbor story as the tale of one human being who, in his brief moment in the spotlight of history, acted contrary to his own aspirations and ideals. He brought about a fatal collision between two countries, one that brought his own country to the brink of ruin and resulted in his own death.

This was not the movie that Elmo Williams was trying to make. For him, the objective was to utilize the 70 mm big screen in full color and stereophonic sound to create a spectacle in which scenes of the Pearl Harbor attack had the power to astound audiences. In achieving this objective, he wanted to portray a factual account of the path to Pearl Harbor from the perspective of each country and explore the inevitability of the destruction of both protagonists.

Utilizing the latest movie technology and giving warplanes, warships, and code-breaking machines roles that would be equal to or greater than those of the people involved, Williams sought to further energize the spectacle of battle. In contrast, for his people-centered drama, Kurosawa aimed to give the audience a tangible feel for the history of these events and for the frightening nature of invisible fate. For him, the battle scene was a curtain rising on tragedy.

CHAPTER
6

STARTING OVER

An Ambush

The most painful arrows of criticism puncturing Elmo Williams's confidence in his screenplay came from an unexpected direction—from another tiger, no less formidable. The critic was the originator of the movie project and Williams's strongest patron, Fox president Darryl F. Zanuck.

After reading the screenplay, Zanuck fired off a telex from Fox's New York headquarters to his son, Fox production head Richard, in California. He said the screenplay was unusable and ordered a comprehensive rewrite. He asserted that the screenplay was rambling and disorganized and as a story it lacked coherence and power. He ordered the number of scenes be cut boldly to create a compact screenplay. Of the 1,133 existing scenes, he pointed to one hundred he thought should be cut.

This was a shock to Richard, who had approved the screenplay without finding particular problems in it. He ordered Williams to analyze his father's instructions and to come up with measures to address them. Williams, too, was astonished. On October 1, he held an emergency meeting with scenarist Larry Forrester and director Richard Fleischer at the Fox studio in Beverly Hills to review the senior Zanuck's points in detail and to begin rewriting the screenplay.

The circumstances demanded haste. Deleting a scene would render unnecessary all the preproduction work for that scene, thereby affecting budget calculations. Multiply that by one hundred and mass confusion seemed inevitable—not to mention the effect that such moves would have on the staff's confidence in the producer. The repercussions on

143

Fox's relations with the Departments of Defense and State also had to be considered. To send the "Final Screenplay" for review and then come back less than two weeks later saying it was being revised would not inspire confidence. Last but not least, it would be necessary to contact Kurosawa quickly to seek his acceptance. Not to do so would only invite further trouble.

During the re-evaluation over the next three days, Williams decided Zanuck's criticisms were for the most part on target. The scenes he wanted cut were mostly political, strategic, or diplomatic portraits of complex relations among the maneuvering nations. Several were light episodes that risked obscuring the movie's theme. Zanuck wanted them to delete scenes that could confuse the audience and to give priority to strength, clarity, and simplicity. The one hundred scenes marked for deletion included twenty-three Japanese scenes and more than triple that number of American scenes.

On October 4, after beginning revisions, Williams reported to Darryl and Richard Zanuck. Seven Japanese and fifty-nine American scenes would be deleted. The remaining thirty-four scenes would be kept to preclude damaging the continuity of the screenplay, but those scenes would be rewritten to make them more compact and to minimize production costs. Williams promised that, if the Zanucks approved, he would reorganize the script and prepare a "Revised Final Screenplay."

Williams said in an interview later that several revised scenes reflected suggestions received in unofficial negotiations with the Department of Defense. One sequence showed that soldiers defending Hawaii were on alert, as they had been trained, and were responding to the situation in an efficient and well-disciplined manner. Including this scene, intended to improve the Army's public image, was an Army prerequisite for providing troops and equipment for filming free of charge. A scene arising from talks with the Navy depicted a band competition that took place on the Saturday before the Pearl Harbor attack. The Navy agreed to provide the Pacific Fleet brass band and a crowd of extras. Williams knew this arrangement would help smooth negotiations with the Navy on the availability of destroyers, tugboats, and facilities needed for other scenes.

Clearly, Williams always had an eye toward procuring people and materials at a lower cost. In addition, the Department of Defense had cautioned that the ending of the movie should not leave the audience feeling intensely sad at America's crushing defeat; rather it should suggest America's ultimate victory. Williams had reflected this view in his final screenplay. Williams wanted to get across to the Zanucks that, as producer, he had to consider the government's position.

After discussion with the Zanucks, Williams submitted a list of the scenes to be deleted to the Departments of State and Defense. But he did not mention that the final screenplay was being extensively revised out of fear that additional confusion could further delay Washington's decision.

Mystery of Postponement

On December 1, 1967, Kurosawa Productions announced a substantial delay in the production of *Tora! Tora! Tora!* The company said it would resume preparations in July 1968, start shooting in November, and complete the movie in 1969. Williams explained the reason in a memo dated November 14, 1967, saying:

> Because Twentieth Century-Fox wants to make "*Tora! Tora! Tora!*" an outstanding, authentic film about the attack on Pearl Harbor, the studio has been forced to postpone the start of production for a few months until it can obtain the best possible combination of talents and facilities to insure the quality of this ambitious undertaking. Due to the difficulties involved in obtaining certain key personnel and equipment we need for the making of this film, therefore, we will be unable to start production in February, 1968, as we had originally planned.
>
> Postponement of this film does not mean that we have any intention of cancelling it. As soon as we have a new schedule, we will give you the exact date when we will go into production.

Run under headlines such as "Another Kurosawa movie postponed" (*Asahi Shimbun*), Japanese newspapers expressed doubts about the prospects for *Tora! Tora! Tora!*, citing the previous year's postponement of *The Runaway Train* that had ended in cancellation. The prevalent view held Kurosawa responsible for the earlier postponement as well as this one.

It appears, however, that Fox took the initiative on this postponement, with Kurosawa Productions not having been involved in the decision. For Kurosawa, who was exhausted to the point of collapse with preparation problems, the Fox proposal for a delay was a stroke of luck. He quickly notified Fox of his acceptance and thus had managed to avoid repeating the nightmare of *The Runaway Train*.

The claim of inadequate preparation time notwithstanding, speculation in Japan held that something must have occurred on the American side. Among the rumors, one that seemed plausible was that the intensifying Vietnam War caused the Department of Defense to withhold permission to use Pearl Harbor for filming until the fall of 1968 or later. Tetsu Aoyagi noted this in private explanations to journalists and it was generally accepted among insiders in the Japanese movie industry. The source of this "most plausible" explanation was Williams, and Aoyagi accepted it.

A Skeleton in the Closet

More than Defense Department reluctance, the key to postponing *Tora! Tora! Tora!* production was a reason Fox was not willing to make public. Twentieth Century-Fox had financial problems. The production division had bled red ink from 1964 through 1967. In 1964, Fox released twelve feature films, with nine ending in the red and only three in the black. Of the seventeen features in 1965, eleven were in the red and six in the black. Fox had a record-breaking hit that year with *The Sound of Music* but the movie division lost money. In 1966 nineteen features were released, with eleven in the red and eight in the black. Williams was executive producer of *The Blue Max*, which made money, and Richard

Fleischer was director of *Fantastic Voyage*, which did not. The year 1967 saw eighteen Fox features released, with twelve in the red and six in the black. Fleischer directed the production of the adventure musical *Doctor Dolittle*, which generated record-breaking losses by making it only half-way to the breakeven point.

With the movie production division at Fox struggling under these losses, deciding priorities for new projects was a heavy responsibility. Richard Zanuck was the executive overseeing the production of *Tora! Tora! Tora!* He made the difficult decision to delay the project. From the start, Zanuck Junior had been unenthusiastic about this movie. He felt *The Longest Day* had been a hit because it was the record of a victory, even if tenuous. The Pearl Harbor story was a record of America's defeat, the greatest in American naval history. As such, he thought, it was just not going to be a hit and that was sufficient justification for pushing back the start of production. Fox executives set July 1, 1968, as the deadline for deciding whether to restart *Tora! Tora! Tora!* production. Darryl F. Zanuck reluctantly gave his consent to the proposed postponement .

Hardships Bring New Strength

Later, Williams said in an interview that the time he began to trust Kurosawa and to reach some compromises was, ironically, during the time of greatest uncertainty, the six months when everything was in limbo. Both Kurosawa and Williams began this trying time with doubt and suspicion but emerged with each having learned to trust the other.

Kurosawa was guaranteed a large retainer so he had almost nothing to lose financially. In his shadow were freelance people who had been invited to work on the movie, but Kurosawa apparently did not feel responsible for what happened to them. Williams, on the other hand, was hard pressed to deal with problems arising from the postponement. He did not worry about Fox's staff but had to cut outside people who had been hired by contract. This included laying off screenwriter Larry Forrester, with whom he had been working for a year and a half.

STARTING OVER

The layoff that hurt the most, however, was that of Williams's friend, veteran pilot Jack Canary. The retired military pilot handled aircraft procurement and pilot training and had become Williams's right-hand man. He would be hard to replace. Williams explained the reason for the layoffs and promised to call Canary back to work as soon as things were ready. Another headache was negotiating with the armed forces that earlier had committed themselves to provide materials and facilities. To keep ships available until a decision to restart production, he agreed with the Navy to pay mooring fees and periodic inspection costs for the retired destroyers and submarines the Navy had promised to provide.

There was, however, some light during those dark days. Williams was encouraged to move forward by Darryl Zanuck's promise of total backing. At this point Zanuck showed his intention to ensure that *Tora! Tora! Tora!* would indeed be made. In addition, he indicated he would take responsibility for the work that remained to complete the screenplay. As a first step, Zanuck told Williams that he wanted to visit Japan and to speak directly with Kurosawa. Thinking that such a meeting could cause a real breakthrough for the project, Williams hurried to set it up.

Zanuck had confidence in his ability to discern the good and bad aspects of a screenplay, as he was an accomplished screenwriter. After being hired as a writer by Warner Bros., he wrote nearly twenty scripts each year. The screenplays of the popular *Rin Tin Tin* silent movies were written by Zanuck. In World War I, an injured German shepherd dog left in a trench by German troops was saved by a young American soldier, which was the basis for the *Rin Tin Tin* adventures that enthralled fans around the world. As an experienced scenarist, Zanuck evidently saw the completion of the screenplay as critical for *Tora! Tora! Tora!* and therefore sought to take command himself.

The Big Boss Comes to Tokyo

Even under the current circumstances, however, it was rare for the president of a major Hollywood studio to take it upon himself to visit the president of an independent production company in a foreign country.

ALL THE EMPEROR'S MEN

Left to right: Darryl F. Zanuck, Akira Kurosawa, Elmo Williams, Tetsu Aoyagi
At the Imperial Hotel suite in Tokyo; January 1968 (Photo courtesy of Elmo Williams)

Zanuck knew that his presence in Japan would put pressure on those concerned, as it would be unseemly for him to return with nothing to show for the trip. On December 28, 1967, Zanuck arrived at Haneda Airport to be greeted by Leon Feldum, manager of Fox's Far East operations, and Williams, who had arrived the previous day. Zanuck was known for his love of travel, both business and pleasure, but this was his first visit to Japan.

Williams and Aoyagi saw the Tokyo meeting of Zanuck and Kurosawa as a "summit conference." *Sherpas* are famous as the mountain people who serve as guides for mountaineers climbing in the Himalayas. Serving as '*sherpas*' for the Zanuck-Kurosawa summit, Williams and Aoyagi engaged in blunt negotiations to ensure that agreement could be reached. Each day they reported the results to their respective bosses to get approval and iron out problems. The actual summit to approve the final results was held just after the New Year's holidays in January 1968. The venue was Zanuck's hotel suite, the Imperial Suite at the Imperial Hotel. Williams and Aoyagi were there as note takers.

Handwritten on legal-size paper, Williams's notes on points made

STARTING OVER

by Zanuck have been preserved. Zanuck told Kurosawa he was aware, through Williams, of the details concerning various points so he would confine that day's talk to generalities. He explained at length his view that they should consider the reasons *The Longest Day* had been a global hit, take the lessons learned from the film and make good use of them in *Tora! Tora! Tora!* The film should be historically accurate, but to keep the story from becoming too stiff and formal, Zanuck said, he wanted to include humorous episodes and human touches. He pointed to specific episodes from *The Longest Day,* emphasizing the degree to which they entertained the audience while telling an accurate story. This opening statement went on for some time. Unfortunately, Williams's memo does not record Kurosawa's response, but Zanuck sent a telex message to his son Richard on January 11:

WE HAD WONDERFUL AND LENGTHY CONFERENCE WITH KUROSAWA AND NOW WE ALL SEE EYE TO EYE ON EACH EPISODE AND WE HAVE NOW SENSATIONAL CLIMAX.
ELMO IS FOLLOWING UP ON TECHNICAL DETAILS WITH KUROSAWA AND WE ARE NOW ALL CON-VINCED "TORA" CAN BE MADE TECHNICALLY PER-FECT BY TRICKS ELMO USED IN "MAGNIFICENT MEN" AND "BLUE MAX" PLUS OTHER DEVICES WHICH ABBOTT AND ELMO HAVE DEVISED AND KUROSAWA AGREED WITH ALL OF THEM.
HAVE APPROVED ELMO TO LEAVE IMMEDIATELY TO GO TO STUDIO TO COMBINE THE THREE VER-SIONS OF THE SCRIPT WE NOW HAVE AGREED UPON AND THEN TO GO TO HONOLULU WITH SKETCH ARTIST TO WORK ON PRODUCTION PLAN FOR TRICK EFFECTS. OF COURSE WE CANNOT ESTIMATE COST UNTIL NEW SCRIPT COMPLETED AND TECHNICAL ELEMENTS SOLVED.
WE HAVE EVEN TALKED CASTING WITH KUROSAWA

AND WE WILL PROBABLY NEXT MEET WITH HIM IN
EITHER HONOLULU OR AT HOLLYWOOD STUDIO.
WHAT WE ACTUALLY HAVE DONE TO SCRIPT IS TO
FOLLOW "LONGEST DAY" FORMULA AND INTRODUCE
NEW ELEMENTS INCLUDING CERTAIN LIMITED
AMOUNT OF HUMAN INTEREST COMEDY BUT ALSO
EMPHASIZING THE BACKSTAGE DIPLOMACY AND
POLITICAL MANEUVERS WHICH WENT ON RIGHT UP
TO THE MOMENT OF PEARL HARBOR ATTACK AND
THESE ELEMENTS ARE ALL AUTHENTIC.

As spokesman for Kurosawa Productions, Aoyagi explained to the Japanese media that the *Tora! Tora! Tora!* screenplay would be reworked along Kurosawa's original story line. They would revisit the draft screenplay of May 1967 in which Kurosawa developed his concept of the film. They would respect Kurosawa's intent to portray "the tragic way in which war wastes the energy of honorable human beings" and present "Isoroku Yamamoto as the main character in this tragedy." The latter part of the movie, from the assembly of the attack force in Hitokappu Bay in the Kuriles, then under Japanese control, to the battle itself would be action centered and present the familiar story of the attack. According to Aoyagi, the overall emphasis would be on the earlier portion of the movie, which would faithfully portray the actions of Admiral Yamamoto, "indicating that wars customarily start with a surprise attack and clarifying the international situation at the time, including the American and British economic blockade that forced Japan down the path that led to the Pearl Harbor surprise attack."

The record thus suggests that Zanuck's visit to Japan led to great progress, with Fox and Kurosawa agreeing with respect to revisions of the screenplay. In production-related issues, Kurosawa Productions explained their plan to film the scene in which the ships of the attack force assembled in Hitokappu Bay on location in Hokkaido and their plan to construct full-scale replicas of the battleship *Nagato* and the aircraft carrier *Akagi* on the coast of Kyushu.

A major change after the Zanuck-Kurosawa summit was that the two leaders engaged in a direct dialogue, going over the heads of lieutenants Williams and Aoyagi. In February and March 1968, Zanuck and Kurosawa exchanged letters in which they touched upon essential aspects of the theme of *Tora! Tora! Tora!*

A dedicated reader, Zanuck read much about the Pearl Harbor attack and Yamamoto. Williams was impressed by the way Zanuck, despite his crowded schedule, managed to read many books and other documents and even commit to memory the details and dates of key events. On February 22, 1968, Zanuck sent the first long letter directly to Kurosawa giving his impressions of several books on Admiral Yamamoto. He wrote:

I now consider myself at least a "high school" authority on Yamamoto, particularly the Pearl Harbor incident.

I find Yamamoto one of the most interesting characters in history. Here was a fighting man who was actually a pacifist, a man who knew America, had gone to Harvard University and had spent several years in Washington as Naval Attache—yet in spite of his personal impression and knowledge of the United States, he was fundamentally one million percent Japanese, devoted to his Emperor and to his Nation. That is why I say that the role of Yamamoto is probably one of the most interesting in the history of drama, especially because of the "inner conflict" he certainly endured.

Admiral Kimmel is also a unique, dramatic and, at times, "frustrating" role. He knew the fleet should not be in Pearl Harbor and, like his predecessor—Richardson—he felt the fleet belonged in San Diego. Yet, as a "good sailor" he followed the order of the President.

Dramatically, Kimmel will never become quite as important as Yamamoto but in order to balance the drama of this film, we must be aware that these two contrasting characters are actually our "leading men."

Over a thousand words long, the letter talks about supporting roles and mentioned roles in the American sequences that Zanuck found particularly appealing: Lt. Commander Alvin D. Kramer of Navy intelligence and Lt. Colonel Rufus G. Bratton of Army intelligence, both of whom had pivotal roles in the code-breaking operation. In the Japanese sequences, Zanuck singled out Pearl Harbor attack leader Commander Mitsuo Fuchida, Commander Minoru Genda, and Captain Kameto 'Gandhi' Kuroshima as having particularly dramatic roles. In addition, he explained his policies about the characterization of the main roles in the movie, rethinking the compatibility of the Japanese and American sequences, and completing the rewrite of the final screenplay.

Kurosawa's reply in English was a formal note of only a dozen lines:

Dear Mr. Zanuck,
    I was extremely delighted and honored to have such a wonderful letter from you. Furthermore, I am deeply impressed by knowing how hard you have been studying and analyzing the materials in connection with the Pearl Harbor incident. I certainly agree with the points which were mentioned in your letter of February 22nd, 1968.
    I am very anxious to have the revised screenplay with your suggestions. As soon as I receive it, I will polish our part of the screenplay.
    Again, it was a great pleasure and honor to have met you in Tokyo last December and I am looking forward to seeing you again in the nearest future. All my associates join me in sending warmest regards to you, Mr. Zanuck Jr., Elmo and Mr. Fleischer.
                                    Sincerely yours,
                                    Akira Kurosawa

This reply was written by Tetsu Aoyagi, who was delegated by Kurosawa to handle all foreign communications. Kurosawa himself only signed his name to the note, which was sent February 28, 1968. The next night, Kurosawa wrote Aoyagi a handwritten note in black felt-tip pen; Kurosawa signed his name in Roman letters. Translated, it said:

The letter you sent to the elder Zanuck yesterday was a not-at-all satisfactory load of platitudes. You must do a better job of communicating my thinking. To be specific, it is necessary to delve more deeply into the *Tora! Tora! Tora!* theme, the contrast between Yamamoto and Kimmel, and the mindset of this tragedy.

Yamamoto's way of life was tragic, but he lived 100 percent! Kimmel, on the other hand, only lived 10 percent and that, in itself, was a tragedy!

I think that these organization and communication differences that existed between Japan and America are the tragedy of the Pearl Harbor story.

I think the only way to go about making this movie is to treat Yamamoto and Kimmel as the stars and portray them in a balanced manner.

This century's leadership style of politicians treating career military men as cards in a deck is a real problem.

Here we find the tragedy of our world!

Both the emperor and president are jokers in the deck, and being all-powerful they themselves do not act. Our century has been constructed on top of this kind of organization and these kinds of human limitations! That this strange and unacceptable state of affairs is determining what happens in our world is something that should make us very afraid! And would it not be Kimmel who had the most visceral experience of this reality? From this perspective, *Tora! Tora! Tora!* must be a scary, scary, scary story.

The D-Day Normandy invasion was without a doubt an

extraordinarily difficult undertaking, but I see it as being a single monumental show directed by Ike.

The same kind of thing cannot be said about Operation Pearl Harbor.

This was a tragedy for both Japan and America. It was not a show, it was a tragedy! I want Zanuck to understand this. Until people understand it, the Vietnam idiocy will continue! (President) Johnson is doing this because he wants to look good strutting around in a military uniform! This stupid, stupid feeling is playing havoc with the world!

It may not be necessary to go this far when talking to Zanuck, but if we do not act with total determination, "Tiger! Tiger! Tiger!" is going to end up as "Kitty! Kitty! Kitty!"

If you are going to act, act decisively! Do what needs to be done!

I may be a little drunk, but I speak the truth. The end!

Kurosawa admitted to being "a little drunk" and some of his points were not clear but he went directly to the point that he wanted Zanuck to understand his concept that *Tora! Tora! Tora!* was a "tragedy" rather than a "show." Kurosawa seemed irritated because the letter in English was formal and did not convey his true intentions and passion. A reading of the records of that period shows that Zanuck wrote Kurosawa letters that expressed his thoughts and feelings in a free, open, and magnanimous way. Kurosawa always seemed frustrated at not being able to express to Zanuck his inner thoughts and feelings. This problem notwithstanding, a new sense of trust and respect gradually formed between Zanuck and Kurosawa.

Story Doctor

On March 22, 1968, the next version of the *Tora! Tora! Tora!* screenplay, dubbed the "shooting script," was completed. The printed copy has

716 scenes, which compared with the screenplay dated September 20, 1967, showed that the scene count had been cut by forty percent. Screen time had been slimmed to a little over the three-hours Fox specified. A detail worth noting in this version is that Fox had adopted Kurosawa's opening scene, the traditional ceremony in 1939 when Admiral Yamamoto arrived to take his post as Commander-in-Chief of the Combined Fleet.

Halfway through this screenplay, the large clock on Aloha Tower in Honolulu chimes eleven o'clock on Saturday night December 6, 1941. Then there is a fade-out to intermission. At this point, the flagship *Akagi* and her task force were pushing through fierce winds, rough waves, and pitch dark in the north Pacific, getting closer to the sleeping island of Oahu. After a fifteen-minute intermission, the fade-in returns to the Aloha Tower clock, which now chimes twelve midnight, the start of Sunday, December 7, 1941. Hawaii rested peacefully.

After the victorious Pearl Harbor attack, the news sparked excitement among some Japanese, dread among others who noted that Japan had already been at war in China for four years. The face of the man who commanded the forces that executed the Pearl Harbor attack, Admiral Yamamoto, is shown with a gloomy expression presaging the dark fate that awaited his nation. This ending is identical to that of Kurosawa's draft screenplay.

Darryl Zanuck and Williams spent a week adding finishing touches to the script. On the title page is a note indicating that it was prepared based on discussions in New York with President Darryl F. Zanuck. Below that are the date March 22, 1968, and the name Elmo Williams. In a letter dated March 13, Zanuck told Kurosawa that Fox had moved a considerable distance towards Kurosawa's concept when they made their final adjustments to the manuscript. In the president's office at Fox headquarters in New York, Zanuck dictated a letter to Kurosawa while Williams was present. In that letter, about 1,200 words long, was this final paragraph.

The more I read and study the script the more excited I

ALL THE EMPEROR'S MEN

become about the potentialities for a great critical success and a great box-office attraction on a worldwide scale. It is something that we all will be proud to be associated with. In my last letter I mentioned that there were two stars in the picture, Yamamoto and Admiral Kimmel. In the revisions we have made to date there is only one actual star in the film and that is Yamamoto. Stark, Halsey, Short, Kimmel, Kramer, Bratton, etc., remain very important roles but none of them are in the same star category with Yamamoto. This was not done deliberately but in our development of characterizations it just turned out that way.

The writer credits on the screenplay include Akira Kurosawa, Hideo Oguni, and Ryuzo Kikushima for the Japanese sequences, and for the American sequences Larry Forrester plus Mitchell Lindemann, a name appearing for the first time. Lindemann appeared in the writer credits of three more manuscripts: a revised screenplay on May 29, another revised script on July 23 and still another revised screenplay on December 3. Lindemann, however, does not appear in the screen credits of *Tora! Tora! Tora!* released in September 1970. The person who used this pen name was a "story doctor," a skilled craftsman who specialized in rewriting but who normally operated behind the scenes. On instructions from Zanuck and Williams, Lindemann played an unsung role in the restructuring of the screenplay.

Beverly Hills Summit

On May 27, Zanuck and Kurosawa met in Beverly Hills, California, for their second "summit meeting." In a densely forested section of the spacious grounds of an ultra-high-class hotel was a stylish structure built to resemble a mountain cottage. Zanuck was staying there with his young lover, Geneviève Gilles. Wearing large black-rimmed sunglasses and with his trademark cigar in his mouth, Zanuck was alone when Kurosawa arrived. Zanuck's appearance was casual: a *batik* robe worn over pajamas and slippers. He appeared to be resting after having weathered the biggest ordeal of his business year, the Fox shareholders meeting the previous week.

The original plan had called for Williams and Richard Fleischer to be present, but at Kurosawa's strong request it became instead a one-on-one conversation with Zanuck as they conversed through an interpreter (the author of this book).

Zanuck launched into talking about the screenplay. Speaking explicitly but at a leisurely pace, he indicated he really liked the March 22 screenplay but that it was still too long. An expert had figured that it was seven minutes over the three-hour limit, so additional cuts were needed. Zanuck said the portrayal of the political, diplomatic, and military realities before the attack generated more dramatic tension and would be better in the Japanese sequences than in the American sequences. Overall, more human touches and humor needed to be woven in so the audience would establish an emotional bond with the characters.

After making each point, Zanuck paused to allow the interpreter to finish before going on to the next point. Kurosawa listened in silence, occasionally nodding his head. When Zanuck asked Kurosawa whether he had any objections, Kurosawa said, "Overall, I understand your points very well. I would like to carefully consider the details to make good use of them. With regard to the length, since I always shoot after fully rehearsing, I shorten the time considerably as I am shooting. With this in mind, I would like to ask you to not worry too much about the length."

Zanuck asked Kurosawa to come again at ten o'clock the following morning, saying he wanted to read through the screenplay one more time. This additional meeting had not been included in the plan but Zanuck's tone made it sound like refusing would not be an option.

Kurosawa was surprised by the next day's meeting. Arriving at the appointed time, he found Zanuck again alone and his wet hair showed that he was just out of the shower. Looking haggard, Zanuck said he had not slept a wink, spending the entire night reviewing the screenplay. Zanuck, showing even greater determination and gravity than the previ-

ALL THE EMPEROR'S MEN

ous day, commented:

> There are of course practical considerations of economics
> and running time. But more important is a tight construc-
> tion and the ruthless elimination of all extraneous and
> irrelevant material. Our epic story should unfold with more
> clarity, added suspense and heightened drama woven with
> touches of human interest. We must contain this mammoth
> historical episode in a continuity which is clean and exciting
> from beginning to end. We have no use for any stereotyped
> scenes or something we've seen before.

Kurosawa listened, a serious expression on his face.

Next, Zanuck considered individual scenes, giving detailed views on
how they should be played and asking for Kurosawa's opinions. Among
the problems Zanuck addressed were two sequences that Williams had
described as Kurosawa's "pet scenes." They had been criticized as irrelevant by Williams and other Fox people who had read the script. One
was a comic-relief scene between two cooks aboard the aircraft carrier
Akagi on its way to Pearl Harbor. They talked about the International
Date Line, by which Japan is thirteen to nineteen hours ahead of the
United States. One cook wisecracks: "It's no use shelling the enemy on
the other side of the line…there's no way for today's shell to reach yesterday's enemy."

Zanuck bluntly dismissed the scene as "irrelevant" and said it should
be eliminated. Kurosawa immediately resisted and cited two reasons
why the scene should be retained. First, he said, the audience should
know why the Pearl Harbor attack took place on Sunday, December 7,
in U.S. history while the day is remembered as Monday, December 8,
by the Japanese. More importantly, he insisted the scene was based on
an old Japanese saying, "yesterday's enemies, today's friends," and this
saying went straight to the heart of the significance of *Tora! Tora! Tora!*
Zanuck did not offer a refutation but said he would think it over.

The other was a scene in which Admiral Yamamoto visited the Imperial Palace to receive an imperial order to send the fleet to war against the United States. Zanuck considered the scene relevant only to Japanese audiences. Kurosawa insisted on the significance of the scene that took place between a war-reluctant emperor and the admiral only five days before the Pearl Harbor attack. Zanuck said he particularly did not like the way the scene ended with Yamamoto and a chamberlain waiting in a hall alone. He knew they could never show the emperor on screen but he said the scene would look as if the meeting between the emperor and Yamamoto had been cut out.

After Kurosawa said he understood the point, Zanuck recommended that he use dramatic camera work. Zanuck hit upon the idea of the camera moving in for a big close-up of the stern face of Yamamoto while the audience heard the off-camera footsteps of someone, presumably the emperor. Kurosawa said that might work and promised to rewrite the scene.

This exhaustive consideration of details went on for nearly three hours. At the end, the two shook hands and Kurosawa said: "Leave it to me. I will do my best. I have no intention of staging a Pearl Harbor attack on Fox."

When this last comment was translated, Zanuck grinned, jokingly raising both arms, shrugging his shoulders, and looking up at the ceiling. For a moment, the cigar in his mouth pointed upward. After taking his leave, Kurosawa laughed about Zanuck's funny face framing his black sunglasses.

On the plane returning to Tokyo the next day, Kurosawa said to the author: "That Zanuck is a good guy. Straightforward." The Japanese expression translated as "straightforward" is *zukatto shite iru,* and was a distinctive Kurosawa expression of praise. Years later in the movie *Kagemusha (Shadow Warriors),* the same expression appears in dialogue that can be translated: "The late Lord Shingen was straightforward. He stepped straight into the hearts of others." Another comment by Kurosawa was, "Just as you would expect, he really knows movies. In the way Darryl thinks about filming scenes and transitions, I sense the touch of John Ford." Zanuck produced many famous Ford pictures and was deeply involved in the editing of those films.

After returning from Hollywood, Kurosawa suffered, perhaps brought on by fatigue, a recurrence of a long-time problem with the veins in the back of his neck and was admitted to the Sanno Hospital for a week. Kurosawa Productions suppressed public mention of the hospitalization. Just after his release, Kurosawa sent a telegram to Zanuck:

DEAR MR ZANUCK:
MOST DELIGHTED TO KNOW THAT YOU FEEL
EXACTLY SAME AS I DO REGARDING LATEST SCRIPT
REFRESHED AT MEETINGS WITH YOU STOP CANNOT
THANK YOU ENOUGH FOR FASCINATING COMMENTS
AND MOST DEEPLY IMPRESSED BY YOUR YOUTHFUL
LIMITLESS ENTHUSIASM AND ENERGY FOR MOTION
PICTURE STOP AGAIN I AM MOST ENTHUSIASTIC AND
HONORED TO WORK WITH YOU TO MAKE IMMORTAL
PICTURE STOP MY DEEP GRATITUDE AND RESPECT-
FUL REGARDS
AKIRA KUROSAWA

This telegram was written by Aoyagi but, while it does contain flattery, it reflected the feelings of Kurosawa.

In late June, Kurosawa Productions received a screenplay reworked by Zanuck. On the title page is a printed note: "This script was re-edited and finalized in conferences in Beverly Hills May 27 and 28, 1968, attended by Mr. Darryl F. Zanuck and Mr. Akira Kurosawa." Compared to the screenplay of March 22, several American scenes had been deleted but nothing had been cut from the Japanese sequences. Even the Japanese scenes that Zanuck asked Kurosawa about cutting were still there.

Notification of Fox's decision to restart production of *Tora! Tora! Tora!* arrived at Kurosawa Productions on June 28, a few days after the revised screenplay had been delivered. After notifying Kurosawa, Aoyagi sent a short telegram to Williams:

STARTING OVER

RECEIVED YOUR CABLE TO CLIMB MOUNT NIITAKA
STOP WE GO ON TETSU

Mount Niitaka is the Japanese name for Mount Yu Shan, the highest peak in Taiwan, which was under Japan's colonial rule from 1895 to 1945. "Climb Mount Niitaka 1208" was the top-secret message that ordered the Imperial Japanese Navy to strike Pearl Harbor on December 8 (Japan Time).

ALL THE EMPEROR'S MEN

PHANTOM FLEET

Storyboards

An essential facet of movie-making is image transmission. The image in the writer's mind becomes a screenplay that generates images in the minds of the producer, director, production staff, and eventually images on the screen. In this process, graphics often transmit more information than text and can be effective in communicating emotional images. That's where storyboards come in.

The Japanese term for the storyboard is *e-konte*, which translates as 'picture continuity,' meaning a sequence achieved through pictures. The *e-konte* is used in Japan as a graphic organizer—a series of illustrations displayed in sequence to visualize a motion picture, animation, motion graphic, or interactive website. These illustrations guide the production staff—the actor's size and movements, the position in which the actor enters or exits, and whether the camera is fixed or moving. The storyboard is an integral part of visual production in Japan and elsewhere.

It is not clear when Kurosawa began making sketches and showing them to his staff before shooting. Eventually he went from occasionally using sketches to always using them and his drawings evolved into information-rich, colorful storyboards. In an interview with director Nagisa Oshima, Kurosawa explained: "I want to communicate my images to the staff, that's all. It is enough if they just grasp the feeling. I am not an articulate person so I cannot skillfully say it in words. It is better for me, and easier for the staff to understand, if I just show them the storyboards and say 'Like this.'" He added: "When I draw storyboards, I think about many different things. I cannot create a picture of a scene without considering a wide range of elements in concrete detail, such as the setting at the site, the state of mind and feelings of the people there, their movements, the camera angles for capturing those movements, the light, and the costumes and props. Actually, it might be more accurate to say that I draw the storyboards to think about such things. In this way, I assemble, fill in, and get a firm grip on the image of each scene in the movie so that I can see it clearly."

Kurosawa said he considered the sketches to be practical tools and he was not trying to draw skillfully. Rather, he said, "After finishing the day's shooting and going back to the hotel, there is a period of about an hour and a half before dinner. While everyone else uses that time to relax, I quickly sketch out pictures for the next day's shoot."

Kurosawa's storyboards soon became not only movie-making tools but fine art. In the latter half of the 1980s, appreciation of Kurosawa's art had grown with exhibitions and the publication of collections of his images. They were exhibited in New York in the 1990s, and since 2004 the Akira Kurosawa Storyboards Exhibition has toured Tokyo and six other cities in Japan; Beverly Hills, USA; Paris, France; Istanbul, Turkey; São Paulo, Brazil; and in Bilbao, Spain in January 2011. Moreover, picture books included superb images from the movies *Kagemusha, Ran,* and *Yume (Dreams).*

At the opening of the 2004 Akira Kurosawa Storyboards Exhibition in Tokyo, his son, Hisao, explained: "First, my father was a painter; and secondly, he was a film director… He loved painting so much all his life." Prior to becoming an assistant director at the age of twenty-six, Kurosawa studied painting in hopes making a name for himself as a painter. Kurosawa wrote in a book of pictures from the movie *Ran*: "Before entering the movie world, I intended to become a painter. Through a strange turn of Fortune's wheel, however, I set out on the path to becoming a movie director instead. To leave the painting part of my life behind, when I started in movies I burned all the pictures I had drawn or painted up till then. For a long time I did absolutely no painting or drawing, but once I became a director, I began to sometimes make rough sketches so that the staff would understand the images I had drawn in my head."

ALL THE EMPEROR'S MEN

For the production of *Tora! Tora! Tora!*, Kurosawa drew more than two hundred storyboards, some in full color, when he secluded himself at his vacation house in Gotemba at the foot of Mount Fuji. The whereabouts of those storyboards was unknown for thirty years after his removal as director and it was generally thought they had been lost. In 2000, two years after Kurosawa's death, however, it turned out that many of those originals had been held by Yoshiro Muraki, a film art director who had worked with Kurosawa on *Tora! Tora! Tora!* Some were published in 2001. Then, in 2002, the Margaret Herrick Library of the Academy of Motion Picture Arts and Sciences (AMPAS) in Los Angeles was found to have held 160 storyboards that Kurosawa had drawn for *Tora! Tora! Tora!*

These storyboards show workmanship worthy of someone who once intended to be a professional artist. They all show a dynamic use of color and evince a sense of the excitement and emotion that Kurosawa must have felt at making the first color film of his career. All of Kurosawa's 23 films prior to *Tora! Tora! Tora!* were in monochrome.

The *Tora! Tora! Tora!* storyboards were mostly drawn on small sheets of paper, the unlined stationery imprinted with the letterhead of the Tokyo Prince Hotel, where Kurosawa Productions had its office. That was the stationery furnished to hotel guests. Many Americans who have seen them have shaken their heads in disbelief that such wonderful storyboards had been drawn on such humble stationery. The sheets were turned sideways and a line was drawn to create a frame of the same 5:2 proportion as a Panavision screen. The frames are filled with sketched line and pastel drawings. In 1968, Kurosawa's storyboards were sent to Fox, where they impressed Williams and his professional artists.

While Kurosawa was drawing storyboards at his mountain villa in Gotemba, at least four other people were there: cameraman Takao Saito, art director Yoshiro Muraki, second-unit director Junya Sato, and chief assistant director Yutaka Osawa. "A stay was at most around a week and I went maybe two times," Osawa said. Osawa described the scene: "A sheet of vinyl was laid across a large table and on top were models of all of the thirty or so ships of the Pearl Harbor task force. While pondering the best camera direction for shooting, Kurosawa drew storyboards from different angles. Even the art director's drawings were no match for Kurosawa's… Ideas were pitched one after another. Thinking that some mist would add to the atmosphere, I was told to go down into the town of Gotemba to buy some dry ice. Even now I can't forget the look of excitement on Kurosawa's face as he was rapidly sketching the view while we made clouds of mist from the dry ice waft over the models."

The time spent drawing those storyboards must have been a blissful moment for Kurosawa even though he said later he had been "coerced" into drawing them. Williams said it was not true that Fox requested Kurosawa to prepare *Tora! Tora! Tora!* storyboards himself. He thought the storyboards would be prepared by sketch artists hired by Kurosawa Productions.

Battleship Arizona *in the Bombsight*

For Americans, the symbol of the tragedy of Pearl Harbor is the battleship USS *Arizona*. She was sunk by an Imperial Japanese Navy dive bomber with the loss of 1177 American sailors and marines. To this day the ship lies on the bottom of Pearl Harbor, still leaking oil. The *Arizona* Memorial, built in 1962, is a long white bridge with a chapel on one end sitting directly above and across the ship. Viewed from above, the memorial and ship form a cross.

From the beginning, Kurosawa and Williams intended to portray the sinking of the *Arizona* realistically and accurately, based on authentic records. Fox invested much money to build in Hawaii a full-scale replica of the ship 600 feet long. A second-by-second shooting plan sought to capture in action the moment the superstructure of the warship collapsed in flames and black smoke. Kurosawa made extensive drawings of Japanese attack aircraft that were to be combined into the *Arizona* scene through special effects technology.

In the screenplay, a five-plane formation of the Japanese Navy's bombers attacked from an altitude of 10,000 feet. The three-man crew of the lead plane included pilot Akira Watanabe, bombardier Yanosuke Aso, and radioman Tadao Saotome. Aso's eye was glued to the bomb-sight and when he pulled the bomb release, the 1,760-pound armor-piercing shell fell to hit the *Arizona* on target. Piercing the forward deck where the armor was relatively thin, the bomb penetrated the powder magazine deep in the ship. The resulting explosion blew open the deck and the ship's hull in a huge eruption of flames and smoke. Tipping forward, the *Arizona* broke in two and quickly sank. The screenplay:

INT. WATANABE'S PLANE—DAY
The bombardier ASO is poised over his sight in the bomber as they make their run on Battleship Row. He holds the release button; pasted up in front of him is a blowup print of his target. He gives directions to the PILOT over the voice tube.

                    ASO
   More to left…a bit more…just a bit more
   Steady, steady…

BOMB-SIGHT SHOT
Ten thousand feet below, the *Arizona* is creeping into view, with the small repair ship Vestal moored outboard. Both vessels are partly obscured by dense black smoke.

The *Arizona* creeps toward the cross-hairs of the bombsight.

                    ASO'S VOICE (O.S.)
   Steady…

CLOSE ON ASO
His thumb presses the bomb release.

Bombs away!

BOMBERS

Finned bombs are falling simultaneously from the bombers behind Watanabe's plane.

FALLING BOMB

Aso's bomb—the armor-piercing shell with special fins attached—plummets down, whistling.

The first wave of the Japanese bomber attack comprised 49 aircraft organized into formations of five planes each, with only the lead plane having a bombsight. All five planes were to drop their bombs on the signal of the lead plane. This tactic was intended to cover the target so that at least one bomber would score a direct hit. Built by the Nakajima Aircraft Company, the Nakajima B5N bomber carried only one 1,760-pound armor-piercing bomb slung under its fuselage. This bomb was a modified version of the armor-piercing shells used by the main guns of *Nagato*-class battleships.

The bombsight was a Type-90, a domestically manufactured version of a German bombsight built by Goertz. The bombardier, who served as navigator and observer, sat in the second of the three seats. While looking through the bombsight, he called out course and altitude corrections to the pilot in the front seat so the plane would pass exactly over the target. Since rapport between pilot and bombardier was vital, they were kept together in training and assignments.

Once the plane was on course, the bombardier concentrated on timing the bomb release. The bombsight was calibrated with data on aircraft speed and release altitude. With a timer, the bombardier determined the instant to release the bomb. The falling bomb continued to move in the same direction of the plane, with the plane moving faster than the bomb's downward trajectory. Thus the bomb impact occurred moments after the plane had passed over the target.

Williams said Kurosawa's storyboards were both beautiful and useful as they carried much information for the pre-production work. Williams said Kurosawa's storyboards were particularly useful for special effects scenes when Fox placed orders for miniatures and other props. The sinking of the *Arizona* seen in the Twentieth Century-Fox version of the film completed in 1970 was based on those storyboards, which Fox owned.

Open Casting Call for "Isoroku Yamamoto"

"Age range: 42 to mid-fifties. Height: 5 feet 2 to 6 inches. Resemblance to Admiral Isoroku Yamamoto."

These qualifications were the only ones specified when Kurosawa issued a casting call for someone to play Admiral Yamamoto. Applicants needed no acting experience; Kurosawa wanted someone whose face was not known, because an established actor might cause audiences to identify him rather than Yamamoto. People could apply themselves or could recommend candidates.

After the selection of the successful candidate, the person who recommended him was to get one million yen (about $2,800 at the Y360 to $1 exchange rate then) as a reward. Applicants were asked to send a photograph and brief profile to Kurosawa Productions in Tokyo. This casting call was issued in early July 1968, just after the decision to restart the *Tora! Tora! Tora!* project, following a seven-month delay.

The reaction was swift. In ten days, 250 applications were received. Candidates who impressed Kurosawa, however, were in short supply. Casting for other roles proceeded in parallel. Kurosawa wanted performers who were authentic former navy men who would not be overwhelmed by ships and planes and other war machines. Thus most roles of the Imperial Navy's senior officers were to be filled by former military men. Kurosawa said he was looking for people who would, even when standing still, project an aura of dignity and the disciplined character of

Kurosawa Storyboards for *Tora! Tora! Tora!*

Courtesy of the Margaret Herrick Library, AMPAS in Los Angeles, California, USA.

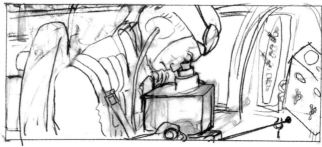

Storyboard#495   Watanabe's Plane / Bombardier Aso

Bombardier Aso keeping his eye to the bombsight. On the instrument panel is pasted a photograph of the Arizona. *Aso shouts to the pilot : "Two degrees to port ... Steady..."*

Storyboard#496-1   Lead aircraft and Fuchida aircraft

Fuchida aircraft crew watch over lead aircraft piloted by Watanabe. The crew watch the 1760-pound armor-piercing bomb carried by Watanabe's plane.

Storyboard#496-2   Watanabe's plane & the bomb : Fuchida's point of view

Fuchida and his crew look intently at the huge armor-piercing bomb under the fuselage of Watanabe's plane. The close-up of the bomb follows.

ALL THE EMPEROR'S MEN

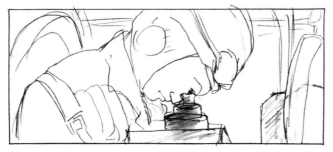

Storyboard#497   Bombardier close-up
Aso looking into the bombsight for the final run. This storyboard and the next two present the sequence of action up to the dropping of the bomb.

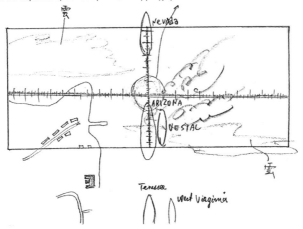

Storyboard#498   Bombsight view seen by bombardier
View through the bombsight partly obscured by clouds. Through the calibrated crosshairs and a bubble, the column of ships is seen below.

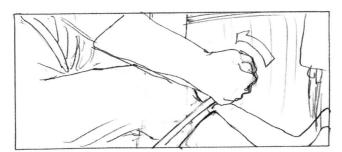

Storyboard#504   Instant of the bomb drop
Bombardier Aso shouts : "Bombs away!" Pressing the release button with his thumb, Aso pulls back hard on the lever.

professional warriors. Kurosawa's idea was to use professional actors in supporting roles.

Chief assistant director Yutaka Osawa went out daily to the Shirogane district of Tokyo to visit Suikosha, a fraternity of former Imperial Navy officers. Osawa gathered information and built a network of contacts there. He asked for assistance in gathering talent from several core members, primarily from the Imperial Naval Academy's class of 1945.

Next, came a banquet in August at a Chinese restaurant in the Akasaka district of Tokyo. Invited were sixty candidates, former navy personnel who were mostly naval academy graduates. Kurosawa attended along with his wife, Kiyo, Yutaka Osawa, and a photographer who took pictures of everyone, one by one. The event resembled a class reunion or meeting of a veterans association, with laughter filling the room as everyone ate, drank, and talked the evening away.

Casting moved forward as Kurosawa reviewed the photos and profiles collected at the banquet. For some candidates the decision on a role came immediately, for some it took more time, and some were left out. These men were at an age when they might have been expected to have heavy work and family responsibilities. Indeed, some were asked to play a role but declined. Others went through considerable trouble to arrange for time off work so they could appear.

The Big Fish That Got Away

The search for someone to take the key role of Admiral Yamamoto dragged on. The screening narrowed the field to several candidates and interviews were held, but Kurosawa could not make up his mind. Then one day he picked up a magazine in the Kurosawa Productions office. Flipping through the pages, his eyes lit on the photograph of a businessman who looked like the Admiral Yamamoto that Kurosawa envisioned.

This was Tokusaburo Kosaka, president of Shin-Etsu Chemical Co., a major Tokyo corporation. Born in Nagano Prefecture in 1916, Kosaka grew up in a family of politicians and business executives. His father,

ALL THE EMPEROR'S MEN

Junzo, had been a member of the national legislature and his brother, Zentaro, held several ministerial posts.

Early in his career, Kosaka was on track to become an elite naval officer. After graduating from Tokyo Imperial University (now Tokyo University), he enrolled in the Imperial Naval Paymasters' Academy. But he decided not to join the navy, going to work instead for *Asahi Shimbun,* one of Japan's top five newspapers. After ten years, he joined the family business and became a captain of industry.

The day after seeing Kosaka's picture, Kurosawa was unable to resist going to Kosaka's office to ask him to play Admiral Yamamoto. But Kosaka flatly refused. No matter how Kurosawa pleaded, no matter how many times he explained the historical significance of *Tora! Tora! Tora!,* the answer was still "no." All the same, talking with Kosaka only strengthened Kurosawa's conviction that this was the man. After imploring him to reconsider, Kurosawa went home.

A couple of days later a letter was delivered to Kurosawa. Brushed in graceful Japanese calligraphy, Kosaka politely and regretfully apologized that due to commitments at work there was no way he could appear in the movie. Kurosawa reread this letter again and again, sighing at the big fish he had failed to land. He could not have known then that his "big fish" would soon be a major player in the government. "He has a special aura," Kurosawa said. "This is no ordinary man."

In 1968, Kosaka was fifty-two years old and had decided to make the jump from business into politics. He was elected to the House of Representatives in December, 1969, and four years later joined the cabinet of Prime Minister Zenko Suzuki as Minister of Transportation.

An Isoroku Yamamoto from the School of Hard Knocks

In the fall of 1968, Kurosawa finally made the casting decision for the main role. The search had bogged down and just as Kurosawa was beginning to feel pressed for time, a friend of assistant Yoichi Matsue sent in a profile and photo of his company president because he thought the man resembled Yamamoto.

175

Kurosawa was immediately interested. This was Takeo Kagitani, president of Takachiho Koeki, an electronics trading firm. At their first meeting, Kurosawa explained his intentions in making the film and said, "We do not have anyone else; I really want you to appear in the film." Kagitani accepted.

Born in 1912, Kagitani was fifty-six and his age rang a bell in Kurosawa's mind in what he saw as another mysterious connection in numbers. Kurosawa noted that Kagitani was then the same age as Admiral Yamamoto had been when he planned the attack on Pearl Harbor. Moreover, Kurosawa once described Kagitani as "a man who had pissed blood." In Kurosawa's way of giving compliments, that meant someone who had endured hardships, driving himself to the limits of his mind and body.

A native of Hyogo Prefecture, in 1930 Kagitani graduated from Kansai University in Osaka with a degree in commerce and joined the Asano Bussan trading firm, where he worked for 12 years. After managing an ironworks and a public works contracting firm, in 1951 Kagitani formed a business alliance with the American computer manufacturer Burroughs (now Unisys). In rising from the manager of blue collar workers to the founder of a pioneering company in the computer age, Kagitani became a wealthy businessman.

Kurosawa decided to use Kagitani even without a camera test. Liking the look of Kagitani's face and eyes, Kurosawa relied on his intuition that this person fit the required image. But Kagitani turned out to have several drawbacks that caused problems for many weeks.

One was Kagitani's Kansai accent, Kansai being the region around Osaka in central Japan. Yamamoto had an accent from the Echigo region in northeastern Japan. This was a big difference that most Japanese would immediately recognize. Could anything be done to fix Kagitani's pronunciation and way of speaking?

Then, in Kurosawa's screenplay, Yamamoto had many faces; sometimes solemn and full of dignity, sometimes spirited and full of anger, sometimes playful and full of jest. Yamamoto's elusive personality would have been reflected in his manner of speaking. Could Kagitani portray the personality traits of Yamamoto?

Still another problem was the vagueness of Kagitani's military service record. In recruiting the cast through Suikosha and the Navy Club, a check of the personal background of each candidate was intrinsic, so service records would be known. The search for the character Yamamoto, however, was handled by Kurosawa and his assistant, Yoichi Matsue. In screening several hundred applications, divided about half and half between people applying for themselves and people being recommended by others, it was impossible to check the profile data thoroughly.

The person who recommended Kagitani may have claimed he had been in the navy, or Kurosawa and Matsue may have jumped to that conclusion. It turned out, however, that Kagitani was not an alumnus of the Imperial Japanese Naval Academy. His name was not listed on the rosters of people who had attended the academy and, according to official records, Kagitani had been enrolled at Kansai University at the time. In 1932, Kagitani would have undergone a physical examination for possible conscription because it was a national duty. But less than twenty percent received draft notices, called *akagami* (red postcards), for induction so it is possible that Kagitani was spared military service altogether.

After the announcement of the cast for *Tora! Tora! Tora!*, Kurosawa Productions was secretive about Kagitani's background and refused media requests to photograph and interview him. Newspaper reports on Kagitani's service record were vague and confusing. One article said he was a sailor first class, another that he was a private first class in the infantry. The former navy men in the cast thought Kagitani had been in the army. After the start of filming, the navy veterans got together for dinner and drinking almost every night at their Kyoto lodgings but Kagitani never put in an appearance.

At Fox were strong misgivings about Kurosawa's plan to use amateur actors. Williams's opposition was particularly strong. The plan was approved, however, because Darryl Zanuck decided that, with Kurosawa being so stubborn, they might as well see what he could do.

Commanding Presence

In Tokyo on November 26, 1968, Kurosawa was visibly tense. He wore an understated dark suit and, unusual for him, had on untinted glasses rather than sunglasses. His cheeks were flushed and his normally calm and amiable eyes were piercing and grim.

Darryl Zanuck, on the other hand, was relaxed and enjoying himself. He wore the military attire given him by the American Legion as an award for *The Longest Day*. It included a white shirt, black tie, black pants, and a white jacket with epaulettes. On the left breast were five decorations. As always, he wore dark sunglasses with thick black frames. His mustache was carefully trimmed and his face was wreathed in a relaxed, bright smile.

Elmo Williams was, as usual, quiet. His benign smile never wavering, he had the appearance of someone looking forward to being a spectator at the soon-to-begin Kurosawa show, a theater piece performed by two big bosses of Japanese and American cinema.

At two o'clock in the afternoon, lined up in a hotel banquet room were the Commander-in-Chief of the Combined Fleet, Admiral Yamamoto, and thirty-seven senior officers of the Imperial Japanese Navy at the outbreak of war between Japan and the United States. With the filming of *Tora! Tora! Tora!* scheduled to start in a week, the principal members of the Japanese cast were being presented to a hundred media people from inside and outside Japan.

Those cast as senior officers of the Imperial Navy wore navy-blue uniforms, regulation caps, and white gloves. They wore rank insignia on their collars and medals on their chests. Staff officers wore aiguillettes, the ornamental cords that indicated their duties. Everyone looked tense as they sat without the slightest stirring. Facing a battery of cameras, no one blinked even as the flashes went off.

Of the thirty-seven members of the cast, only two were professional actors: Tsutomu Yamazaki as Commander Minoru Genda and Susumu Fujita as Vice-Admiral Gun'ichi Mikawa. (Eijiro Tono, playing Vice-Admiral Chuichi Nagumo, was absent.) Everyone else was an amateur

ALL THE EMPEROR'S MEN

Darryl Zanuck and Akira Kurosawa appearing together at the press conference in the Hotel Okura in Tokyo when the Japanese cast was announced on November 26, 1968. In the background are 'Kurosawa Fleet' commanders. (Photo courtesy of Tokyo Shimbun*)*

Kurosawa Fleet commanders: Front row from left: Commander Minoru Genda (Tsutomu Yamazaki), Rear-Admiral Takijiro Onishi (Shigeru Ando), Admiral Isoroku Yamamoto (Takeo Kagitani), Rear-Admiral Matome Ugaki (Yoshio Miwa), Vice-Admiral Gun'ichi Mikawa (Susumu Fujita). (Photo courtesy of Sokichi Matsumoto)

PHANTOM FLEET

without acting experience. With the exception of Kagitani, most of the new "actors" were alumni of the Imperial Japanese Naval Academy who had become company presidents or senior executives. Everyone looked at home sitting up straight in his navy uniform. Their commanding figures were intended to reflect the dignity of eminent actors.

At the front of the room was a narrow table covered with a white cloth. Darryl Zanuck sat in the center with Akira Kurosawa to his left and Elmo Williams to his right. The cast sat in three rows facing the front table or at inward-facing rows to the left and right of the three movie executives. Each member of the cast stood up and saluted as he was introduced in Japanese, then would lower his hand and sit down after the introduction was repeated in English.

This continued one by one until the final member stood: Takeo Kagitani as Admiral Yamamoto. Once the barrage of camera flashes had abated, Kagitani sat down but Kurosawa motioned him to stand up again.

Holding a microphone, Kagitani spoke about how he had come to take this role. "Earlier this fall, I had a message that Director Kurosawa would like to meet with me. He told me about the difficult time he was having casting for the role of Admiral Isoroku Yamamoto for this movie and asked me to take the role. For no well-defined reason, I ended up accepting. Through this role, I hope to show many people throughout the world something of the anguish of Admiral Yamamoto, who intended to open the war between Japan and the United States with a surprise Pearl Harbor attack that would not be considered an illicit sneak attack, but who saw those intentions go unrealized."

Then Zanuck stood and said, "Among the American people, there is a great deal of interest in this movie. I think it is very significant that movie people from both the United States and Japan are working together to tell the Pearl Harbor story, and on a personal level I am proud to be able to work with Kurosawa."

Next, the guests were introduced and stood one by one to face the camera flashes. Participating as an advisor on military matters was Minoru Genda, the member of the House of Councilors, the upper

ALL THE EMPEROR'S MEN

house of the national Diet, who had been the planning officer for the attack on Pearl Harbor. Acting as aviation advisor was Kameo Sonokawa, who had been an aviation officer in the sea battle off of Malaya in Southeast Asia. As advisor on diplomacy and playing Foreign Minister Shigenori Togo was Kazushige Hirasawa, a media commentator on diplomacy who had been Japan's consul general in New York at the start of the war.

Everything proceeded in accord with the stage direction of Kurosawa. The unveiling of the unusual cast was successful. In the photograph taken of Kurosawa and the entire cast in the garden of the hotel, his expression is relaxed and he appears relieved. Zanuck and Williams also look satisfied. At that point, everyone seemed to think that all would go well.

Puppets Come to Life

It did not take long for an unforeseen incident to occur. Once the introduction of the cast had been completed, everyone moved to another room for a buffet. Freed from the tension, the cheerful cast proceeded to eat and drink heartily and to enjoy themselves in lively conversation. Crowds gathered around Zanuck, Takeo Kagitani (Yamamoto), Tsutomu Yamazaki (Genda), and Susumu Fujita (Mikawa), lining up to shake hands and have their pictures taken. When the real Minoru Genda and actor Tsutomu Yamazaki posed shaking hands at the request of a photographer, an even larger crowd formed.

Standing against the wall a little apart, Kurosawa watched intently, his face growing increasingly grim. He called producer Tetsu Aoyagi and told him: "They should not be forgetting their roles and ranks and behaving in such a sloppy and undisciplined manner. I want you to immediately stop the picture taking and remove the film from the cameras of the media people who have been snapping photos."

Not believing his ears, Aoyagi thought he must have misunderstood Kurosawa's whispered instructions. Moreover, he could see no way to carry out this order. After an exchange of words, Kurosawa angrily stalked from the room. No one else noticed so a major uproar was avoided.

In retrospect, earlier events foreshadowed the problem. On the previous day, perfectionist Kurosawa had summoned the cast to the office of Kurosawa Productions. Renting a large banquet room in the hotel for three hours, Kurosawa held a full-dress rehearsal of the upcoming ceremony. The cast put on their uniforms with all the accouterments and sat in their specified seats, with Kurosawa giving instructions. He had them practice the movements and timing, from standing when names were called to saluting and sitting down again. They were warned to keep their eyes open and not to blink, even when the camera flashes went off. Kurosawa told them: "When you are sitting, please keep your body stiff like an unmoving puppet. When the character's name is called, you awaken into your role. From that point onward, you should stay in that role. Understand?"

In the ceremony the next day, Kurosawa intended that each member of the cast be in character from the moment his character's name was called. This seemed too much to ask of amateurs not trained in acting. This miscalculation by Kurosawa exploded with a vengeance once filming started. The inability of amateur 'puppets' to become the assigned character seriously frustrated Kurosawa during the shoot and ultimately wrecked the initial stage of the filming.

Something else may have contributed to the irritation Kurosawa showed at the buffet, something to do with Takeo Kagitani as Isoroku Yamamoto. The commander-in-chief of the "Kurosawa Fleet" was the only amateur actor in the cast who did not have an Imperial Japanese Navy background. From the time the cast had been announced until that day, Kurosawa had refused to allow Kagitani to be interviewed. His nerves may have been on edge because he feared that media questions about the background of his main player would divest him of his mystique.

Neither producer Tetsu Aoyagi nor Chief Assistant Director Yutaka Osawa suspected this because they knew little about Kagitani beyond what they were told by Kurosawa and Matsue. More than thirty years

ALL THE EMPEROR'S MEN

later, Aoyagi and Osawa acknowledged that they still mistakenly thought that Kagitani was an alumnus of the Imperial Naval Academy. Williams said he had no reason to doubt that Kagitani was a navy veteran.

Full-scale Warship Replicas

On November 27, the day after the presentation of the cast, Kurosawa flew to the southwestern island of Kyushu to inspect the outdoor set, the full-sized replicas of the battleship *Nagato* and the aircraft carrier *Akagi*. After Kyushu, he planned to fly to Hokkaido in northern Japan to oversee the shoot of a refueling scene of the task force in rough seas. The shoot was to be done by second unit director Junya Sato. About the same time, Darryl Zanuck was scheduled to arrive in Kyoto because he wanted to be present at the start of filming by Kurosawa. Everything seemed be in order for the start of the photography of *Tora! Tora! Tora!*

In Kyushu, Kurosawa was pleased when he saw the monumental outdoor sets built on the scenic seashore facing an arm of the Japan Sea known as the Hibiki Sea, also called the Genkai Sea. The Ashiya shore is an expanse of white sand and green pines stretching east to west. The full-scale replica of the battleship *Nagato* was 164 feet tall and 734 feet long. Nearby was the replica of the front half of the aircraft carrier *Akagi*, which was 328 feet long.

The building of those outdoor sets had come only after a tug-of-war between Kurosawa and Twentieth Century-Fox. Kurosawa felt that the life-size sets were indispensable. So in September 1968 he requested the construction of the sets. Twentieth Century-Fox took a dim view of Kurosawa's request and Williams was reluctant to approve it.

The Americans were constructing a full-scale replica of the battleship *Arizona* on Ford Island, inside Pearl Harbor. Built by the Dillingham Corporation of Honolulu, the hull was 600 feet long with a superstructure 280 feet long and a tower 220 feet tall. This set was necessary for the movie's climatic scene, a huge explosion followed by the *Arizona* listing and sinking.

On the other hand, it seemed the *Nagato* and *Akagi* replicas would not be used for much more than filming the opening scene. Kurosawa did not explain the need for them and how he would have used them for filming. How he would have combined the miniature shots to create special effects in the final footage is unknown. The schedule allocated ten days to opening-scene filming and Kurosawa did not disclose even to Williams a detailed plan for what he intended.

Did this set justify spending $500,000? Williams was not sure it was worth it. If standard industry practices had been followed, the outdoor sets would have been discussed with the special effects and art directors, and after a detailed shooting plan had been drawn up, decisions would have been made. Then, because of the costs involved, the director would have discussed the scope of the sets with the producer to get his approval. None of these things had happened. Kurosawa had insisted that Fox approval should come before detailed planning started.

The Japanese production unit for *Tora! Tora! Tora!* had no special effects director as Kurosawa intended to handle this himself. It appears that Kurosawa or Kurosawa Productions privately discussed the special effects of *Tora! Tora! Tora!* with Eiji Tsuburaya, a top special effects director who had read a draft of the *Tora! Tora! Tora!* screenplay and praised it as riveting. Tsuburaya was a leader in the Japanese movie industry and had gained an international reputation for his *Godzilla* movies. Film critics say his special effects were comparable in film history to those of Stanley Kubrick's *2001: A Space Odyssey*. In Japan, his advice was considered essential for innovations, camera handling, model design, and miniatures.

Despite dissent from Williams, Darryl Zanuck gave the go sign again on the ground that if Kurosawa wanted it so much, they would have to gamble on his talent. The sums of money spent on replicas produced sighs among Japanese movie people since they could have produced four or five movies for the same amount of money.

The ships were built from the waterline up. Both the *Nagato* and *Akagi* were pointed towards the sea with hulls jutting out from the land. The Genkai Sea can be rough, and the ship foundations were built

ALL THE EMPEROR'S MEN

on soft sand so the hulls did not extend out enough to be washed by waves. Construction began with driving two thousand red pine posts, each about 30 feet long, into the sand as the foundation for assembling an iron framework to which plywood sheets were attached to form the hulls of the ships. For the *Akagi*, aircraft were to be lined up on deck for filming, so thick boards capable of carrying that weight were put in place. Painting was important in determining whether the replicas would impress viewers as magnificent "iron castles" afloat on the sea.

Kurosawa was pleased with the gigantic sets and they became the talk of the town. From close up the ships looked almost unbelievably large. Once a week on Saturday afternoons, the public was allowed to come take a look. Thousands of people came in an unending stream until dark.

On November 29, 1968, Elmo Williams sent Fox head of production Richard Zanuck a telex saying that *Tora! Tora! Tora!* preparation in Japan was complete and they were waiting for the filming to start on December 2. Zanuck sent back a telex:

DEAR ELMO:
AFTER ALL OF THE MONTHS OF FAITHFUL DEVOTION
AND HARD WORK "TORA TORA TORA" IS FINALLY
COMING TO LIFE STOP I KNOW WE WILL ALL BE
REWARDED BY A STUNNING CONTRIBUTION TO FILM
MAKING AND THE HISTORY OF OUR TIMES STOP BEST
OF LUCK AND GOOD WISHES DICK

From the beginning, Richard Zanuck had not been enthusiastic about this project and had clashed with his father over the cost. Williams had suffered from being caught between the father and son and so was gratified by those encouraging words. In his experience as a producer, each movie had a particular moment of revelation when he became convinced the project would succeed. For *Tora! Tora! Tora!*, that moment was when he read the telex from Richard Zanuck.

CHAPTER
8

COUNTDOWN TO
THE FALL

Timeline of a Fiasco

On Christmas Eve, 1968, in the ancient city of Kyoto, three weeks after the filming of *Tora! Tora! Tora!* had commenced, Twentieth Century-Fox dismissed Akira Kurosawa on grounds of ill health.

For decades since, rumors swirled through the movie communities in Japan and America. There was a scarcity of facts. Few records were available and people who should have known were tight-lipped about Kurosawa's illness and his 'strange' and 'erratic' behavior as reported in the scandal-hungry tabloids. Authentic records were long considered lost.

Today, verifiable evidence helps to determine what really happened. Twentieth Century-Fox kept memos that recorded the events leading up to Kurosawa's dismissal. Producer Elmo Williams compiled detailed reports on what transpired and sent them to Fox headquarters. Stanley Goldsmith, Fox's production supervisor in Japan, kept daily logs and sent other detailed reports to Fox headquarters describing incidents he had witnessed. From these American sources, coupled with credible records and eyewitness accounts from Japanese sources, a timeline of events at the Toei Kyoto Studios in December 1968 can be reconstructed.

In August 1968, four months before the start of filming for the Japanese sequences of *Tora! Tora! Tora!*, an English-language shooting schedule was delivered from Fox to Kurosawa Productions. It listed the shooting arrangements authorized by Fox based on the draft of a shooting plan put forward by Kurosawa Productions. After adjustments by

COUNTDOWN TO THE FALL

the American and Japanese producers, a shooting schedule was settled upon in November.

Filming in Japan was to begin in early December and would last for 130 days, or 18 weeks. Of those 130 days, nine were allocated for rehearsals and shooting preparations, eight for travel to locations, four for the New Year holidays, 82 for shooting, and one day off per week, which sometimes overlapped with travel.

Shooting was scheduled to start at Toei Kyoto Studios. Eighteen sets would be built on four stages, with shooting commencing on Monday, December 2, 1968. This would last until mid-January, with three days (including travel) on location in Hiroshima and the New Year holidays squeezed in between. From Saturday, January 18, 1969, there would be a shoot on the big open sets of the battleship *Nagato* and the carrier *Akagi* on the coast in Kyushu in southwestern Japan. This would last for a month. On Monday, February 20, the U.S. second unit would bring the footage they planned to shoot in Hawaii and carry out 'front projection' photography, which was a special effects technique for combining foreground performances with pre-filmed backgrounds. This composite photography was to be done at the World Trade Center building in Osaka. All was to be directed by Kurosawa. Additional location shoots in Hokkaido (for a refueling scene at sea), Tokyo (Imperial Palace and Navy Ministry), and Kagoshima (for a torpedo plane training scene) would be handled by the second unit director, Junya Sato. The Japanese shoot was to be wrapped up on March 24.

Filming during the first half of the schedule would not be affected by weather since all was to be shot indoors. But there would be only a limited time to shoot the 'Manning the Rails' ceremony and other outdoor scenes in Kyushu involving 600 extras because of the unpredictable weather. The 'front projection' special-effects photography in Osaka would be another major undertaking and intricate construction would take at least a month. Fox expected that the initial Kyoto shoot would be the easiest and would go smoothly. If the schedule was to run longer, that would happen in Kyushu or Osaka.

In reality, the schedule fell into disarray as soon as the Kyoto shoot began. Fox was quick to insist that Kurosawa was responsible for the confusion at the Toei Kyoto Studios. In his report to Twentieth Century-Fox headquarters, Goldsmith summarized the statistics: "The production record of Mr. Kurosawa is in twenty-three days of work he has been able to deliver only seven days of shooting, totaling 7-1/8 script pages which cover 18 scenes. During the period from December 2 to December 24, 1968, there were three company rest days."

At least that was the plan, put forth by people who couldn't or wouldn't recognize all of the unpredictable forces arrayed against it. Goldsmith said that during three weeks of the Kyoto shoot Kurosawa filmed only seven or eight minutes of usable footage. As Gordon W. Prange says, "The unexpected can happen and often does." What actually happened in Kyoto led to a tragic loss for the art of film that strangely reflects the story of great human tragedy that Kurosawa had wanted to tell.

The Big Boss Comes to Kyoto

On November 30, 1968, Darryl Zanuck, who was visiting Japan at the time with his young girlfriend, actress Geneviève Gilles, arrived in Kyoto. He had fielded press interviews in Osaka the day before, chatting in high spirits. That afternoon, showing no signs of fatigue, Zanuck met with Kurosawa in his suite at the Kyoto Hotel, where they discussed the final revisions of the screenplay for *Tora! Tora! Tora!* This meeting lasted for four hours and included Williams and Aoyagi. As usual, Zanuck rambled on as he gave his opinions in a booming voice, gesturing with animation.

Those who were there agreed that Kurosawa seemed tired, yet appeared to be in good spirits. Before arriving in Kyoto, he had visited Kyushu to inspect the life-sized *Nagato* and *Akagi* sets and had flown to Hokkaido to observe Junya Sato's second unit's operations. From the coast, they were shooting a refueling scene on the rough seas with a 500-mm telescopic lens and were buffeted by strong winds. In the middle of the filming, Kurosawa suddenly lost consciousness and collapsed. It

COUNTDOWN TO THE FALL

caused a commotion but the crew was ordered not to talk about it and it was kept secret.

In the morning, Williams and Goldsmith visited Stage 18, where rehearsals were to begin the next day, to ensure that everything would be ready. They noticed, however, that work on the sets had stopped. Surprised, they asked Aoyagi what had happened. He told them the builders were striking over a discrepancy in pay. The stage hands were under contract to Kurosawa Productions so Fox was not responsible for paying them. Williams and Goldsmith asked whether it would be possible to begin shooting even though the set walls had yet to be painted and wallpaper was not hung. Aoyagi answered that it would be all right and that the work would be completed on time. The two Americans left, unsatisfied.

Williams and Goldsmith arrived at Stage 18 at 9 A.M. for the shoot of a scene at the Japanese Embassy in Washington in which ambassadors Saburo Kurusu and Kichisaburo Nomura contemplate a top-secret telegram from Tokyo. Lighting and camera equipment had been brought in but the set was still incomplete.

Kurosawa arrived shortly after 9 A.M. and discovered wrinkles in the wallpaper that was still wet. He said he could not begin filming with the set in this state and demanded that the new wallpaper be hung at once. Eventually rehearsals were held in the costume room. No shoot took place.

Williams was frustrated because he could not show the set to Zanuck and sent him a message at his hotel saying Kurosawa wanted him to come the following day because preparations were not yet complete. He apologized for the delay.

At his hotel, Zanuck began to worry because trouble had begun on the first day of the shoot. He sent a telex to his son Richard in Hollywood saying the shoot might fall into confusion when Williams left Kyoto. He said Fox should bring in a production manager from California to oversee the Japanese operation. Meanwhile, Williams proposed to Darryl Zanuck that it might be best for them to go back to the United States and return to Japan later to visit the Kyushu shoot. The Kyoto shoot would have comparatively few problems and if trouble was to happen it would be at the shoot in Kyushu at the open sets. He suggested there was no point for them to stay in Kyoto waiting for the newly hung wallpaper to dry.

TUESDAY, DECEMBER 3 (DAY 2 OF SHOOTING):

When Williams arrived at the stage at 9 A.M., Goldsmith seemed unimpressed by the crew's slow preparations. Scheduled were three scenes at the Japanese Embassy in Washington. Although shooting was set to start at 9 A.M., the crew arrived just at that time and were beginning to set up. Aoyagi and the crew had to be told firmly that they must strictly abide by the schedule. Kurosawa had still not appeared by 10 A.M. and, when he did, he began rehearsals on the same scene he had worked on the day before.

Zanuck arrived at the studio at noon. Williams took him to his office, asked him to wait there until later in the afternoon, and stayed chatting with him. After lunch, they once again killed time in Williams's office but Zanuck could not suppress his irritation, so Williams asked Aoyagi to take them to the set at once. They received a message from Kurosawa asking them to come to the set in thirty minutes.

On the stage, Kurosawa welcomed Zanuck, Williams and Goldsmith. He sat them near the camera and, after some rounds of rehearsal, shot several takes with the camera rolling. After their visit was over, Zanuck and Williams were impressed by Kurosawa's spirit and ability and his meticulous style that saw him pay attention to even the minutest detail. Zanuck told Williams, "It's interesting that he's using a multicam setup (shooting a scene simultaneously with several cameras) on such a small set." Shooting continued until 8:45 P.M.

That night, Zanuck sent a telex to his son telling him that, after all, there would be no need to dispatch another production manager and to cancel the request he sent the night before.

Scheduled was another scene at the Japanese Embassy in Washington. Williams arrived again at 9 A.M. Perhaps because of his strong words the day before, the crew arrived on time and were intently preparing for the day's shoot. Kurosawa, however, had still not arrived. It was later discovered that he had been drinking the night before until well into the early morning and had taken sleeping pills. When he did turn up, he was irritable and yelled at the crew.

Zanuck had come to the studio to observe the shoot again that morning but waited in Williams's office for four hours. When his patience finally ran out at 2:30 P.M., Williams pressed Aoyagi to take them to the stage. After a while, Aoyagi received word that an accident had occurred: part of the lighting equipment had fallen from a catwalk, barely missing Kurosawa. He was not injured but was shaken. At 4 P.M., shooting was called off for the day. Zanuck gave up and returned to his hotel.

Zanuck and Williams watched the shoot on stage 18 all day. Both sensed that Kurosawa was back on track and would be all right if he kept to it. Kurosawa completed all five scenes at the Japanese Embassy in Washington scheduled for the day.

Zanuck and Williams had dinner together and Zanuck praised Kurosawa's directing methods and unique style. Williams surmised that Kurosawa might be nervous because Zanuck was looking over his shoulder and that it would perhaps be better if they left him alone. Williams would later regard this day as the only one when shooting went smoothly.

FRIDAY, DECEMBER 6 (DAY 5 OF SHOOTING):

Scheduled was the rehearsal of a scene in which Prime Minister Fumi-maro Konoe and Admiral Yamamoto discuss the prospects of the impending war with the United States. Kurosawa, who had had a sleepless night, came to the stage at 9 A.M. in an ugly mood.

During the rehearsal, Kurosawa noticed something wrong with Admiral Yamamoto's uniform. In particular, he saw that removing medals from the jacket left small holes in the white summer uniform. The spare uniform also had pin holes. Kurosawa flew into a rage, stopped the rehearsal, and expelled all the assistant directors from the stage to punish them for carelessness. The rehearsal was halted for the day.

On this day, Zanuck left Kyoto and began his journey home via Tokyo.

SATURDAY, DECEMBER 7 (DAY 6 OF SHOOTING):

An all-day rehearsal was conducted for the Konoe-Yamamoto scene carried over from the previous day. None of the assistant directors were present and nothing was filmed.

Goldsmith's daily log said filming was one day behind schedule. On this day, Williams left Kyoto for Tokyo, where he boarded a flight for Honolulu.

SUNDAY, DECEMBER 8 (DAY 7 OF SHOOTING):

In the morning, the Konoe-Yamamoto scene was rehearsed and shot. In the afternoon, rehearsals were held for another scene. None of the assistant directors were present. Goldsmith's daily log says the status is one day behind schedule, unchanged from the previous day.

MONDAY, DECEMBER 9 (DAY 8 OF SHOOTING):

Company day off. No call. But Kurosawa and the crew gave up their day off and one scene was shot during the morning. With Kurosawa's 'special pardon,' all the assistant directors were back on duty.

During the filming, Kurosawa raged at a camera assistant whose operation of the clapper board to assist in the synchronizing of picture and sound was deemed sloppy in timing. He rolled up his script and hit the assistant on the head, screaming, "You're fired!"

The scene was set at a naval hospital where the convalescent Vice Admiral Zengo Yoshida was in bed reading get-well letters from Yamamoto and others. Between shots, Kurosawa inspected props. He picked up a pile of the letters that had been left on Yoshida's bedside table and checked them one by one. When Kurosawa found a letter prop from a Toei Studio *yakuza* gangster film, his fury was out of control. Again he held the assistant directors responsible for their lack of discipline.

"All you assistant directors, line up. Spread your legs. Grit your teeth. Osawa, hit them," he yelled. To which chief assistant director Osawa replied, "I can't hit them, sir. It's my responsibility. Please hit me instead." Without saying a word, Kurosawa stormed off the stage and secluded himself in the staff room. Witnesses said Kurosawa was alone, crying. Later, Osawa was expelled from the crew for disobedience.

When shooting resumed in the afternoon, Kurosawa noticed something wrong elsewhere: the curtains on the naval hospital set were creased because they had just been purchased. Kurosawa rebuked the crew harshly, telling them, "I can't continue filming under such slack circumstances. This kind of thing never happened before in my life. Fix it right now." Shooting was canceled for the rest of the day.

Goldsmith's daily log said the filming was one day behind schedule, unchanged from the previous day.

TUESDAY, DECEMBER 10 (DAY 9 OF SHOOTING):

The company day off carried over from the previous day. The studio was visited by war-hero-turned-politician Minoru Genda, who was given a guided tour. On sets built to recreate Admiral Yamamoto's quarters, Genda pointed out: "The room's interior was not like this. It was spot-

ALL THE EMPEROR'S MEN

lessly clean and the brass rail was well polished, the walls were regularly repainted, and the paintwork had no drip marks." The crew had tried to give the set a well-used feel by dirtying it up, but this had backfired. Art director Yoshiro Muraki hastily began redoing the set.

Goldsmith's daily log said the project was one day behind schedule, unchanged from the previous day.

Wednesday, December 11 (day 10 of shooting):

Scheduled for the day's shoot was the scene of a luncheon held in the admiral's quarters aboard the battleship *Nagato* to send off Admiral Yamamoto's staff officer, Shigeru Fukudome, who had been reassigned to naval headquarters.

Preparations were complete and the cast and the staff were standing by on time at 9 A.M. But Kurosawa did not show up. The crew was forced to wait without knowing what was going on. Kurosawa had been discovered unconscious in bed by a chambermaid employed at the inn at 6 A.M. and had been admitted to Kyoto University Hospital, where he rested until evening. Kurosawa Productions hushed up the news. In his report, Goldsmith described Kurosawa's condition as a "nervous breakdown." His daily log said the project was now two days behind schedule.

Thursday, December 12 (day 11 of shooting):

Scheduled for filming was another scene in Yamamoto's quarters aboard ship. At 10 A.M., 22 actors and six extras were assembled and led onto the stage where they were told to stand by. Kurosawa failed to show up, as he was convalescing at his lodgings. Only lighting and camera rehearsals took place. The day's shoot was called off at 6:30 P.M. No explanation was given to the cast and the crew.

Goldsmith's daily log said the filming was now three days behind schedule. He was panicky, unable to control the confusion on the stage and the shooting delays. He made an urgent telephone call to Williams in Honolulu for help: "Kurosawa's behavior is abnormal and he isn't working well with the crew. Shooting hasn't progressed since December 9 and everything is going badly." Williams instructed Goldsmith to put his report in writing and send it to him.

After returning to the Pearl Harbor set in Hawaii, Williams was swamped with preparations for shooting the crucial battle scenes. But he continued to receive disturbing reports of troubles in Kyoto. He grew impatient and angry with Goldsmith for failing to keep things under control and his nerves wore thinner each day. The shoot in Kyoto should have been a cinch: everything was taking place on indoor sets where actors were required only to say their lines. Williams was angry with Goldsmith, Aoyagi, and most of all Kurosawa. He felt they should be resolving such trivial problems.

On this day, Williams sent a telex to Aoyagi at the Toei Kyoto Studio:

SINCE KUROSAWA APPARENTLY SHOOTING VERY
SIMPLE DIALOGUE SCENES WITH LIMITED NUM-
BER OF PEOPLE, AM CONCERNED AND SO IS STUDIO
BECAUSE FILMING TO DATE AVERAGES APPROX HALF
PAGE ONLY STOP PLEASE ADVISE WHAT THE PROB-
LEM IS AND LET ME KNOW WHAT I CAN DO TO HELP
ALSO PLEASE USE GOLDSMITH TO FULLEST IF YOU
ARE HAVING CONSTRUCTION OR OTHER PROBLEMS
WITH TOEI STUDIO STOP EVERYTHING HERE GOING
EXTREMELY WELL AND OUR WASHINGTON UNIT
IS PRODUCING MAGNIFICENT RESULTS AND ARE
AHEAD OF SCHEDULE STOP REGARDS ELMO

FRIDAY DECEMBER 13 (DAY 12 OF SHOOTING):

As on the previous day, 22 actors and six extras were assembled and came onto the set at 9 A.M. At 10 A.M., Kurosawa appeared with the stench of alcohol hovering about him. During the shooting of the luncheon scene in the admiral's quarters, Kurosawa developed an aversion to two new assistants and fired them on the spot. Shooting ended at 7:30 P.M.

ALL THE EMPEROR'S MEN

Goldsmith's log says the filming was now three days behind schedule, unchanged from the previous day.

At 9 P.M., Aoyagi brought Kyoto University Hospital neurosurgeon Dr. Hajime Handa to the inn to examine Kurosawa. That night Kurosawa, who was feeling uneasy about his personal safety on the set, demanded that Aoyagi get him a helmet, two bodyguards for himself, and eight guards who were to be posted outside the crew's common room on a 24-hour basis.

For the second day in a row, Goldsmith called Williams in Honolulu to report: "The situation is worsening and Kurosawa is becoming paranoid, afraid of his own crew and Toei Studio actors dressed like *yakuza* gangsters." Although Williams was shocked, he remained skeptical and suspected Goldsmith might have been overreacting. He began to wonder whether Goldsmith's reports were exaggerated.

SATURDAY DECEMBER 14 (DAY 13 OF SHOOTING):

Kurosawa had been drinking all night without sleep until 7 A.M., then turned up on the stage at 10 A.M.

Scheduled shoot for the day was the scene in which staff officer 'Gandhi' Kuroshima was in his quarters, tormented by the plan to attack Pearl Harbor, which he opposed as foolhardy. Unhappy with the performance of amateur actor Kiyoshi Makita as Kuroshima, Kurosawa was in an irritable mood all day.

In the course of incessant rehearsals, Kurosawa found fault with the bookcase in the admiral's office and demanded that the set manager "replace the books with those that Yamamoto would most likely have read at the time, such as books in English, books about marine and naval affairs." Fortunately, the set manager knew someone at the Kyoto Public Library and managed to borrow the required books. The filming lasted until 8:30 P.M. None of the scheduled shoot for that day was completed, however, and Goldsmith's daily log said the filming was now four days behind schedule.

In the afternoon, Goldsmith received a written note from Aoyagi

COUNTDOWN TO THE FALL

about Kurosawa's demands for helmets and bodyguards. Goldsmith visited Dr. Handa, the neurosurgeon at Kyoto University Hospital who had examined Kurosawa the previous night. The doctor said his opinion was that "Kurosawa is able to work, but he shouldn't be pressured too much. Stressful tasks are out of the question. Kurosawa is easily agitated so the people around him must make an effort not to anger him." The doctor had prescribed tranquilizers for Kurosawa.

Goldsmith relayed this doctor's opinion to Williams in Hawaii over the phone. Dr. Handa had suspected that Kurosawa might have a brain tumor but then thought he might be mistaken, so he asked Dr. Hitoshi Murakami, a neuropsychiatrist colleague, to examine the director.

After hearing from Goldsmith, Williams called Richard Zanuck to report that Kurosawa's crew was on strike demanding an improvement in working conditions. Filming had ground to a halt. He contended that Kurosawa was mentally unstable and had made a stupendous demand that Fox purchase a 50% stake in Toei's Kyoto studio to keep *yakuza* actors at a distance. Zanuck gave permission for Williams to go to Japan to get the situation under control.

SUNDAY DECEMBER 15 (DAY 14 OF SHOOTING):

Kurosawa had again been drinking well into the morning hours. He arrived on the stage at 9 A.M. without having slept and reeking of alcohol. The production staff and cast refused to work with him and the day's shooting was called off at 10 A.M.

The production staff held a meeting at the stage and put together a letter to Kurosawa Productions and Twentieth Century-Fox to voice their opinion that it was impossible to work with the director in his present condition. None of the scheduled shoot was completed and Goldsmith's log said the project was now five days behind schedule.

Williams called Goldsmith from Honolulu to tell him that he would leave Hawaii immediately to fly to Kyoto.

ALL THE EMPEROR'S MEN

Although a day off had been scheduled, Aoyagi suggested to Kurosawa that they should try to make up for lost time. Kurosawa agreed and attempted to continue rehearsals for scenes left unfinished from the previous two days. They included the scene in which 'Gandhi' Kuroshima agonizes in his quarters and where Yamamoto speaks to his men about his visit to the Imperial Palace to receive from the Emperor the formal order to attack Pearl Harbor. Rehearsals were repeated endlessly with little progress.

The crew presented Aoyagi with a list of demands requesting that Kurosawa control himself and act reasonably. Since this was a day off, Goldsmith's log said the work was five days behind schedule, unchanged from the previous day.

On this day, Aoyagi requested that Dr. Murakami of Kyoto University Hospital come to Kurosawa's lodgings to examine him. At the same time, he asked Kurosawa's wife to come to Kyoto to help restore her husband's mental balance. When Dr. Handa, who had examined Kurosawa three days earlier, and Dr. Murakami went to Kurosawa's lodgings to examine him, Kurosawa refused to see them.

Williams arrived back in Japan and headed for Kyoto as Kurosawa's wife made her way there herself.

When Kurosawa turned up on the set at 10 A.M., the crew demanded an apology for the problems he had caused. Williams and Goldsmith were present when Aoyagi read the crew's list of demands. Kurosawa refused to apologize, left the stage, and returned to his lodgings.

Williams and Goldsmith asked the crew and the seven assistant directors to tell them what was wrong. Roughly, their assertions were: "Kurosawa is not himself. He abuses members of the crew. He makes demands that have nothing to do with the shoot. He has forced the crew to give military salutes, to replace costumes without good reason, and to construct set elements that will not appear on camera. He has also fired crew members for not wearing their staff jackets." Williams proposed a break in shooting until Kurosawa calmed down but the crew were steadfast in their demand that he apologize. Eventually, they went on strike.

Goldsmith's log said: "No shooting due to Kurosawa's ill health." The filming was now six days behind schedule. This was the first time Goldsmith said the cause of the delay as "Kurosawa's ill health."

In the afternoon, doctors Handa and Murakami, who had tried to examine Kurosawa at his lodgings the previous evening, waited for him at the Kyoto University Hospital but he broke his promise to meet them and failed to turn up.

Late that night, a drunken Kurosawa and his assistant Yoichi Matsue inspected the stages to see if they were being guarded in accordance with his demand to Fox. Realizing that no guards were stationed there, Kurosawa ordered Matsue to smash the stage's windows, which he did. Nobody came. Angered, the two 'surrendered' to police at the Kyoto police station, claiming they were criminally responsible for property damage. They requested that they be arrested but the policemen laughed at them and drove the 'drunkards' away.

WEDNESDAY DECEMBER 18 (DAY 17 OF SHOOTING):

None of the scheduled shoot took place. Kurosawa rested at Kyoto University Hospital, sleeping under the influence of sedatives.

"No shooting due to Kurosawa's ill health" was again noted in Goldsmith's daily report. The film was now seven days behind schedule

Williams and Goldsmith visited Dr. Murakami at the hospital to inquire about Kurosawa's condition. The doctor was reluctant to give details of his diagnosis, but they understood that Kurosawa was mentally and physically exhausted and required rest. The doctor's advice was for Kurosawa to receive four weeks of treatment at a Tokyo hospital, followed by four to eight weeks of rest.

For the first time, Williams heard directly from Goldsmith what was wrong with Kurosawa. Goldsmith said that by talking with Aoyagi he had learned that Kurosawa was drinking heavily every night and using sleeping pills and that he would often become violent and damage things at his lodgings.

Williams was convinced now that the Kyoto production was at a costly standstill. He was told by the accountant that losses each day cost Fox twenty thousand dollars. Williams advised Fox's head of production, Richard Zanuck, that immediate action should be taken. He suggested that even if they had to revise the schedule and give up on Kurosawa, it would still be possible to complete the film on time and within budget. In a message, he said:

Dear Dick: Kurosawa currently suffering from extreme exhaustion due to hypertension. Doctor this morning recommended four to eight weeks rest under clinic care for full recovery but Kurosawa hoping for enough energy to resume work Sunday. If he does, doctor expects another more serious collapse within two weeks. This is best possible time for us to reorganize in view of forthcoming Japanese holiday starting December 30 and ending January seventh. Two of our location sites dictate the decisions we must make now in rescheduling production. Firstly our most expensive set and most important one in Kyushu where battleship *Nagato* and carrier *Akagi* are nearing completion. Key scenes with Yamamoto and Nagumo must be filmed there before stormy season which normally expected to start mid February. Second in importance is building we leased in Osaka for front projection work from mid February through March with no possibility of extension of lease. Believe we can close down until January seventh and still make schedule and stay within budget without sacrificing quality if we accept inevitable and make some changes now. Elmo

No call. Goldsmith's daily report said: "Due to Kurosawa's illness there was no shooting today. Shooting may resume on Sunday, December 21." It said filming was eight days behind schedule. Kurosawa was resting at his lodgings and there was no activity on the stage.

While preparing to wield the axe if worst came to worst, Williams tried to mend the situation and get Kurosawa back on track. In the afternoon, he visited Kurosawa with Aoyagi, carrying the list of complaints given to him by the crew. They spent three hours discussing ways to get the shoot back on track. As a specific measure, Williams suggested that Kurosawa delegate responsibility for the Kyoto shoot to second unit director, Junya Sato, and Kurosawa's chief assistant director, Yutaka Osawa, and allow them to proceed with the tasks at hand to a substantial degree. In other words, Williams had devised a plan in which Kurosawa's work would be continued by Sato and Osawa while waiting for him to recover his health.

Kurosawa acknowledged the crew's complaints and demands but adamantly refused to apologize. It is important to note here that an apology is often more important in Japanese culture than in American. In Japan, an apology does not represent readiness to take legal responsibility. Rather, an apology is a ritual or gesture of face-saving concession to clear the air. At stake was the honor of both parties, in this case the workers on one side and Kurosawa on the other.

In the meantime, Kurosawa agreed to Williams's proposal that rehearsals and lighting setup be delegated to Sato.

Goldsmith's daily report said: "No shooting due to Kurosawa's ill health. However, shooting should resume on December 22." The project was eight days behind schedule, the same as the previous day.

Kurosawa's primary physician, Dr. Domaru Mikochi, arrived in Kyoto from Tokyo and examined him at the Tawaraya Inn, where he was lodging. He diagnosed Kurosawa as having no serious problems with his health except for his being mildly stressed, but he found it necessary to prescribe tranquilizers for the director.

Kurosawa arrived in the morning appearing nervous and weak but personable. He met with the crew and first had a discussion with them. They responded to his statement that he understood their demands by calling off their strike for that day and began preparing to shoot for the first time in three days.

In the afternoon, Kurosawa demanded of Williams via Aoyagi: "The person playing Admiral Yamamoto needs a more decent greenroom." That was the dressing room or place to rest reserved for star players. Kurosawa said: "The room of the actor Kagitani must be refurnished to look more like the authentic C-in-C's office on the *Nagato*." That would require dismantling part of the set, which was deemed impossible. Instead, they prepared a new greenroom on the fourth floor of the actor's building in the Toei Kyoto Studios. At Kurosawa's request, they laid a red carpet from the first floor entrance to the room on the fourth floor and installed a new, immaculately polished, brass handrail in the staircase. A refrigerator to be stocked with selected beverages was brought in. Kurosawa barked at the crew to find out what the teetotaler Yamamoto drank aboard ship.

Goldsmith's log was the same as the previous day: "No shooting due to Kurosawa's ill health. However, shooting should resume on Sunday, December 22." The shoot was now nine days behind schedule.

Williams telexed Richard Zanuck to report on the three-hour discussion he had with Kurosawa the previous day. Both his discomfort with becoming entangled in the chaos in Kyoto and his distress over the lack of preparation for the battle scenes scheduled to be shot in Hawaii were evident. Further, his fatigue from making several long journeys between the United States and Japan, plus the stress from his work, led him to lament that he would not return home for the Christmas holiday. But he would soldier on.

> Dear Dick:
> After extensive meetings with Kurosawa he requested to

205

start shooting again this Sunday. He also agreed to iron out differences with crew and to revise shooting schedule move to Kyushu location January seventh thereby eliminating weather hazard. Kurosawa also agreed to let second unit director stage rough rehearsals and to pre-light on one stage while Kurosawa shoots on another to speed up operation. He also agreed to let another assistant help make most of foreground projection scenes to stick to present schedule. Have had three meetings with unions and production crew to get them to call off strike against Kurosawa and expect to resolve that situation satisfactorily today. My biggest worry now is lack of preparation time in Hawaii where we must start shooting on January twentieth to supply foreground projection material to Kurosawa unit on time. Important that I coordinate this work with Kellogg to give Kurosawa material he needs and prepare this big operation in Hawaii for Fleischer. Excessive travel plus long hours and strain of this past three weeks has been exhausting and I had hoped for at least two days rest over Christmas but will stay here as requested and will give you report Monday.
Regards, Elmo

SATURDAY, DECEMBER 21 (DAY 20 OF SHOOTING):

Company day off. No call. The project was nine days behind schedule.

SUNDAY, DECEMBER 22 (DAY 21 OF SHOOTING):

At the meeting three days earlier, it was arranged so that second unit director Sato would handle the pre-lighting setup and rehearsals, and Kurosawa would come in to direct the filmed takes. Full of expectation, Williams arrived on set at 9 A.M. But Sato was not there for reasons unknown. With no preparation done, Kurosawa appeared on set at 10 A.M. In high spirits, Kurosawa exhorted the crew and the shoot got

ALL THE EMPEROR'S MEN

underway.

In the afternoon, Kurosawa invited Williams to observe the shoot. A red carpet had been laid from the stage entrance to the set, a fanfare was played, and the crew stood at attention like honor guards to greet him. Although Williams always took off his shoes when stepping on the stage, today he was told to keep them on. Escorted to a chair by the camera, he was told by Kurosawa: "Put on your helmet. Some lighting equipment might fall on you." At that moment, a hat fell (or was dropped) from the catwalk and landed at Williams's feet.

Before the filming, Kurosawa made sure that the fanfare was played properly. He changed the position of the speaker stand and adjusted it numerous times, eventually returning it to its original position. Kagitani, as Yamamoto, moved from the entrance of the building where his greenroom was to the entrance of the stage by car, despite the short distance that would have been covered in two minutes on foot. A fanfare was played and Kurosawa and the crew saluted in unison. When the filming had finished, Kagitani was escorted off the stage. When he got in the car, Kurosawa and the crew stood at attention and saluted to send him off. When Kurosawa returned to the set, the crew greeted him with a salute. He had forced the staff to do this for other actors as well. At 7:05 P.M., Kurosawa's shrill voice rang out: "Today's shooting is now over!"

Williams was uncomfortable with Kurosawa's behavior but he appreciated the seriousness with which he approached filmmaking. That night, he telexed Richard Zanuck with the message: "Kurosawa did a full day's work today. It'll work out if he keeps it up." The number of incomplete shooting days decreased by one; the work was now eight days behind schedule.

That night, Williams decided to let Kurosawa handle things a little longer as he had the desire and the ability to complete the film. All the trouble would be worth it if he produced the expected result. He did not inform Richard Zanuck about the director's unusual behavior on the stage. There was no mention of a fanfare, the red carpet, or military salute in Williams's report.

COUNTDOWN TO THE FALL

CHAPTER
9

SOUND AND FURY

The Fall

The finale of this sorry tale began on Monday, December 23, 1968, on what should have been the 22nd day of shooting the Japanese sequence of *Tora! Tora! Tora!* The crew entered the stage at 8:30 A.M. with shooting scheduled to start at 10 A.M. Without having slept the night before, Kurosawa arrived at 10:30 A.M., obviously fatigued and in a bad mood. Soon after the rehearsal opened on a scene in the admiral's quarters on the battleship *Nagato*, Kurosawa suddenly called a halt, claiming that "the color of the walls isn't right." He ordered that walls be repainted and quickly picked up a brush and began repainting the walls himself. Unable to stand there watching without doing anything, the rest of the crew joined in.

Williams was holding a meeting with Aoyagi in his office at the studio when Aoyagi received a handwritten note. After a glance at it, he was dumbfounded and moaned: "Kurosawa's once again lost his mind and he is now repainting the set." Williams and Aoyagi jumped from their seats and rushed to the stage.

The white walls of a senior commander's quarters in the Imperial Japanese Navy were repainted once every month. Kurosawa's argument was that the entire set should be repainted to reflect that naval practice. Williams desperately tried to stop Kurosawa. He argued that the color of the repainted walls would differ from that of the luncheon scene that had already been shot, making it unusable; that repainting now was a crazy idea that was out of the question; and that he wanted him to cease immediately. After all, Williams continued, from a technical standpoint,

211

the color white is an important standard in color films but it is never possible to get whites absolutely perfect. This can be influenced by lighting equipment, film stock, or the bulb used by a projector in a cinema. The idea of making something whiter was in itself mistaken. Williams told Kurosawa that he should have known better.

All of this, however, only angered the director further. Kurosawa refused to listen, ordering the crew to continue. Then he began to paint the walls black, not white. Williams and the crew were astonished and speechless. Presumably Kurosawa was using a Japanese technique in *Negoro-nuri* lacquerware in which black was painted as an undercoat to bring out more depth in the color of the overcoat. Kurosawa knew about this traditional lacquerware and was a collector. But this was beyond the comprehension of Williams and the crew. Williams was confounded and now was convinced Kurosawa had truly lost his mind.

Kurosawa did not stop. He turned his attention to the doors on the Shinto altar in the admiral's quarters, which had been made of plywood. He asserted that they were cheap-looking and demanded that they be replaced with others made from authentic material. Art director Yoshiro Muraki balked, saying it would take at least two days to find an appropriate alternative. Kurosawa ordered him to "just go and find some real boards with a straight grain right now."

After lunch, more chaos erupted when a multi-camera shoot rehearsal began. Kurosawa suddenly ordered the destruction of a wall of the set and had two cameras placed there. As he began a camera rehearsal with several assistant directors as stand-ins, he changed his mind again and had another wall taken down. Then he told the crew to rebuild the wall he had previously ordered demolished.

That night, Kurosawa ordered the crew to "find a folding screen to hide the missing set wall, but it must be a screen with artistic value." A splendid screen, most likely ordered by art director Muraki, was delivered to the set a few hours later. Seeming to be standing at attention as he gazed at it, Kurosawa scrutinized it carefully and exclaimed in admiration: "This is definitely the kind of wonderful screen that is perfect for a room with an altar. If his majesty the Emperor could see it, I'm sure he would praise it. Pack it up immediately and send it to the Imperial Palace!" he yelled. The crew was speechless.

Kurosawa repeatedly yelled: "If you don't get the preparations exactly right, you'll have a harder time with tomorrow's shoot," and made the crew run around until 11 P.M. Aoyagi waited until midnight before seizing the opportunity to take Kurosawa by the arm and ease him off the stage. With that, an end was finally called to the day's work.

The exhausted members of the crew were angry. They could not fathom the reasoning behind all this and stood there at their wits' end. Some of them were heard to mumble, "Can't take any more of this." Goldsmith's log notes: "Due to reoccurrence of Mr. Kurosawa's illness, the company was not able to shoot." He reported that filming was nine days behind schedule.

TUESDAY, DECEMBER 24 (DAY 23 OF SHOOTING):

Shortly after midnight, Williams sent a telex to Richard Zanuck: "All my hopes in Kurosawa have been dashed. Please call my room at the Kyoto Hotel on December 24 at 2 A.M. Japan time."

He asked Aoyagi and Goldsmith to be with him when he received Zanuck's call. Williams had come to the conclusion that they could not allow Kurosawa to go on making the film and that the time had come to replace him. At 2 A.M., they received a call from hotel's front desk. Kurosawa was in the lobby and wanted to see Williams at once. Williams had to wait for Zanuck's call, so he sent Aoyagi and Goldsmith down to find out what the director wanted.

Kurosawa had moved to the Kyoto Hotel the previous night. He had been staying at an old inn, Tawaraya, but was forced to leave after he became drunk and violent, lifting a big urn from a corner of a corridor and throwing it into the garden, yelling, "I don't want such a sham." Hearing that Kurosawa had nowhere to stay, Williams secured a suite at the Kyoto Hotel. In heavy rain, Kurosawa, his wife Kiyo, and their daughter Kazuko had arrived at the hotel by taxi late at night.

At 2:30 A.M., Goldsmith and Aoyagi returned to Williams's room.

They said Kurosawa had only wanted to tell him that the security provided by the Kyoto City Police was insufficient.

Williams then received the expected call from Richard Zanuck in Acapulco, Mexico, where he had been honeymooning. Williams told Zanuck junior about the disruptive incidents such as the wall repainting, the demand for new Shinto altar doors, the destruction of the walls, and the order that a folding screen should be sent to the Imperial Palace. Williams urged Zanuck to dismiss Kurosawa as quickly as possible. Zanuck was shocked and, for reassurance, asked Goldsmith and Aoyagi to take the phone to tell him personally what had happened. Aoyagi told Zanuck there was no way they could allow Kurosawa to remain as director of the Japanese sequences.

After listening, Zanuck became convinced that Kurosawa was a "madman" and agreed he should be fired. He issued three instructions to Williams. One: dismiss Kurosawa. Two: the film project itself is to continue. Three: release an explanation to the press in a manner that would not damage Kurosawa's reputation.

Williams had publicity manager Ted Taylor draft a statement to be issued to the press and decided it would be released as soon as Zanuck had approved it. The draft was completed at 4 A.M. and sent to Zanuck, who quickly gave the go-ahead.

Three-way International Telephone Conference

Williams then called Fox headquarters in New York but was told that Darryl Zanuck was on vacation and could not be contacted. Williams stressed to the secretary that it was a matter of utmost urgency, after which he was told Zanuck was on the French Riviera. Williams contacted him immediately. Zanuck senior was astonished and disappointed but said he felt concerned for Kurosawa's well-being.

Williams's secretary, Christa Streichert, set up a three-way international conference call to connect Darryl Zanuck in France, Richard Zanuck in Mexico, and Williams in Kyoto and their deliberations began. Unknown to Williams, the Zanucks had discussed the issues before the conference call and had reached a tentative decision. When informed of this through the heavy static on the phone line, Williams was taken aback. The *Tora! Tora! Tora!* project was to be shut down. They would not allow a cent more to be spent on it.

Williams implored them to reconsider. Half of the budget had already been spent on items related to set construction, procurement of ships and aircraft, property and equipment rental, staff costs, freight costs, transport costs and more. The Hawaii-based unit was fully operational, on schedule, and starting to produce fantastic results. They had able staff working on the Japanese shoot, including excellent technicians from whom a high standard of work could be expected. The only problem was Kurosawa and if they were to replace him, all would be solved. Shutting down the project would be a slap in the face to the Japanese and American governments who had been so cooperative, inevitably resulting in a negative influence on future relations. Williams desperately tried to convey this to the Zanucks.

Neither would budge easily, but they finally consented to allow Kurosawa to be replaced. But it would still be necessary to consider how the entire project should proceed. The Kyoto shoot was to be called off, all production was to be shifted to Ford Island in Hawaii, and the remaining Japanese sequences were to be filmed there. Williams objected, saying it would be impossible. If the Japanese sequences were filmed in Hawaii, he argued, they would most likely have to cast many Chinese and Hawaiians to play the officers and men of the Imperial Japanese Navy. That would not be desirable for a film that strove for authenticity. He urged them to think back on why *The Longest Day* had been praised as a masterpiece. That film had adhered to historical fact and had an authenticity that silenced even Americans who opposed the project. Wasn't that also the aim of the *Tora! Tora! Tora!* project?

Even so, neither father nor son would listen. They stood firm in their insistence that the Japanese shoot be wrapped up and shifted to Hawaii. Here Williams argued that Fox had already invested a massive sum in the shooting of the Japanese sequences. If they were to call it all off now, then changed their minds and resumed production, the amount

SOUND AND FURY

of money wasted would be enormous. Would they consider delaying a decision and holding a later conference?

The Zanucks finally acquiesced. "All right. Let's wait until after Christmas," was their decision. For Williams, who had gone without sleep to save the project, Christmas Eve 1968 dawned without joy.

Search for a Replacement

Although it had been decided that Kurosawa was to be replaced, no one in Kyoto apart from Goldsmith and Aoyagi knew what was afoot. At 9 A.M. on Tuesday, December 24, the cast and crew arrived on time but there was no sign of Kurosawa. It was the 23rd day of shooting. Goldsmith's daily report noted: "Due to Mr. Kurosawa's inability to be on the set, because of illness, there was no shooting today (December 24). Because of illness, there will be no call tomorrow (December 25)." (Christmas is not a holiday in Japan.) The project was recorded as being ten days behind schedule. It would become apparent later that the "ten-day delay" was of crucial importance under the shooting contract.

Before dismissing Kurosawa, Williams needed to decide on a replacement and arrange for the shooting to continue. He already had Junya Sato in mind to take over as director. Williams had been told by Aoyagi that Sato would accept. Apart from him, Williams urgently needed to choose those he wanted to remain from the cast and crew and explain the circumstances to secure their commitments.

When he received word that Kagitani (playing Yamamoto) and Ando (playing Onishi) had arrived, he and Aoyagi visited them in their green-rooms to ask them to stay on. Kagitani was the only member of the cast that Fox had taken out cast insurance on (in case of illness or accident during production). He had Kagitani's English-proficient secretary sit in on the meeting. Williams explained that Fox had backed Kurosawa but now believed they had no choice other than to dismiss him in the light of his ill health. Kagitani and Ando understood the position Williams was in, and they believed he had acted with sincerity, so they agreed to continue in their roles.

ALL THE EMPEROR'S MEN

Williams went on to speak with a selected few of the crew about remaining in their jobs. He stated repeatedly that it was impossible for Kurosawa to continue. His explanation persuaded them to agree that the film could not be completed as things stood.

The Sting

At noon, Williams called Kurosawa's room. His assistant answered and said the director was still asleep. Williams had intended to speak with some other crewmembers after lunch to explain the situation. Before he could, however, Kurosawa awoke and sent a message that he wanted to meet Williams as soon as possible.

If Williams had followed American business practice, the notification of dismissal could have been as simple as delivering a sheet of paper saying Kurosawa's services were no longer required and thus avoided the stress of informing him face to face. But Kurosawa might already have heard about the decision from Kagitani, Ando, or the few crew members Williams had spoken to that morning. Williams decided that he should speak to Kurosawa personally and inform him of the decision with respect.

After he had given Ted Taylor permission to release the announcement of Kurosawa's dismissal to the press, Williams met Kurosawa at his Kyoto Hotel suite at 3 P.M. Williams later sent a detailed report to Twentieth Century-Fox headquarters on what happened on the day of dismissal. In that report, "I" refers to Williams:

> I then joined Tetsu and visited Kurosawa in his room at the Kyoto Hotel. Kurosawa was full of excuses but the ones he offered made no sense to me, so I decided to tell him the studio's decision.
>
> I told Kurosawa that I was sure he could understand that we could not continue to start and stop a production as expensive as *Tora! Tora! Tora!* the way we had been doing. Kurosawa agreed that this could not continue and he apologized to me for it.

However, when he started talking about again repainting the set and telling me that he had to have a complete new crew and that he wanted to move to another studio, I had to reaffirm to him our intention of finding a way of making the picture without him because I insisted that his first duty was to take care of his health and to look after his family.

When it became clear to Kurosawa that Fox was displeased with his actions, he immediately threatened to take away the entire cast. I told him that this would be regrettable but that if we had to, we could recast the picture.

Kurosawa then wanted to know what we would do with the film that he had shot and I reminded him that he had only shot about eight minutes of screen time and that, if necessary, we could reshoot it. I told him this would be less costly to us than to continue with the operation the way it had been going. Kurosawa agreed with me.

He then offered to go personally to the cast, to ask them to continue working with me, even if he was removed from the picture. I thanked him for his generous offer and started to leave, telling him to please return to Tokyo where I thought he could best look after his health.

Kurosawa now asked for permission to film all of Yamamoto's scenes separately and to let someone else film the balance of the picture but I told him this did not seem a very practical idea.

Kurosawa then threatened suicide, but as I felt he was acting, I told him that whatever he did must be his own affair but that suicide to me had always been a coward's way out of a problem.

Seeing that he was getting nowhere, Kurosawa stood up as if to dismiss us and escorted us to the door, saying he understood the situation and accepted my judgment when I told him that what Fox was doing was in the best interest of the picture that both Kurosawa and I had always believed in.

This exchange between Williams and Kurosawa was vividly documented but there is no guarantee it is entirely accurate. For example, this report said Aoyagi was in the room when Williams notified Kurosawa of his dismissal. If Aoyagi had been in the room, he would have been a credible witness. But the report is ambiguous about Aoyagi's presence.

Thirty-three years after Kurosawa's dismissal, Williams related in more detail what happened. Williams said Aoyagi was waiting in the hotel lobby and Kurosawa's interpreter conveyed the dismissal notice in Japanese. Besides Kurosawa and Williams, it seems certain that two other people were in the hotel suite: Yoichi Matsue and the unidentified interpreter. Matsue confirmed that he was in the room but said he had no recollection as to who interpreted for Williams, stating that "I myself wasn't very composed at the time." An undated document written by Williams's secretary, Christa Streichert, was also unclear on this point: "Kurosawa's aide opened the door and invited Williams inside, gave him a chair, and interpreted for Kurosawa, also interpreting Williams's words to Kurosawa." This 'aide' was never identified.

Letter of Farewell

Having delivered Kurosawa's dismissal, Williams wrote a farewell letter to Kurosawa in which he revealed his mixed emotions. It is a lucid piece of writing that confirms the reasons for Kurosawa's dismissal and discloses glimpses of his personal feelings. In its entirety, the letter said:

> Dear Mr. Kurosawa:
>
> I regret the state of your health which has worried me for some time. When the strain of this assignment proved too much for you ten days ago, we all hoped that a week of rest would restore your vitality enough to let you continue your work so we closed our production down. After several days' rest I checked with three different doctors to ask their professional opinion about your ability to go on. Unfortunately, the doctors did not agree.

One of them reported you showed signs of fatigue and tension but he thought nothing would suppress your determination to carry on. Therefore, he thought you could continue but he warned that you would have to watch the build-up of tension and anxiety.

The other doctor thought you should have from four to eight weeks of complete rest, otherwise he felt there was danger of a serious nervous breakdown that would impair your health—perhaps permanently.

My own observations were that you were not physically very strong and the burden of responsibility was weighing much heavier on you than it should. You obviously were working under mental strain and the only thing that was carrying you along, as I saw it, was your will.

With this second seizure following so close to the first one, I can (sic) but agree with the doctor who said you need extensive rest. As I consider your health of utmost importance to your family, your friends and to your profession, I want you to return to Tokyo to recuperate fully.

We will carry on with the making of "TORA! TORA! TORA!" exactly along the lines we agreed. Because I cannot guarantee the completion of this film unless we adhere to our present schedule, I must find a replacement for you. After discussing this with Mr. Richard Zanuck he agrees with my decision.

For a short while we will again close down actual filming to give us a chance to revise our schedule and to acquaint another director with this project. I will remain here for a while to be sure that the essence of what you and I have prepared and agreed upon is retained. As everyone, crew and cast alike, are devoted to making this an outstanding historical document, rest assured that we will do our best to capture the spirit that you intended in filming "TORA! TORA! TORA!"

Please take good care of yourself. We wish you well. We will also try to make you proud of the final results.
Sincerely,
Elmo Williams

At 10 A.M. on December 25, 1968, Williams handed his letter to Aoyagi. It is not known whether it ever reached Kurosawa.

Comedy in Close-up

A month later, at Kurosawa's first press conference following his dismissal, he attempted to justify his behavior at the Toei Kyoto Studios, asserting that the confusion occurred because his "way of making films" had not been understood by the cast and crew. Furthermore, he said: "It was my first major DeLuxe Color feature, and many of the interior scenes that were to be shot on the Kyoto stage were very important, so I had to make sure that everything was built carefully."

In a memoir published 25 years after Kurosawa's dismissal, Richard Fleischer, the American director of *Tora! Tora! Tora!*, wrote:

The blame for this catastrophic turn of events lay on both sides, although Twentieth Century-Fox must carry most of the burden. Kurosawa had always been his own, completely autonomous, boss. Now he had many bosses, all of whom he surely felt were his inferiors, all of whom were tearing away at his autonomy, his dignity. His way of operating was totally unlike anything they were used to. He had a different set of rules: his own. Kurosawa was a master precisely because he went his own way. They (Twentieth Century-Fox) made a major mistake in how they treated him. It was folly to try to squeeze him into the Hollywood studio mold. You don't hire Kurosawa to give you just another movie or even behave like just another director... You don't hire him to make you go bankrupt, either.

When Fleischer published his memoir entitled *Just Tell Me When to Cry* in 1993, Kurosawa was 83 years old and had just finished his last film, *Madadayo (Not Yet)*, a nostalgic story of an old schoolteacher and his adoring students. But never did Kurosawa agree to answer questions about the *Tora! Tora! Tora!* fiasco a quarter century earlier. It is ironic that Fleischer—who Kurosawa apparently considered to be one of his 'inferiors'—delivered an objective and even sympathetic appraisal of Kurosawa in the debacle. By contrast, Kurosawa never stopped calling Fleischer "the micro guy" or "the ketchup guy."

"Life is a tragedy when seen in close-up but a comedy in long-shot," said the comedian Charlie Chaplin. Kurosawa thought it should be the other way around, with the close-up on the comedy and life's tragedies seen in the long shot. His strange behavior at the Toei Movie Studio in Kyoto in 1968 was, in close-up, indeed a comedy.

As Kurosawa became more eccentric, his staff distanced themselves from him and he became an object of ridicule. He suffered under the intense pressure, much of it self-imposed, of making a great movie. As he grew more frustrated, his efforts became more futile. He became infuriated over trifles. His rage, his drinking, and his reliance on sleeping pills contributed to his ill health and deteriorating judgment. From the outside, Kurosawa's behavior may have seemed eccentric. Those episodes constituted a comedy when seen in close-up but in long-shot were a tragedy, which was Kurosawa's declared theme in *Tora! Tora! Tora!*

CHAPTER 10

WORLD ON HIS SHOULDERS

A Man Called 'Helmut'

The name *'Helmut'* appears frequently in Fox's internal documents on *Tora! Tora! Tora!* that circulated among an exclusive group in upper management. At first, it was unclear who *Helmut* was but it soon became apparent from the context that the name referred to Akira Kurosawa. *Helmut* is a male German name but here was a dig at "a man who wore a helmet." The name derives from the Greek, meaning "a brave warrior who wore an iron helmet." Fox management was probably unaware of that meaning but it was a scathing nickname.

Sometime after the "lighting equipment incident" in the Toei Kyoto Studios, Kurosawa came to the stage wearing a white helmet that he never took off during filming. He was the only one wearing a helmet, which made him look more like a foreman on a construction site than a film director. He did this out of fear that something would drop on him or would be dropped on purpose to hurt him. What made Kurosawa look even more bizarre and conspicuous were the several bodyguards who always shadowed him, even when he took a toilet break. The rest of the staff could be forgiven for imagining him a nut straight out of a comic book.

The helmet and the bodyguards had been provided to Kurosawa after he demanded them from Stanley Goldsmith, Fox's production supervisor. The "Imperative Requirements by Director Akira Kurosawa," a memo written in Japanese, is preserved among Fox's internal documents. It was handwritten by producer Tetsu Aoyagi, then translated into English and signed by Aoyagi. Dated December 13th, 1968, it listed seven items:

225

1. Be sure to have guards to escort Mr. Kurosawa on every
    trip between his hotel and the stage;
2. Give helmets to both Mr. Kurosawa and (Second Unit
    Director Junya) Sato to be worn on the stage;
3. Whenever Mr. Kurosawa goes to the toilet, please have
    a guard escort him;
4. Make his car safely (sic) as much as possible and put
    bullet-proof glass in the car;
5. It is not in perfect condition to put the light equipments
    on the sets, so try to make it (sic);
6. Keep the studio clean;
7. We always have to have somebody to keep guard
    through 24 hours (sic).

In the first item, the words "main staff" in the original Japanese have been deleted, indicating Kurosawa had demanded guards for himself and other principal staff, but the latter demand was presumably dropped during negotiations. The helmets were supplied, with Kurosawa's helmet having three white stripes while Sato's had two. Sato said he never wore it.

About the third item, Kurosawa once said "a *samurai* is most vulnerable to assassins when he is sleeping, having sex, or emptying his bowels." The Japanese version of the fourth item says that Fox must provide Kurosawa with an 'absolutely safe' car and put curtains in its windows. In the English translation, Fox took this to mean a car fitted with "bullet-proof glass" and no curtains would be necessary.

The fifth item suggests that the "falling lighting equipment incident" led Kurosawa to suspect that somebody might intentionally drop something on him. Although the Japanese version states that he demands "absolutely safe conditions," it is unclear as to just what he wanted. The Japanese wording for the sixth item is more specific, saying paths must be cleaned and sprinkled with water and that there should be no trace of trash around. This passage is deleted from the English translation. The original sixth item must have baffled Fox staff but it is not so

ALL THE EMPEROR'S MEN

strange from the Japanese point of view. Sweeping around one's home and garden every morning and sprinkling water were once intrinsic to Japanese lifestyle. Perhaps Kurosawa sought peace of mind from that ritual cleansing. The Japanese version of the seventh item suggested that Kurosawa wanted the stage and the offices of his production company to be guarded around the clock as safety precautions.

Threats of Assassination

Kurosawa may have suffered from chronic paranoia, especially as the leading character of the film he was directing had been threatened in his real life. Kurosawa had a tendency to identify with the protagonist of that movie, as many in his coterie have testified. Second unit director Sato said:

> When he was shooting *Tora! Tora! Tora!*, he really took on the role of Isoroku Yamamoto. Yamamoto's war with the United States became his own war. It seemed he [Kurosawa] was determined never to yield to America.

Similarly, in 1950, when Kurosawa was filming *The Idiot*, adapted from Dostoevsky's novel, people close to Kurosawa said he seemed to be in agony as if he was under pressure from the author. He said: "I was stressed and felt great pain. I felt as if Dostoevsky were riding on my shoulders." It is possible that Kurosawa was feeling that Yamamoto was riding on his shoulders when he was making *Tora! Tora! Tora!* Elmo Williams said:

> Kurosawa had involved himself so deeply in the picture that he was actually carrying the responsibility for the last war on his shoulders… the same responsibility Admiral Yamamoto had carried. I think Kurosawa was actually reliving that phase of Yamamoto's life.

On the other side, Williams said he received death threats from Americans angry that he was making a movie of the Pearl Harbor attack:

> Several times, my life was threatened while I was making this film. I began receiving death threats after hiring Minoru Genda as a technical adviser... the orchestrator of the actual attack on Pearl Harbor. I had a guy who called me one day and said: 'Every day when you leave the studio, I'll have you in my gun sight.'

Williams said he didn't think the threat was genuine but he believed anything could happen. From then on, he kept his friendly relations with Genda low key.

Army vs. Navy

In Japan, a theory about what the Japanese call the Pacific War holds: "The Army was bad; the Navy was good." The Army pushed for the war, while the Navy tried to prevent it. Admiral Yamamoto, the head of the fleet, was a tragic hero. He was sure Japan could never win but found himself in a position where he was forced to start the war. On the other hand, Army veterans rejected this theory.

A rumor ran through the staff that anti-Navy extremists were around the studio in Kyoto where Kurosawa was filming. It spread among the Japanese and American staff but the source was never discovered. It was whispered—half seriously, half jokingly—that if you favored the Navy too much in this controversy, you would find yourself in serious danger. Both Williams and Kurosawa appear to have been aware of the rumor. A letter, undated, from Aoyagi to Williams suggested that Kurosawa might have felt the same way. Aoyagi wrote:

> Some parts of the screenplay you sent us for reading are a problem. Very seriously, it is a fact that ex-Navy and ex-

ALL THE EMPEROR'S MEN

Army people here in Japan are against each other even now. They are still blaming each other for defeat in war. If we say something which leads either group to think that they have been insulted, it is going to cause a terrible situation here. You may not take this seriously, but it could result in assassination. We know this from our experience of being blackmailed... I am not kidding. We would like you to give your strongest consideration to this matter.

It might be worthwhile here to touch on the situation in 1939 surrounding Yamamoto, who was then Navy Vice-Minister before he was appointed Commander-in-Chief of the Combined Fleet. Journalists dubbed him one of "the navy leftwing trio" who stubbornly resisted the conclusion of the Tripartite Pact among Japan, Germany and Italy that was promoted by the army. The other two were Navy Minister Mitsumasa Yonai and his confidant, Shigeyoshi Inoue, who was the head of the ministry's Naval Affairs Bureau. The army and right-wingers believed that Yamamoto, who had openly declared that "the Japanese navy is no match for that of the U.S. and Great Britain," was the instigator of opposition to the Tripartite Alliance. Anonymous documents were circulated in an attempt to have him excluded from politics. There was even a credible plot to have him assassinated.

In May 1939, Yamamoto seems to have resigned himself to the possibility of sudden death. His will titled "Statement of Beliefs" was dated May 31, 1939, three months before he was sworn in as Commander-in-Chief of the Combined Fleet. Only after he was killed in action in the South Pacific in 1943 was his will found. It had been kept in the safe in the Navy Vice-Minister's office.

In part it read:

To give up his life for his sovereign and country is the military man's most cherished wish: what difference whether he gives it up at the front or behind the lines?... They may destroy my body, yet they will not take away my will.

Elmo Williams's report to Fox headquarters explaining the events that led to Kurosawa's dismissal ends with this passage:

> I had heard several times over the past four months (since August, 1968) that Kurosawa felt that he was doing all of the work on the picture, that the Americans were lying down on the job, that none of us had the ability to produce the kind of quality that he wanted, and he was anything but complimentary about Richard Fleischer's work and ability.

A case in point concerns the scene that shows the takeoff of fighters, dive bombers, and torpedo bombers from the carrier *Akagi* bound for Pearl Harbor. According to historical records, the takeoff started at 6 A.M. Hawaiian time. The scene begins with a voice ringing out: "Commence takeoff!" With a deafening roar, Zero fighters, Val dive bombers, and Kate torpedo bombers ascend into the dawn sky. Blue exhaust floats in the cold morning air; eardrum-piercing noises wrench the air; purple clouds at sunrise drift across the darkened sea.

The Fox version of *Tora! Tora! Tora!* has been celebrated for the beauty of this scene. Williams said this sequence was so successful that the footage has been borrowed and re-used in documentary and feature films the world over. He described this scene as a veritable "gift from the goddess of good luck." It was shot over two days—December 3rd-4th—with the American aircraft carrier *Yorktown* standing in for the *Akagi* and was the proud work of second unit director Ray Kellogg. It was the culmination of Williams's formidable efforts behind the scenes.

The U.S. Navy had originally agreed that the decommissioned aircraft carrier *Valley Forge* could be dressed as the *Akagi* for filming. After concerns were raised about the strength of its deck and other safety issues, the naval authorities declared they would permit aircraft to take off but not land on her. They did not want to be responsible for possible accidents. But if *Valley Forge* could not be used for scenes of aircraft landing, that would be a problem. Neither side would compromise, which brought negotiations to a temporary halt.

Another obstacle: The Federal Aviation Administration (FAA) had not granted permission for old-model American aircraft to be refitted to resemble Japanese craft and then take to the air. The FAA insisted that each plane undergo a flight test to confirm that it met safety requirements. Until the FAA granted licenses, the remodeled aircraft could not be flown in American air space, and the pilots who would fly the planes during the shoot could not be trained as long as clearance from the FAA was delayed.

Help arrived from an unexpected savior. One day in November 1968, Williams heard that the mission of the carrier USS *Yorktown* had suddenly changed and that she was returning from the central Pacific to port in Hawaii to refuel and give her crew shore leave. The *Yorktown* had been steaming in the mid-Pacific to retrieve the three-man crew of the *Apollo 8* space module upon its return to earth and splashdown. The postponement of *Apollo*'s launch from the Kennedy Space Center to December 21 meant the carrier would not be required until then. Williams sprang into action.

He immediately phoned the Pentagon to confirm the relevant schedules and sound out the possibility of using USS *Yorktown* for the *Tora! Tora! Tora!* shoot. The DOD response was positive. The ship had space to hold an additional 30 aircraft. It would be possible to grant permission for crew members on leave to participate in the shoot.

Knowing that he shouldn't let this opportunity escape, Williams pressed the FAA to rush flight licenses for the converted aircraft and received them a week earlier than scheduled. He asked Ray Kellogg to assemble a film crew in time for the *Yorktown*'s arrival in Honolulu, which required clearance with the DOD. The scene was ultimately filmed after Williams had employed every means possible.

Williams was so happy about the success of this scene that he carried the rushes to Kyoto because he wanted to please Kurosawa. Williams arranged a preview screening at the Toei Kyoto Studio and invited Kurosawa and the production staff. Williams described Kurosawa's reaction in his report to Fox:

> After we screened this film, Kurosawa gave me no reaction
> at all. I was sitting in the theater when the screening was
> over and he just nodded his head, got up and left the build-
> ing. Later I heard that he had told members of his staff that
> the entire sequence was shoddy, the quality terrible, it was
> not what he had visualized and he fully intended to re-film
> the entire takeoff sequences.

Williams was horrified to learn of Kurosawa's intention, as shown in the English translation of Kurosawa's written instructions that Williams kept. After the preview, Kurosawa told art director Yoshiro Muraki to reinforce the flight deck of the life-sized set for the carrier *Akagi* under construction in Kyushu so that real aircraft could use it to take off and land. Additionally, he ordered that a workable elevator be constructed inside the carrier to haul aircraft from the internal hangar to the flight deck. None of this was done as Aoyagi and Williams disregarded Kurosawa's instructions.

This episode reveals the definitive rift that had opened between Williams, the pragmatic producer, and Kurosawa, the artist, who had assumed, mistakenly, that he was the 'headman' who could pursue his vision while holding costs and other worldly restraints in contempt.

False Start at Cross-purposes

Something had been wrong from the beginning but no one in Japan was aware of it. Many of the Japanese staff had taken much for granted, as did Kurosawa. In April 1967, Japanese newspapers splashed headlines such as:

> "Akira Kurosawa, '*Sokantoku*' of *Tora! Tora! Tora!*" (*Nippon
> Keizai Shimbun*)

"Akira Kurosawa to work with Fox, named '*Sokantoku*' of *Tora! Tora! Tora!*, Shooting starts in Japan and America next spring" (*Yomiuri Shimbun*)

"Kurosawa, '*Sokantoku*' of *Tora! Tora! Tora!* on Pearl Harbor attack, Shooting on location in Washington and Hawaii" (*Daily Sports*)

The key word was the Japanese term '*Sokantoku*.' '*So*' means 'supreme' or 'overall' and '*kantoku*' means 'director.' There is no exact equivalent in English as there is no position equivalent to '*Sokantoku*' in Hollywood. The closest equivalent of the Japanese term is 'Principal Director.' If more than one director works on a film, the producer supervises. Under the contract, Kurosawa was to be the director of Japanese sequences. His jurisdiction did not extend to the American side. When the production was announced, the director of the American sequences had yet to be named. Even so, it was obvious that Kurosawa and the unnamed American director held equal status.

At the news conference to announce the production of *Tora! Tora! Tora!*, two sets of handouts were distributed, one in Japanese and the other in English. The text was the same in most aspects but subtly different in others. The two were alike in that "the picture will be an authentic representation of history" (Japanese version) and "will give a strictly factual, wholly objective account of the attack—and of events leading up to it—'from both points of view'" (English version).

They diverged, however, in reference to the directors. The Japanese version lists Kurosawa as '*Sokantoku*' and also "director of the Japanese sequences" and the (unnamed) American director as "director of the American sequences." The English text said: "The Japanese sequences will be directed by Akira Kurosawa and the American scenes by a leading American director." It said nothing to indicate that Kurosawa would be the Principal Director, nor did it say the American director would be a co-director in a subordinate role.

In addition, a newsletter released by Fox said only that Kurosawa would direct the Japanese sequences. An Associated Press dispatch and four English-language newspapers in Japan—*Japan Times, Asahi Evening News, Daily Yomiuri*, and *Mainichi Daily News*—made no mention of Kurosawa as '*Sokantoku.*'

One Director Is Enough

Tetsu Aoyagi was Kurosawa's trusted manager and interpreter and in a position to reassure Kurosawa that he was the '*Sokantoku.*' Kurosawa was often heard to say that one director is enough for a film. The majority of the Japanese mass media never doubted Kurosawa's claim that he was the Principal Director. *Asahi Shimbun* ran a long article on November 17, 1968, two weeks before shooting was scheduled to begin, saying:

> Fox is paying all the expenses but the '*Sokantoku*' is Kurosawa. He is to complete shooting the Japanese sequences by next March. After that, Richard Fleischer will begin shooting the American segment. Kurosawa will head for the United States to supervise the shooting. He will then take part in all aspects of making the film, including editing and dubbing.

Asked about his aspirations as the '*Sokantoku*' of the film, Kurosawa said: "I do not want to make a simple anti-war film. I will present facts exactly as they were. All I want to do is to show how wasteful war is. The rest is up to audiences to judge."

Some journalists expressed doubt. The weekly magazine *Shukan Yomiuri* asked Aoyagi who would be responsible for making *Tora! Tora! Tora!* The magazine pointed out that Fox was to pay all expenses, Richard Fleischer was to direct the American sequences, and the producer would be Elmo Williams of Fox. A reporter asked how far Kurosawa could be assured of his artistic freedom as the director.

Aoyagi answered: "This is not a co-production in the usual sense of the word, as Fox will pay for everything. But Fox President Darryl

ALL THE EMPEROR'S MEN

F. Zanuck makes it clear that Fox will sell the film around the world as a Kurosawa film. Kurosawa and Fox will have a fifty-fifty say." No evidence has been found, however, to corroborate Aoyagi's claim that Zanuck said Fox would sell it as Kurosawa's film.

Further, *Shukan Yomiuri* quotes Kurosawa as saying: "I'll be in charge of the shooting, editing and dubbing (creating, editing and re-recording dialogue, music and sound effects) for the Japanese sequences, then I'll take them to the U.S., and will observe the filming of the American sequences as much as time allows. Editing as well. That's how it'll go."

The final section of the article delivers the coup de grâce. In response to the reporter's question, "Will the Japanese and American versions of the film differ when it is released into theatres?" Kurosawa casually pronounced: "No, they won't." This was a critical mistake that revealed how little Kurosawa understood the limits of his authority.

On the other hand, second unit director Sato had a more realistic understanding. During the selection of the second unit director, Kurosawa viewed films by several candidates. Sato's *Rikugun Zangyaku Monogatari* (*A Cruel Army Tale*) was his 1963 debut film for Toei's Tokyo Studio and caused a sensation with its vehement anti-militarism. It won the Blue Ribbon award for best new director, which caught Kurosawa's attention and led him to give Sato the job in June 1967. Sato had been told by Aoyagi that Kurosawa would be Principal Director and that about five Japanese directors would handle the filming.

That Kurosawa believed he was the Principal Director when he was not in Fox's eyes was a cause of the troubles that led to Kurosawa's dismissal. This mistake was ironic since he was devoted to the tragedy of the Pearl Harbor epic that he saw as a culmination of misunderstandings between the United States and Japan. In the end, he personified those misunderstandings.

Misplaced Confidence

Kurosawa's rehearsal of scene 93 was going well on Stage 11 at Toei Kyoto Studio at 1 P.M. on December 6, the fifth day of filming. Although it

WORLD ON HIS SHOULDERS

was a simple dialogue scene, it was important to the Pearl Harbor saga. Admiral Yamamoto had been secretly invited to the private residence of Prime Minister Fumimaro Konoe in the suburbs of Tokyo to discuss the grim prospects of an imminent war with the United States.

Darryl Zanuck and Elmo Williams sat side by side in directors' chairs and watched Kurosawa conduct the rehearsal and Kurosawa was apparently conscious of the observers. Chief Assistant Director Yutaka Osawa said Kurosawa may have been playing a role that day—himself as the 'world-famous master of cinema.' He was tense and energetic, wearing a purple beret pulled down over his forehead and dark sunglasses. Using three cameras on dollies, he coached his cast carefully—Koreya Senda, a professional actor, as Prime Minister Konoye and Takeo Kagitani, the amateur actor, as Yamamoto. Kurosawa's directions were crisp and authoritative. He looked confident and dignified and fit the image of a great director in total control. Zanuck and Williams looked on, impressed.

During a break shortly after 2 P.M., Zanuck stood up, approached Kurosawa, spoke a few complimentary words with a big smile, shook hands, and left. Williams followed. Zanuck departed from Kyoto a few hours later and headed for America the following day on December 7, the eve of Pearl Harbor Day, Japan time. This was the last time Zanuck and Kurosawa ever saw each other. Eighteen days later, Zanuck approved Kurosawa's dismissal.

One week after Zanuck left Japan, he was staying in southern France on vacation at the Hotel du Cap in Côte D'Azur, a resort facing the Mediterranean Sea. From there, Zanuck sent a telegram to Kurosawa that reflected his concern about reported troubles at the Toei Kyoto Studio. Zanuck was an autocratic and relentless CEO but the tone of his telegram belied that image. He was polite and sounded as if he was pleading with Kurosawa. The telegram, a copy of which is in the UCLA library, was undated but its content suggests it was sent around December 14, saying:

My dear Kurosawa,
Am eagerly awaiting to see your first rushes which were
to be airmailed to me in Rome or London but studio has
notified me today that they have not yet received even your
first day's work. Am particularly anxious to see the episodes
that were shot when I was on your set and also eager to see
the first sequence between Yamamoto and Prime Minister.
I appreciate your system of advanced rehearsals and then
photographing the rehearsed sequence the following day
but I note that in the first week we have slipped two days
behind your shooting schedule and while this is not alarm-
ing considering it was the first week I notice that even
though you photographed late at night and apparently one
scene on Sunday that we are still continuing to drop behind
schedule. I am confident this will not continue because it
would certainly be financially disastrous if we continue to
lose a couple days each week and I am confident you are as
aware of this as I am. It may seem presumptuous for me to
express my concern at this early date but I am sure that you
are aware that both Dick Zanuck and I are responsible to
the board of directors and it took me many weeks before I
obtained the approval of the budget but I know that when I
reach New York I am going to be asked questions and particularly regarding TTT (sic meaning *Tora! Tora! Tora!*) and
it is as you know the most expensive undertaking in the history of Fox.
Affectionate regards, Darryl

Whether Kurosawa read Zanuck's telegram is unknown and there is
no evidence that he sent a reply. When the telegram arrived, Kurosawa
was in a state of confusion. He was having a hard time controlling the
crew and the non-professional actors. While on the set, he was irritated
and nervous, often shouting at staff over trivia. Both cast and crew were
distancing themselves from him. His health was deteriorating; he was

suffering from insomnia and fatigue, and was drinking heavily. Zanuck was unaware of what had happened to Kurosawa since they had last met.

Reap What You Sow

Looking back, Williams said Kurosawa's misguided casting was responsible for most of the trouble. The preparations for *Tora! Tora! Tora!* were exorbitantly expensive, so much so that Williams realized that they had no money left to hire stars. Zanuck and Williams agreed they could not afford the caliber of actors in *The Longest Day*. Instead, they assembled a top-notch company of Hollywood veteran supporting actors and bit players to minimize costs.

Kurosawa surprised Fox when he minimized the hiring of professional actors and brought in former members of the Imperial Navy to play key roles. This, however, backfired as it was nearly impossible to elicit believable performances from amateurs. Fox staff, skeptical of Kurosawa's casting, circulated a rumor that Kurosawa's real intentions were to flatter those businessmen to secure financing for future films.

Williams, having decided that Kurosawa's decision was a dangerously bad idea, pointed out to Kurosawa that the screenplay for *Tora! Tora! Tora!* contained lines and scenes that demanded skillful performances. "Perhaps Kurosawa became frustrated, demanding too much from non-professional actors," he surmised. In an interview, Williams said:

> At one time when Kurosawa became very difficult, I told him... I said, Mr. Kurosawa, I think you have brought all those troubles upon yourself, because I don't think you can get performances out of these people... amateurs. And I think that worries you... You don't know what to do about it. You employed those people... They are important people... See, I don't think you can fire them without causing a lot of trouble. And on the other hand, you can't get performances out of those people. I said you've painted yourself into the corner.

Kurosawa felt differently. Even after he had been dismissed, he insisted he was correct in his casting decision. At a news conference on January 21, 1969, he claimed that the non-professional actors had given far better performances than he had expected and he was sure the film would have exceeded expectations if it had been finished. Kurosawa never called the non-professionals "amateurs" but referred to them as "actors who are full-fledged members of society."

This infuriated Toshiro Mifune, who was then among the foremost actors in Japan. At a party two days later in the Imperial Hotel in Tokyo to mark completion of *Furin Kazan*, a movie about a legendary feudal lord, Shingen Takeda, Mifune expressed his anger in a statement released to journalists. He said: "Kurosawa gave most of the roles in *Tora! Tora! Tora!* to rank amateurs. This is tantamount to throwing down a challenge to all of Japan's professional actors. His disregard of professional actors has left us with a huge problem. I will never act in Kurosawa's films again. No other actor should do so either, if they take pride in their work."

On the same day, professional actors who had been cast in *Tora! Tora! Tora!* sought to hold Kurosawa responsible for their loss of employment. About fifty had been told on December 25th that shooting had been suspended and they received no compensation from Fox or Kurosawa Productions. The suspension caused them tangible and intangible losses and they were angry. On January 23rd, the managers of seven companies with which the actors were affiliated agreed to demand compensation from Kurosawa Productions.

Five months later on June 24, an informal party at the Akasaka Prince Hotel was intended to cheer Kurosawa up. Entitled "Kurosawa, Make Movies Again," it was organized by members of Kurosawa's former crew at Toho Studios. Around thirty people attended, among them director Kajiro Yamamoto, Kurosawa's mentor, and Toho's managing director Sanezumi Fujimoto. Actor Toshiro Mifune was one of the party's organizers even though five months earlier he had said he would never act in a Kurosawa film again. He showed up at the party because Mifune was to Kurosawa what John Wayne was to John Ford: a disciple-to-mentor relationship. But the two would never meet in film-making for the rest of their lives.

Addressing the guests, Kurosawa declared he had been filled with a fresh zeal to work again and that he was writing a new screenplay. He said he had ideas for five new movies and that he was putting the *Tora! Tora! Tora!* incident behind him. But he said he still believed he was right in trying to use non-professional actors:

> The performances of the non-professionals who had a wealth of experience as active members of society were of a much greater quality than those who had worked for many years as professional actors. Despite having worked as a director for as long as I have, I was still amazed by how good they were. The experiences and conditioning as members of society outweighed those of the actors and that which they had obtained over the course of their acting careers. I want professional actors and professional filmmakers to give this serious consideration.

The party fell silent, apparently either impressed by Kurosawa's words or offended by them.

Stranger in Kyoto

Kurosawa loved everything about Kyoto. Even so, he had difficulty working there because his ways were not Kyoto's ways and he was often considered an outsider in a city that prided itself on being the soul of Japanese culture.

Kyoto had been the capital of Japan for more than a thousand years before the Emperor was moved to Tokyo during the Meiji Restoration of 1868. The *shogunate* had been overthrown and governance was returned, at least ostensibly, to the emperor. Many Japanese contend that the cultures of Kyoto and Tokyo differ in subtle ways, with traditional Kyotoites tending to look down on upstart Tokyoites. Perhaps those subtle cultural differences played a part in his downfall. In her memoir, his daughter, Kazuko, wrote:

[After his dismissal], my father refused to go back to Kyoto for a time. However, perhaps thanks to time soothing his hardened, distressing memories, one day he said, 'We've been away from Kyoto for some time. Shall we go there?' It was quite a relief.

Kurosawa's attachment to Kyoto began when he was young. Every year, he stayed for a time at his favorite inn and wrote screenplays. He liked to visit the Imperial Palace as well as Kyoto's many temples and shrines. He browsed the antique shops and strolled along the alley of Nishiki-koji, a narrow stone-paved arcade lined with shops selling fish, vegetables, fruit, groceries and cooked foods in a neighborhood known as "Kyoto's kitchen." When he grew tired, he rested at an old coffee shop in Sanjo-Sakai. Being a gourmet, he frequented a famous restaurant serving turtle cuisine. In Kyoto, Kurosawa found peace of mind.

In 1994, Kurosawa was awarded the Kyoto Prize that had been established by the Kyosera Corporation's Inamori Foundation in 1985 to commend "those who have made significant contributions to the progress of science, the development of civilization, and the enrichment and elevation of the human spirit." The prize had three categories: two for natural science, and one for humanities. Kurosawa was awarded the prize in humanities for "Mental Science/Expressive Arts." Having expressed his love for Kyoto, he was gratified to win an award with a strong connection to the city. The question remains, however: was Kurosawa, a man from the east, loved by the people of Kyoto as much as he loved them?

In the last years of his life, Kurosawa patronized a small inn named Ishihara, which had only six rooms. He wrote screenplays there, including *Ran*. In March 1995, when he was writing a screenplay for *Ame Agaru (After the Rain)*, he slipped on a *tatami* straw mat and had a bad fall, suffering a broken hip. He spent three months in a Kyoto hospital and was confined to a wheelchair when he returned to Tokyo. He never

241

fully recovered and died three years later in September of 1998.

Shadows of 'Rashomon'

It is usually not easy for a director to establish leadership in a new environment, but when Kurosawa came to Kyoto to film *Rashomon*, he was not worried about potential difficulties. He had been invited to shoot the film by the Daiei Motion Picture Company after Toho's Kinuta Studio in Tokyo was locked down in a round of labor strikes in 1948. He and other directors, such as Kajiro Yamamoto, Mikio Naruse, and Senkichi Taniguchi were unable to make films with Toho so they left and founded an independent association to make themselves available for films with other companies.

Kurosawa said later: "It wasn't difficult at all to work for a different company. Film people are just as good no matter where you go. Whatever the company, people making a living from film are the same. No matter what company I worked for, there was never a time when I couldn't do my job freely."

The people who made *Rashomon* were young up-and-coming filmmakers. When shooting began in June, 1950, Toshiro Mifune, cast in the leading role of Tajomaru, was 30; Masayuki Mori, who played the samurai, was 39; cameraman Kazuo Miyagawa was 42; and Kurosawa was 40.

Kurosawa already exuded an aura that captivated the hearts of young and enthusiastic professionals. He was tall and masculine and worked with irrepressible passion and tremendous concentration. This inspired young actors and staff and they sought to satisfy him. When *Rashomon* was released on August 26th, 1950, the reception was less than enthusiastic among the general public and knowledgeable critics. The common complaint was that the story was too esoteric and too complicated to understand. Daiei was disappointed and hesitated to ask Kurosawa to make another movie. Then, in August 1951, the unexpected happened when the movie won the Golden Lion, the highest award of the Venice International Film Festival. Overnight, this brought Kurosawa interna-

ALL THE EMPEROR'S MEN

tional recognition.

A vital contribution to Kurosawa's success with *Rashomon* was the work of cameraman Kazuo Miyagawa. Kurosawa handpicked him even though they had never met. Miyagawa was born in Kyoto and began learning traditional Japanese ink painting when he was 12. A sense of beauty cultivated through this art enabled him to make beautiful black-and-white images with his camera. Before he met Kurosawa, however, he had been held in rather low esteem by Daiei, the company regarding him as too slow.

Miyagawa functioned as a buffer between Kurosawa and the Kyoto staff during the making of *Rashomon*. Kurosawa was demanding in the way he directed. When he failed to get what he wanted, he shouted angrily at the crew. Miyagawa recalls that Kurosawa usually regained composure and explained why he had to shout. He said that even if Kurosawa refused to accept other people's objections, at least he showed respect to those who dissented. Miyagawa must have helped Kurosawa communicate with the crew as those from Kyoto tended to be less than open with an outsider such as Kurosawa.

Since the early years of his career, Kurosawa had distinguished himself with what the Japanese call "*jidai geki*," or "period films," perhaps better known outside of Japan as samurai movies, with warriors engaged in both individual and massed battles. If cowboy movies in America are called "Westerns," samurai movies might be called "Easterns."

Kurosawa's irresistible samurai action comedies—*Yojimbo* in 1961 and *Sanjuro* in 1962—became the director's record-breaking hits. With those films, Kurosawa had boldly defied the Kyoto film industry's traditions, so the people at Toei Kyoto Studio saw Kurosawa's arrival with mixed feelings of excitement and skepticism.

Moreover, that *Tora! Tora! Tora!* was a war movie made Kyoto crews uneasy. Gaps between generations regarding war are common around the world and Japan is no exception. Among generations of the Japanese are three deep divides: among those born in the Meiji and Taisho eras of 1868 to 1926, those who experienced World War II, and those who became adults after the war.

Kurosawa was in the first generation. He was born in the Meiji period and brought up in the Taisho period, eras when the Japanese had imperial aspirations for their nation and believed in its military power. As Kurosawa revealed in *Something Like an Autobiography*, he had evaded the draft and never served in the military services. That may have invited antipathy from members of his crew who had experienced war in the armed forces or as civilians.

Besides, there was something snobbish about *Tora! Tora! Tora!*, a story of elite military men. The actors playing admirals and other senior officers were graduates of the prestigious Naval Academy and were successful businessmen who tended to look down on their social inferiors. It was not surprising that the Kyoto crew gave them the cold shoulder.

Kurosawa treated the non-professional actors with respect. He was strict and relentless while coaching on set but off-stage he endeavored to be sociable. For amusement's sake, he often had them wear their military uniforms and took them out to Ponto-cho, a famous old entertainment district in Kyoto. Ponto-cho was known for its Japanese-style restaurants where *geiko* and their juniors, *maiko*, entertained guests with refined conversation and traditional performing arts. First-class establishments accepted no new customers without a referral from a regular patron. As business leaders, the amateur actors were well aware of this. Kurosawa told them to wear Navy uniforms because he wanted them to become comfortable and enhance the authenticity of the film. The sight of 30 men strolling into the geisha quarter in navy uniforms more than twenty years after the end of World War II, however, raised the eyebrows of Kyotoites.

Work Ethics and Labor Rights

Another obstacle for Kurosawa to overcome was the difference in working conditions between Toho's Studio in Tokyo and Toei's Studio in Kyoto. Members of the staff in Tokyo were full-time employees with guaranteed monthly salaries. Toho had introduced a time-card system that ensured employees received overtime pay. After labor disputes,

Toho's unions had won agreements far more favorable than those of other companies. One requirement, for example, said all employees would be given eight hours of rest after their day's work. Thus Kurosawa's unit would not have complained if they had to work overtime. People were known for going out of their way to work for him, and critics said it was Kurosawa's devoted staff that made his films so exceptional.

At Toei Kyoto Studios most of the staff was made up of freelance workers on short-term contracts. In 1964 when Toei shifted its production from period films to *yakuza* films, the company cut its work force from two thousand full-time employees to nine hundred. The *yakuza* is the Japanese version of the mafia, gangsters in organized syndicates, and movies about them were often popular. At Toei, veteran staffers were transferred to subsidiary companies and many retired or were forced to resign. Even so, the head of the studio, Shigeru Okada, decided those nine hundred employees were still too many and turned many into temporary staff so the company would not have to pay overtime. Those who wanted to stay in Kyoto and continue working had to resign and become freelancers.

The freelance crew on *Tora! Tora! Tora!* had signed contracts with Kurosawa Productions. This was a time, during the 1960s, when labor movements were active around the world. Around 40 of the freelance crew working on *Tora! Tora! Tora!* filed demands with Kurosawa Productions to improve their working conditions. They held Kurosawa responsible, not as director of the film, but as president of Kurosawa Productions. It was still unusual in 1968 for freelance film studio workers to join forces and present their demands to their employers or to go on strike in a conservative place such as Kyoto.

Kinji Fukasaku, another director who was later hired by Fox to complete the Pearl Harbor movie, was no outsider to Kyoto but even he had a hard time in making a movie there. Unlike Kurosawa, he was lucky to have the authoritative support of local staff to smooth things out. As to how the Kyoto crew reacted to Kurosawa, Fukasaku said:

Toei's Kyoto Studio was at the peak of its production of

yakuza gangster films, so there were all these guys saunter-
ing around in *setta* sandals, and then these Naval officers
come along looking all prim and proper, so the Kyoto tough
guys say "Look, what the hell do you think you're doin'?"
(laughs). They knew the actors were getting into character
before stepping on set, so they started joking around within
earshot saying things like "Wow, it's the famous Kurosawa
team," and then Kurosawa blew his top... All these actors
dressed as naval officers and saluting in that peculiar way
with their elbows pulled tight was a big laughing stock for
those '*yakuza*' who were around at the time.

Kurosawa's idea of making his non-professional actors act like
authentic navy men even when they were off-stage only invited ridicule.
Kurosawa no doubt keenly felt an atmosphere of antipathy towards him
in the Kyoto Film Studio. The real sadness is how much this hurt him,
prompting him to over-react and ultimately to push himself beyond the
point of no return.

CHAPTER 11

WAS HE MAD?

News Spreads Like Wildfire

When Fox dismissed Kurosawa, citing his poor health, a press release was prepared in the early morning of December 24, 1968, several hours before Williams informed Kurosawa of Fox's decision. That afternoon, Williams gave Ted Taylor, a public relations staffer, permission to release the announcement written under Richard Zanuck's instructions that Fox must present the facts in simple terms and without harm to Kurosawa's reputation.

It was released in English and Japanese under the names of Twentieth Century-Fox and Kurosawa Productions. Copies were sent from a post office near Toei Kyoto Studios to wire services, newspaper publishers, and broadcast networks by express mail.

The American news agency, United Press International, was the first to react. At 2:30 P.M. on December 25, UPI's Tokyo Bureau dispatched bulletins on the replacement of Kurosawa as the director of *Tora! Tora! Tora!* Another worldwide news agency, the Associated Press, followed. Japan's leading wire service, Kyodo, translated Williams's statement carried by the AP and sent a Japanese version to its subscribers. Leading national dailies, television and radio in Japan gave the news a small play, while tabloids had a field day splashing stories not only about Kurosawa's dismissal but also suspected scandals and conspiracy rumors.

The key passage of Williams's statement:

Mr. Kurosawa gave up his duties as director of the Japanese

249

scenes of *Tora! Tora! Tora!* because of fatigue. It is a great loss to us and we deeply regret it, as the movie has an epoch-making and historic significance. But it is a matter of health and that comes first. Doctors attending him have prescribed extensive rest. We will proceed as quickly as possible to continue filming the production exactly as it was planned and conceived.

The Japanese text was prepared by Kurosawa Productions with subtle departures from the English text. The Japanese version said "resigned" instead of "gave up" and "overwork" in place of "fatigue." The Japanese text was intended to suggest that Kurosawa had resigned of his own will.

The short announcement triggered an uproar because it left many questions unanswered. It was public knowledge that Kurosawa was committed to making *Tora! Tora! Tora!* Why would he "bow out," "give up," "resign," or "withdraw" from the project of his own will? If the great director was really ill, what ailed him? How serious was his condition? Did his departure have anything to do with the eccentric behavior that had been rumored since the filming of *Tora! Tora! Tora!* had begun?

Reporters rushed to the headquarters of Toei Kyoto Studios but Aoyagi and Kurosawa had disappeared. The Japanese and American staff members who might have been able to give answers had also disappeared in anticipation of a media onslaught. Toward evening, Taylor met with reporters after having been cautioned by Williams to be careful about his comments. He offered little clarification, saying: "Fox is worried, as there are few other directors as good as Kurosawa. But the production has got this far, so Fox hopes to name new directors as soon as possible."

Nervous Breakdown?

Then, a surprising remark came from the public relations manager of Kurosawa Productions, Kosuke Ito. Speaking to reporters at the Kyoto

Hotel, he said Kurosawa had suffered a nervous breakdown as a conse-
quence of sustained stressful conditions. Reporters seized on this remark
and December 26 newspapers printed headlines:

"Kurosawa resigns from *Tora! Tora! Tora!*, Hit by nervous
breakdown" (*Mainichi Shimbun*)
"Kurosawa has nervous breakdown, resigns from Japan-US
joint movie, *Tora! Tora! Tora!*" (*Sankei Shimbun*)
"Kurosawa resigns because of fatigue; Serious nervous
breakdown cited" (*Daily Sports*)
"Kurosawa steps down with fatigue, Perfectionism pushes
him into neurosis" (*Hochi Shimbun*)

The next day, the Fox production manager, Stanley Goldsmith,
informed the Japanese and American staffs that Fox planned to go
forward; about 80 of the 100 staffers were present. Goldsmith said it
was Fox's decision to dismiss Kurosawa and that the director had been
informed of the decision, which contradicted the announcement that
Kurosawa had resigned of his own will.

Kurosawa had not been seen since December 25 but the media knew
only that he had not returned to Tokyo. Kurosawa, his wife, Kiyo, and
their daughter, Kazuko, were secretly sheltered at Takeo Kagitani's
villa near Osaka. Kagitani, who played Admiral Yamamoto, sought to
deceive the press on December 27 when he blithely told reporters: "I
have talked with Kurosawa over the telephone. He intends to continue
his work on *Tora! Tora! Tora!* He is not suffering from neurosis nor has
he resigned as director. Such rumors are groundless."

The director of the second unit, Junya Sato, acknowledged that he
had talked with Kurosawa by phone. He said: "Kurosawa has not with-
drawn from the movie. He himself has not heard any such thing from
Fox. Fox made that announcement without telling him anything. As far
as I can tell from the telephone conversation, Kurosawa sounded healthy
and certainly didn't appear to be suffering from a nervous breakdown."

These remarks found their way into headlines:

WAS HE MAD?

"Was Kurosawa sacked? Did he resign? Puzzle deepens just as on the eve of Pearl Harbor attack" (*Hochi Shimbun*) "Kurosawa virtually dismissed, Fox unhappy about slow progress of shooting" (*Tokyo Chunichi Shimbun*)

In sum, it seems that the statement issued by Fox and Kurosawa Productions was released without Kurosawa's knowledge. It also seemed that Kurosawa would not admit that he knew anything about Fox's claim that, on doctor's orders, he needed treatment and weeks of rest.

Pandemonium

On December 30, 1968, the contract between Fox and Kurosawa Productions was terminated in the wake of Kurosawa's dismissal and Kurosawa Productions ceased to have any legal part in the movie. The confusion over Kurosawa's dismissal was compounded by bizarre twists at the beginning of 1969. Public attention shifted from the rift between Fox and Kurosawa to scandals within Kurosawa Productions.

Kurosawa and Tetsu Aoyagi started to exchange accusations in public. On January 16, Aoyagi, scenario writer Ryuzo Kikushima and accountant Sadahiro Kubota stepped down as executives of Kurosawa Productions, saying there had been irreparable damage to their relations with the president, Kurosawa. On January 20, they met 30 reporters at the Tokyo Prince Hotel in a hastily arranged news conference; they had heard that Kurosawa planned a press conference of his own the next day.

For two and a half hours, Aoyagi did most of talking. He claimed Kurosawa had resigned of his own free will and stressed that it was because of illness. He said three doctors had examined Kurosawa. Aoyagi further asserted: "Kurosawa was on the verge of falling into extreme fatigue and neuropathic disorders. He might have managed to continue shooting a little more while at Toei Kyoto Studios. But if he had gone on with shooting schedules under continued stress, there was a possibility that his condition could have worsened to the point of no return when he was shooting on location in Kyushu or directing special-effects photography in Osaka. So, we asked the three doctors to examine him. One of them, Professor Hitoshi Murakami of neuro-psychology at Kyoto University Hospital, was of the opinion that Kurosawa needed treatment and four to eight weeks of complete rest. We consulted with Elmo Williams of Fox and decided that Kurosawa should resign."

The following day, Kurosawa spoke out after nearly a month of silence to divulge what he called "the truth." He invited 60 people, including the non-professional actors and business leaders he had recruited, to the Akasaka Prince Hotel in Tokyo. He thanked them for having cooperated with him and apologized for the confusion. After that meeting, he met with 50 reporters, one of whom asked Kurosawa what he thought about Fox's announcement that he had been dismissed because of illness.

Suddenly, Kurosawa's smile disappeared. With trembling lips, he said: "I'm neither neurotic nor sick. I have been examined by a doctor I completely trust (Dr. Domaru Mikochi) and he found nothing wrong with me. He just said it was about time I might begin feeling tired and that there were some rumors, too. I was also examined by two doctors from Kyoto University Hospital. I remember that one of them (Dr. Hajime Handa) examined my eyes for retinal disorders but found none. The other one (Dr. Hitoshi Murakami) conducted no particular test at all. I just talked with him about my condition. It is this third doctor (Dr. Murakami) who said I needed weeks of rest. I've heard that Fox has this doctor's diagnosis. It was never shown to me. You can surely tell whether I was neurotic or not if you examine the footage of rushes I made at the Kyoto studios."

This news conference grabbed headlines:

"Kurosawa speaks the truth: 'I'm not sick. My social credibility undermined.'" (*Daily Sports*)

"Kurosawa says: 'I was made redundant. It's not a health issue.'" (*Tokyo Chunichi Shimbun*)

Curiously, only the tabloids and sports newspapers carried that news.

WAS HE MAD?

The prestigious national newspapers refrained from carrying the news, possibly because of an unmistakable scent of scandal.

Opinions of Three Doctors

Four medical documents on Kurosawa were found in the private files of a retired Fox employee. They were determined to be authentic copies of the original documents, complete with names of the three doctors, their identities, signatures, seals, and dates. The documents were written in Japanese and filed with English translations, apparently as records for insurance claims arising from Kurosawa's dismissal. Medical records demand the highest degree of privacy but Kurosawa's son, Hisao, and his daughter, Kazuko, gave the author permission to release them in this book.

Four documents were pertinent to Kurosawa's dismissal: Dr. Handa's findings on December 14; Dr. Murakami's opinion on December 18; Dr. Mikochi's diagnosis on December 19; and finally Dr. Murakami's diagnosis on December 27.

When Goldsmith, with his interpreter and Aoyagi, visited Dr. Handa at Kyoto University Hospital on December 14th, the doctor told them Kurosawa could work but he should avoid stress. Goldsmith wrote down what Dr. Handa said, evidently thinking Fox would need the information to file an insurance claim. Goldsmith's notes said:

> Dr. Handa said Kurosawa could continue to work but must not be under pressure or strain. He said Kurosawa is a tyrant and highly excitable, so everyone must cater to him. Tranquilizers were prescribed.

Goldsmith wrote that Dr. Handa at first suspected a brain tumor. But brain tumors usually cause headaches, vomiting, nausea, paralyses of limbs, inability to speak clearly, dizziness or epileptic seizures. Dr. Handa found none of those symptoms in Kurosawa and, in addition, considered this to be outside the scope of his practice as a brain surgeon.

He did not write a diagnosis but gave Goldsmith a verbal explanation of his findings and advised him that Kurosawa should see Dr. Murakami, a neuro-psychological expert at Kyoto University Hospital.

At the request of Fox, Dr. Murakami's medical 'opinion' (not diagnosis) on Kurosawa's condition was given in a handwritten note on December 18 when Kurosawa lost consciousness and was admitted to the hospital for the second time. The document titled "Opinion" said:

> Mr. Akira Kurosawa needs at least more than four weeks of rest due to continuous insufficient sleep, anxiety and excitement that are conspicuous. However, his present state is a reactionary excitement caused by his pertinacity by nature and excessive feeling of responsibility to the work he is carrying on. He will recover to normality after the rest recommended.

Dr. Murakami wrote a formal diagnosis on December 27, three days after Kurosawa had been dismissed. The doctor identified himself as professor of neuro-psychology at the Medical School of Kyoto University.

> Name of illness: Neurasthenia. Diagnosis: He is suffering from disturbance of sleep, agitated with feelings of anxiety and in manic excitement, caused by above mentioned illness. It is necessary for him to have rest and medical treatment for more than two months.

Several medical experts said that, to render his diagnosis, Dr. Murakami must have examined Kurosawa after he had been admitted to the hospital and taken some rest. Dr. Murakami is believed to have asked Kurosawa about his main complaints and to have observed Kurosawa's facial expressions, complexion, and reflexes. While talking with Kurosawa, Dr. Murakami evidently observed that Kurosawa had a tendency to be obstinate in his work.

In his news conference in Tokyo on January 21, 1969, Kurosawa

WAS HE MAD?

described what happened when he met Dr. Handa and Dr. Murakami at Kyoto University Hospital on December 18, 1968: "One doctor (Dr. Handa) said there was nothing wrong with me. He asked if there was anything going on at my work place that irritates me. About the other doctor (Dr. Murakami), I just chatted with him."

Experts say that Dr. Murakami's findings were important from a medical point of view. He referred not only to symptoms but to causes and indicated when Kurosawa's symptoms had started. He listed three symptoms, sustained lack of sleep, anxiety, and excitement. He attributed these to Kurosawa's pertinacious nature and excessive feelings of responsibility, indicating Kurosawa's symptoms started after he had begun shooting the movie. When Fox sought insurance payments, a focal point of a dispute between Fox and the insurers was whether Kurosawa had been sick before production started or whether he became sick after he began shooting.

Dr. Murakami said Kurosawa's condition was due to reactionary excitement. He said Kurosawa had a mild mental condition but would recover if he stayed away from work-related stress for about four weeks. Experts say that Dr. Murakami thus denied that Kurosawa suffered from a 'serious' mental disease such as schizophrenia.

Dr. Mikochi's Diagnosis:

On December 19, a day after Kurosawa had undergone Dr. Murakami's examination, Kurosawa's chief physician, Dr. Mikochi, traveled to Kyoto from Tokyo at Aoyagi's request. He examined Kurosawa at the inn and wrote a diagnosis that night. This handwritten document carried his signature and seal and said:

Mr. Akira Kurosawa was examined by me on December 19, 1968, in Kyoto. The examination of the patient resulted in the following findings:

ALL THE EMPEROR'S MEN

1. Physical findings:
   Blood pressure: 150 over 98
   Pulse: 80
   Chest: Normal
   Abdomen: Normal
   Limbs: Normal
2. Neurological findings:
   Cerebral nerves: Normal
   Spinal system: Normal
   Ataxia: None
   Pathological reflex: None
   Pupils: Both of same size, normal reflex to light
   Fundi: Slight signs of arteriosclerosis, otherwise normal
3. Mental condition:
   Orientation: Normal
   Judgment: Normal
   Thinking: Normal

However, the patient shows the slightest signs of mental tension.
Sedative should be taken. From the above findings, I conclude that the patient is quite fit for normal work.

The contradictory diagnoses confused Kurosawa Productions and Fox. On December 18, Dr. Murakami said Kurosawa needed treatment and rest for two months. The following day, Dr. Mikochi said Kurosawa was fit for normal work. Yoichi Matsue, an assistant to Kurosawa, said: "Aoyagi was the only person who accompanied Kurosawa when he met the two doctors. One day, he told the main staff that Kurosawa needed four weeks of rest and they would just have to believe the doctor's words. The next day, he came back to the staff with another doctor's diagnosis that Kurosawa was all right. And he said they had to go back to shooting. The staff just didn't know what to do. They were very angry." Whatever the case, Fox did not hesitate to take the next step once they had decided to replace Kurosawa, which was to file a claim with the insurance underwriters.

Cast Insurance

When Fox signed the contract with Kurosawa, the company had Kurosawa insured for 1.5 million dollars. It is called "cast insurance," which movie companies take out against possible losses if a contracted person becomes sick or incapacitated.

Kurosawa, who declared he knew little about worldly affairs, did not care at all about insurance matters. Records show that Aoyagi was also paying little attention to Fox's obligations on cast insurance. All this eventually led to untoward difficulties between Fox and Kurosawa Productions later.

In the United States and Europe, regulations govern disputes over insurance benefits. Even so, a dispute is often the beginning of a war between insurer and insured. Each has a clear view of the process from negotiation to victory or defeat in court. The players are investigators who can see through padding of claims, brokers who are professional dispute settlers, certified public accountants, and lawyers.

To arrange cast insurance for *Tora! Tora! Tora!*, Fox contracted a consortium of insurance companies who commissioned a group of brokers in a consulting firm to negotiate with Fox. To succeed in its claim for insurance benefits on Kurosawa, Fox had to prove that Kurosawa became sick after he began shooting *Tora! Tora! Tora!* and make a convincing estimate of the damages incurred.

Stanley Goldsmith sent three medical documents concerning Kurosawa, together with their English translations, to Beverly Hills. The packet with documents was addressed to Stan Hough, head of Fox's production department, and a confidant of Richard Zanuck. Goldsmith added his explanation to Dr. Murakami's diagnosis that said Kurosawa had neurasthenia. Goldsmith's often-quoted description of Kurosawa as "not a normal man" appears to have influenced Fox executives' appraisal of the situation:

Dr. Murakami said Mr. Kurosawa was suffering from a continued nervous breakdown. Kurosawa has a mental condition, does not sleep well, nor does he realize he needs treatment. The doctor believes Kurosawa needs four to eight weeks in a hospital in order to recover and even then cannot guarantee that the condition will not happen again. At present time the doctor believes Mr. Kurosawa is not a normal man.

On January 1, 1969, Goldsmith sent another report to Beverly Hills, citing Kurosawa's 'eccentric' behavior and asserting that his illness made it impossible to continue shooting, with Fox suffering losses as a result. Fox's application for insurance benefits was dated December 18, 1968, the day Fox became aware that Kurosawa was seriously ill. Fox said it would submit its estimate of the damage when the assessment of its losses was known but indicated it would be at least one million dollars.

The insurers reacted swiftly, sending two investigators to Japan to collect evidence on which to base their own judgment. When they arrived in Japan in January, 1969, it was not yet clear what Fox would do about the Japanese sequence of *Tora! Tora! Tora!* While Fox was pondering, expenses of $20,000 a day piled up; they included payments for crews, stage-rental, and leases on real and movable properties. If expenses for relocating to Hawaii were added, the insurance claim would be enormous.

It was not easy to calculate Fox's losses. Kurosawa had been behind schedule but did finish some scenes. If this footage could be used in the final print, that work would not be wasted. Would the expensive studio sets and open sets built to Kurosawa's order survive the change of directors and subsequent shooting plan?

Several issues perplexed the insurance investigators. Kurosawa contended he was not ill and denounced Fox for sacking him on false grounds. It became apparent that Fox was not always precise and, further, it became clear to both Fox and the underwriters that if they contested the allegation that Kurosawa was ill, the dispute would drag on

WAS HE MAD?

with no winner even if the issue was brought to court.

The insurers offered a compromise. They were ready to pay $250,000 dollars in settlement, saying they took into account the years of amicable business relations with Fox. Fox rejected the offer. The insurance underwriters raised the settlement offer to $500,000 but Fox quickly rejected that, too. On April 19, 1969, Fox submitted an estimate of its claim to the insurers: $1,435,000. The insurers put their reply on hold and sent more investigators to Japan to conduct a fresh round of inquiries.

Tug of War

On February 4, 1970, a certified public accountant considered neutral by the two sides presented an audit of Fox's insurance claim in front of two adjusters for the insurance company and two lawyers for Fox. The amount allowable by the accountant was $625,000 dollars, or 43.5 percent of Fox's claim.

After the accountant left the room, the insurance adjusters revealed something that astounded Fox. They said an investigator sent to Japan had interviewed 30 people who had worked with Kurosawa and obtained statements in which none said Kurosawa had been ill during the work on *Tora! Tora! Tora!* Twenty-six said "he was not ill at all" and "the remainder declined to give an opinion." The adjusters said the investigator had asked to interview Kurosawa but was unable to meet him because he was busy with a new movie, *Dodesukaden.*

The insurance underwriters looked into Kurosawa's style in making movies and found that he was "a notoriously slow worker" with many eccentricities and peculiar work patterns. They concluded that Kurosawa was "exhausted and drank too much" while filming *Tora! Tora! Tora!*

After this revelation, the adjusters concluded that "Kurosawa had not suffered any illness during the course of filming and was not ill when he was removed from the picture." They concluded that they were "denying any claim for cast insurance." Even so, they suggested that to save time and the cost of litigation and in consideration of the years of friendly relations with Fox, they were ready to offer some payment.

Hearing this, Richard Zanuck was infuriated. His handwritten note among Fox's documents said: "We should fight this all the way. We certainly have plenty of proof. All of our files should be examined. I, for example, have some personal letters from Tetsu which might be helpful. We cannot let the insurance company get away with this."

An angry letter by Stan Hough, head of the production department, on April 13, 1970, said:

> During the years of 1966, 1967 and 1968 we paid premiums of $2,175,000 for cast insurance. Our claims during this same period came to $600,000. Therefore, the insurance companies show a net profit of $1,575,000, which is quite tidy. To be informed over one year later on February 4 that Mr. Reider (Al Reider, an adjuster) did not intend to honor our claim in this case is shabby treatment indeed, particularly to a company which has always vigorously endeavored to keep shooting under the most adverse of circumstances and it is through these efforts that they have been able to net such a high percentage of profit. I realize that it is also to our benefit to keep shooting in such times but the relation of premium and profit does indicate good faith on our part. Mr. Reider is relying upon the fact that Mr. Kurosawa is an idol in Japan, the only truly international figure upon which the stature of their industry depends and therefore few people will step forward to diminish him and therefore their industry as well. The mental illness of a distinguished foreign director may be difficult to prove in a court of law but I would like to try rather than tamely submit to this kind of intimidation.

Negotiations continued until May 6, when the insurance companies gave Fox an ultimatum. They said it did not consider Fox's cast insurance claim to be legitimate and argued that Fox's claim that Kurosawa fell ill while shooting *Tora! Tora! Tora!* was not supported by sufficient medical proof.

Further, the insurance companies questioned the procedures Fox had used to insure Kurosawa. They asserted that Kurosawa's certificate of health, which Fox had attached to its application for insurance, had serious flaws. This certificate had been written by Kurosawa's primary physician, Dr. Domaru Mikochi, on November 30, 1968, and was hand-written with a fountain pen on the letterhead of the Hibiya Hospital in Tokyo, where he served as a surgeon and deputy director. The two-line certificate that carried his signature and seal read:

> Mr. Akira Kurosawa: After close examination, I find that there is no problem in his physical and mental condition.

The insurers claimed that this certificate had flaws, asserting:

1. Dr. Mikochi's certificate of health is more like a diagnosis than a medical examination report and cannot be accepted as a legitimate certificate for the purpose of this contract.
2. Dr. Mikochi is Kurosawa's private physician and not approved by the insurance companies.
3. The certificate carries no medical check-up lists required by the insurance companies, nor their results.
4. The certificate carries no signature of Kurosawa to prove that he underwent the medical examination by Dr. Mikochi.
5. The certificate came late. It reached the insurance companies on January 7, 1969, more than one month after the shooting began.

The insurance companies again offered $150,000 dollars as a gesture of good will but maintained that if Fox intended to litigate the claim, they would respond in court.

Fox was appalled and began another investigation. It soon became clear that they had little evidence for counter-argument and that the insurance companies were right when they said Fox's application was flawed. For the most part, Goldsmith, production chief of the Japanese sequence, was to blame. Goldsmith blamed Aoyagi, saying he had repeatedly asked Aoyagi to produce a health certificate. That did not help Goldsmith, who was held responsible when Fox was late in submitting the certificate to the insurance companies. It appears that Goldsmith just forgot to send it to the U.S.

Fox examined the certificate of health and found problems. On November 30, 1968, when Kurosawa was supposed to have been given a medical examination in Tokyo, he was in a Kyoto hotel room with Darryl Zanuck and Williams for four hours editing the final screenplay. Further, at the Hibiya Hospital in Tokyo where Dr. Mikochi worked, it was mandatory for doctors to conduct urine and blood tests, take a chest X-ray, and measure blood pressure before issuing health certificates. Kurosawa's certificate contains no record of those tests.

Fox still had the option of going to court but capitulated under pressure from the insurers. Fox feared a court case would undermine its corporate image in Japan and eventually jeopardize box-office prospects for *Tora! Tora! Tora!*

In August 1970, a month prior to the scheduled world premiere, Fox received $175,000 dollars from the insurance companies in full and final settlement of the case.

Did Kurosawa Have a Second Chance?

After Kurosawa was fired, Richard Zanuck argued that Fox should suspend all shooting in Japan and move the crews to Hawaii to complete the movie there, contending this would cost less. Darryl Zanuck agreed but Williams opposed, asserting that everything done in Japan would be wasted and that it would undermine Fox's intention of portraying the Pearl Harbor attack from both Japanese and American perspectives.

To sort this out, Richard Zanuck and Stan Hough arrived in Japan on February 12, 1969. For two days, they discussed every aspect of the project with Williams and Goldsmith. In the end, the four agreed that shooting the Japanese sequences should continue in Japan. They accepted a Williams plan for replacing members of the cast and the directors.

At a news conference on March 4, Williams announced that shooting on *Tora! Tora! Tora!* would resume. He said Fox had signed contracts the day before with Toshio Masuda and Kinji Fukasaku as directors. Masuda would take charge of filming at Toei Kyoto Studios and in Kyushu. In Osaka, Fukasaku would be in charge of the innovative front projection system, which involved a special effects process for combining foreground performance with pre-filmed background footage. In the main cast, So Yamamura would play Isoroku Yamamoto, Tatsuya Mihashi would be Minoru Genda, and Takahiro Tamura would play Mitsuo Fuchida, the commander of the aerial attack itself. They were all established actors.

In addition, Richard Zanuck was on a secret mission for his father and had been instructed to see Kurosawa in person. On February 9, Darryl Zanuck had sent a telegram to Kurosawa saying:

> My dear Akira Kurosawa:
> Nothing perturbed me more than the recent unfortunate incident. Much as I would like to talk with you personally I broke my leg while skiing last Christmas holidays. My son Richard who respects you no less will visit Japan on my behalf. Talk it over with him person to person. Believe something satisfactory to all concerned could come out. Contact New York Plaza Hotel in case you want to reach me direct. Darryl Zanuck

According to Kurosawa's assistant Yoichi Matsue, the telegram reached Kurosawa Productions about 8:30 A.M. on February 10. Before the hotel could pass the telegram to Kurosawa, Aoyagi came by the front desk and accepted the telegram on Kurosawa's behalf. The hotel's record has a shortened signature by Aoyagi as "Tetsu." Matsue learned about

ALL THE EMPEROR'S MEN

this later when he found the telegram's number and went to the central Tokyo office of Japan's International Telegram and Telephone Corporation, known by its acronym in Japanese, KDD. He explained that the telegram was addressed to Kurosawa and obtained a copy for Kurosawa who read it on February 19.

Meantime, Richard Zanuck arrived in Japan on February 12. At noon on Friday, February 14, a woman speaking Japanese and identifying herself as an employee of the Tokyo office of Fox telephoned Kurosawa at his home. She said Zanuck wanted to see him and asked him to go to the Hotel Okura at 5:45 P.M. that day. Kurosawa did not know about Darryl Zanuck's telegram and became suspicious. He summoned Matsue to discuss what to do but time was against him. Zanuck apparently thought Kurosawa's lack of an answer was a snub.

The next day, February 15, Matsue telephoned Fox's Tokyo office but that was Saturday and the office was closed. The next day, February 16, Zanuck left for the United States. Matsue later maintained that if Darryl Zanuck's telegram had reached Kurosawa on February 10, Kurosawa would have met with Richard Zanuck and might have had a second chance to be the director.

On February 19, Kurosawa sent a telegram to Richard Zanuck, explaining the situation. The message read:

Richard Zanuck Vice President:
Most regretful missing opportunity meeting you in Tokyo owning to a great misunderstanding. It has been disclosed only today that Mr. Darryl Zanuck kindly cabled me advising your arrival in Tokyo on his behalf and also that the cable addressed to Tokyo Prince Hotel unfortunately stolen and hidden by Tetsu Aoyagi. Tetsu already resigned himself from Kurosawa Productions as you probably know and to my great regret his strange movement since last December caused so many confusions and misunderstanding everywhere. I am still keen to talk over with you person to person regarding resolution Tora problem. Looking forward to hav-

WAS HE MAD?

ing any opportunity of seeing you again very near future. Kindest regards. Akira Kurosawa

When he received the telegram, Zanuck sent it to his father at once, declaring that he would not go to Tokyo again:

Dear Dad: Have just received following wire from Kurosawa. (entire transcript of Kurosawa's cable inserted here) This man is absolutely crazy besides being rude. Whether or not your wire got to him or was stolen by Tetsu is beside the point. He knew I was in Tokyo and we had a definite appointment set up and then he backed out at the last minute. I don't see any point in answering this as we must cut this guy off completely or it will never end and I am not anxious to fly back to Tokyo as I have misplaced my crash helmut. Love. See you later. Dick

"My crash helmut," was, of course, a reference to Kurosawa's wearing a helmet while shooting in Kyoto. In Japan, Kurosawa waited in vain for a reply from Richard. This marked the end of communications between Kurosawa and Darryl Zanuck. Kurosawa and Matsue are believed to have met with Aoyagi on February 22, in the presence of a lawyer, and asked him what happened. Aoyagi is said to have denied that he had intercepted the telegram.

It's not known what "secret mission" Darryl Zanuck had entrusted to his son but one thing is certain: It was not to reinstate Kurosawa as director of *Tora! Tora! Tora!* It is known that Zanuck was personally concerned about Kurosawa. Given detailed reports by his subordinates, the mogul felt sure that Kurosawa was suffering from mental illness. On January 8, 1969, Zanuck sent a telegram from Paris to Stan Hough, confiding in him how he felt:

Dear Stan: Many thanks for the detailed information in your telex on 'TORA' situation which is baffling to say the

ALL THE EMPEROR'S MEN

least and undoubtedly and regrettably Kurosawa is obviously ill and in no physical condition to continue even after eight weeks recommended by psychiatrist and doctors report. Can Bole obtain a copy of medical report that significantly omits any guarantee of non-recurrence of neurasthenia? I agree with Dick that any negotiation with Kurosawa's attorney should be realistic as he has cost us millions and while I personally like him and admire his previous works, it is my strong recommendation that we refuse at this time to negotiate any sort of settlement as this not only indicates that we discharged him from the film. But actually we have no logical way at this time to estimate our own damages and what they may eventually come to through no fault of our own. How can we possibly pay a man, even if he is mentally ill who has put us into a situation that has cost us millions?

Evidently, Darryl Zanuck wanted his son to see Kurosawa to ease along the negotiations between Fox and Kurosawa Productions for screen credits after Fox had completed *Tora! Tora! Tora!* Kurosawa had done much in preparing for the movie and Zanuck might have wanted to give him credit. Zanuck was aware of the power—not to mention the value—of Kurosawa's name. Years later, Williams recalled that Zanuck not only appreciated Kurosawa's ability as a director but liked him as a person. As Williams saw it, Zanuck had shaken hands with Kurosawa as a friend at the studio in Kyoto. Then Kurosawa succumbed to illness and was dismissed. Not surprisingly, Zanuck wanted to give something back to Kurosawa.

Richard Zanuck had a different view. He was an efficient businessman and has been described as dry and merciless in his work. His father's request had nothing to do with the main purpose of his visit to Japan, which was to get things started again, and he might well have been reluctant to do as he had been asked. The appointment with Kurosawa was set a time (5:45 P.M. Friday, February 14, 1969) after the younger Zanuck had completed meetings with Williams and Goldsmith. It is

WAS HE MAD?

possible that he was ready to give Kurosawa only 15 minutes of his time. Zanuck the son did not like Kurosawa. From the beginning, he had distanced himself from the director whom the younger Zanuck believed had ignored him. When Kurosawa's eccentricities were made known, Zanuck made him an object of ridicule, giving him the derisive nickname 'Helmut.' In turn, Kurosawa had little time for Richard Zanuck and underestimated the power of the young executive.

What Made Kurosawa What He Was?

After Kurosawa was dismissed, the Japanese media reported that he might be suffering from neurosis or even a nervous breakdown. Some tabloids bluntly asserted that he was mad.

In 1968, Kurosawa was 58 years old, tall and husky, and looked healthy. But when *Tora! Tora! Tora!* was in pre-production, he was taken ill several times, which was always hushed up. Even so, sometimes incidents happened in public. In May, 1968, when Kurosawa was visiting Hollywood, he was invited to dinner by Robert Wise, director of *The Sound of Music*. As the party began, Kurosawa was sipping whisky and talking cheerfully with other guests. Suddenly, he complained of an acute pain in the neck and retreated to a rest room. Wise offered to call an ambulance but Kurosawa declined and was driven back to his hotel. He slept well that night and felt better in the morning.

In June 1968, after he returned from Hollywood, he again complained of headache and acute pain in the neck and was admitted to the Sanno Hospital in Tokyo. In November, a month before the principal photography was scheduled to begin in Kyoto, Kurosawa collapsed on the beach in Hokkaido while visiting the site of the second unit shoot led by Junya Sato. From Fox's internal documents and what Aoyagi said later, Goldsmith and Williams as well as Aoyagi knew that Kurosawa was prone to seizures.

Kurosawa's family remembers that he often lost consciousness. His daughter, Kazuko, writes in her book: "My father sometimes experienced momentary lapses of awareness. This occurred when he was too excited or over tired." This could happen while they were traveling, and Kazuko tells about an incident aboard a plane: "Soon after the plane took off and my father began sipping red wine, he fell unconscious. I was shocked. But I knew this was not rare with him. He frequently suffered from a shortage of oxygen to the brain."

A decade after he was dismissed, Kurosawa wrote an autobiography titled *Gama no Abura* (*A Toad's Oil*) in 1978, which was translated into English under the title *Something Like an Autobiography*. Kurosawa admitted he had suffered from epilepsy all his life. (Quotes are taken from Vintage Books Edition, 1983.) Kurosawa said: "I learned from having an X-ray taken of the vascular system of my brain that my main artery has a peculiar bend in it. Apparently a normal artery is straight, and my condition was diagnosed as congenital epilepsy. As a matter of fact, I used to have frequent seizures as a child, and Director Kajiro Yamamoto—my mentor at Toho Studios—often said to me, 'you have a habit of falling into a state of distraction.' I never noticed it myself, but it seems I would sometimes have brief lapses during my work when I completely forgot what I was doing and went into a kind of trance. The brain needs a lot of oxygen, and apparently a lack of oxygen to the brain is extremely dangerous. When I am overworked or overly excited, it seems this bent main artery in my brain cuts off the blood supply and causes me to have small epileptic seizures."

On his character, Kurosawa said: "I am short-tempered and obstinate. These defects are still pronounced and when I was an assistant director, they gave rise to some very serious problems." He threw a boxed lunch at a production chief and a "silver-colored glass ball" at a director for whom he was an assistant. He wrote: "Even though I have passed the age of sixty, I haven't been able to cure my quick temper... According to my assistant directors, when I get angry my face turns red, but the end of my nose is drained of pigmentation—an anger that would lend itself well to color film, they say."

Evidence suggests that Kurosawa and his family were aware of his epilepsy when he was a child but not until he was 68 did he acknowledge it. Kazuko quoted her father: "One day, I had my brain examined, and

WAS HE MAD?

was told that the main artery of my brain has a peculiar bend that looks like a question mark. The doctor said if I was operated on, the bend could be corrected and my epileptic seizures could vanish. But then, he said, my own individual talent might be gone too. I refused to take surgery because I didn't want any change in my way of life."

Medical experts say an epileptic seizure might explain why Kurosawa remembers nothing about the meeting with Williams on December 24, 1968, when he was informed of his dismissal. Four weeks later, at a news conference on January 21, he said: "I knew nothing about my dismissal. Fox suddenly announced I would resign because I was sick. I was baffled. With so many people doing so much work for the movie, how can I suddenly resign?"

Medical experts say Kurosawa was probably telling the truth. One theory is that being told of the dismissal shocked him so much that his brain sought to avert the stress by erasing the memory of what he had just heard. Another theory suggests he experienced a momentary lapse of awareness that often happens to those with epilepsy.

Dostoevsky and van Gogh

Kurosawa said a doctor once told him that epilepsy was common among artists and geniuses such as Fyodor Mikhaylovich Dostoevsky and Vincent van Gogh.

Two psycho-pathologists in Japan analyzed Kurosawa's films, screenplays and his autobiography and have concluded that Kurosawa suffered from a particular type of epilepsy, known as 'Temporal Lobe Epilepsy.' In their book, *Kurosawa and Psychopathology*, Drs. Hirotaka Kashiwase and Shin Kato say this is the secret behind the appeal of Kurosawa's movies.

The doctors point to Kurosawa's admission that he often experienced convulsions when he was young. He could have been experiencing lapses of awareness, often marked by staring. These affect part of the brain and in this form of epilepsy, the center of emotion in the brain is affected, causing irritation, anxiety, terror, and anger. This epilepsy is known to

ALL THE EMPEROR'S MEN

cause 'Geschwind Syndrome,' symptoms of disconnection or bad moods. Dr. Kashiwase listed six reasons for saying Kurosawa suffered from Geschwind Syndrome:

1. Kurosawa himself said he often became short-tempered and furious.
2. He was a perfectionist at work.
3. None of Kurosawa's films have love with women as central themes.
4. Kurosawa was careful in presenting smallest details.
5. Humanism was the main theme of his movies.
6. He wrote a large volume of screenplays.

Dr. Kashiwase likened Kurosawa to Dostoevsky in personality and behavior. Kurosawa was devoted to the Russian author and made a film based on his novel *The Idiot* at Shochiku Ofuna Studios in 1951. In a television interview, Kurosawa said: "I like the novel very much so I thought I might make a film of it. But when I was shooting the film, I felt great pain. I felt as if Dostoevsky were riding on my shoulder." His original film lasted for more than four hours. When the studio told him to cut it in half, he blew up: "If you want to cut the film, you might as well cut it in half lengthwise—from beginning to end."

Dostoevsky suffered from Temporal Lobe Epilepsy and medical scientists often advise their protégés to read Dostoevsky as an aid to understanding epilepsy. *The Idiot* recounts detailed descriptions of people suffering from epileptic seizures. Dostoevsky produced masterpieces between seizures, with admirers saying he was able to do so because he was epileptic.

A prolific artist who fought seizures almost every day was Vincent van Gogh, the painter whose work Kurosawa liked. His penultimate film, *Yume (Akira Kurosawa's Dreams)*, has eight episodes. In the fifth, *Karasu (Crows)*, Kurosawa depicts himself as an art student and tells of an imaginative encounter with van Gogh. "I," the art student, is overwhelmed by the works of van Gogh, and he goes into the painting of

The Langlois Bridge at Arles to seek after the artist eternally.

Whenever Kurosawa was lonely in his late teens, he dreamed of being a painter. When he became lonely in his twilight years, he resumed painting to find himself again. Kurosawa identified with Dostoevsky as a writer and van Gogh as a painter. Could he perhaps have identified himself with these two great artists because they shared the lifelong challenge of epilepsy?

CHAPTER 12

CROOKS AND
CONTRACTS

Snake in the Grass

Kurosawa's daughter, Kazuko, once said, "It seems to me my father was cheated by many people." She went on: "My father trusted people and never doubted them. Even when he was taken for a ride, he never learned his lesson. For crooks, he must have been an easy target. It would have been as easy as twisting a baby's arm."

In her book, *My Father, Akira Kurosawa*, Kazuko asked: "What exactly was it about, that *Tora! Tora! Tora!* incident? In those days, from the end of 1968 to the spring of 1969, our family was at a loss. All around us, speculation swirled. 'Sooner or later, it will all be clear,' my father would say in news conferences. But it has never been made clear, still to this day (year 2000). But I think I know what happened. Certain crooks feed on the cinema industry. They caught the scent of money and, driven by greed, got away with whatever they could lay their hands on. This resulted in total confusion."

Years later, Kurosawa remarked, "I don't know why but I was always surrounded by con men." In *Something Like an Autobiography*, Kurosawa wrote: "What lurks at the bottom of the human heart remains a mystery to me. Since that time (1949, early in his career), I have observed many different kinds of people—swindlers, people who have killed or died for money, plagiarists—and they all look like normal people, so I am confused. In fact, more than simply 'normal,' these people have very nice faces and say very nice things, so I am all the more confused."

In *Kumonosu-jo (The Throne of Blood* aka *The Castle of the Spider's Web)*, a film that Kurosawa made in 1957, there is an evil spirit in the form of

275

an old woman like the witch in Shakespeare's *Macbeth*, on which Kurosawa loosely based his work. In a scene in which she sees the feudal lord flinch when he realizes she is aware of his hidden ambition, she says: "A funny thing, human beings are. They are afraid of looking into the depths of their hearts."

The battle between good and evil was a lifelong Kurosawa theme. He was a humanist with his basic philosophy rooted in human love. But the mysterious darkness he perceived to be in the human heart was an undercurrent that permeated many of his works. Perhaps this dark view explains why he was obsessed with a search for the basic agreement between him and Fox. Kurosawa claimed he had never seen it, let alone read it, and he believed his dismissal to have been unjust. He was confident that the details of the agreement were behind his dismissal. Kurosawa was determined to identify the "swindlers" who had deceived him by taking advantage of the agreement. He wanted to confront them, even though this might have been his way of escaping reality.

Kurosawa was president of Kurosawa Productions and thus it might be hard to believe that he had never seen the document called the Agreement. Kazuko said this was typical of her father. "When he was making a movie, he was always so concentrated on the ideas and images around his subject. At such a time, he was in high spirits. But he didn't really care anything about agreements and such. He left that kind of thing to others. In this case, too, he was in the dark as to the details of the agreement with Fox. He knew nothing about what was going on behind the scenes, or who signed what kind of an agreement and with whom. He was simply dedicated to making a good movie. Even if he had been shown the agreement, he wouldn't have been able to make heads or tails of it, as it was written in English."

Many things changed drastically after December 24, the day he was dismissed, mainly having to do with Tetsuo Aoyagi, who had been his trusted right-hand man and his contact with Fox. In Kurosawa's view, Aoyagi suddenly appeared to be a snake he had taken to his bosom, a double-crosser in the guise of a friend. Kurosawa had demanded that Aoyagi give him the agreement with Fox. Aoyagi wouldn't comply,

ALL THE EMPEROR'S MEN

citing this or that pretext. Kurosawa's suspicion grew deeper until he became convinced that Aoyagi was the leader of those who had plotted his dismissal. Late in January 1969, a month after the dismissal, Kurosawa and Aoyagi held separate news conferences to accuse each other in public.

At the Tokyo Prince Hotel, Aoyagi called Kurosawa "an artistic kid" who didn't know anything about the real world. He said: "I've done my best to ensure that Kurosawa can make a good movie. If he says he rewrote the screenplay 26 (sic) times, then I rewrote the agreement 260 times to make the conditions more favorable for him. The fact is, he was so preoccupied with the movie that he didn't know anything about any part of the agreement."

The following day, January 21, Kurosawa claimed in a press conference at the Akasaka Prince Hotel that he had never seen the agreement. "I didn't sign it because Aoyagi said he was still negotiating some part," he said. "I told Aoyagi to send me the agreement by registered mail. But it never reached me." Asked what he saw as the cause of the dispute over the agreement, Kurosawa said: "It may just be my imagination, but it seems everything started with the way Aoyagi handled it. In the first place, he didn't bother to tell us about small requests from Fox. Then he didn't bother to tell Fox about our own small requests. All these accumulated into serious rifts and problems. In the end, we were forced into an impossible situation."

All through 1969 and 1970, Kurosawa continued to investigate Aoyagi's suspected role. The Kurosawa team was led by Assistant Director Yoichi Matsue and included a lawyer. During this period, three executives of the production company who were opposed to Kurosawa—Tetsuo Aoyagi, Ryuzo Kikushima, and Sadahiro Kubota—resigned. On March 7, 1969, Matsue and Kurosawa's wife became executives of Kurosawa Productions. Kurosawa appears finally to have obtained a copy of the agreement from a Fox lawyer in April 1969. As the investigation continued, internal disputes and scandals erupted and the tabloids had a feast.

On June 26, 1969, after Fox's version of *Tora! Tora! Tora!* had been completed and the dispute appeared to have abated somewhat, Kurosawa gave a party at the Akasaka Prince Hotel for the amateur actors to thank them and apologize to them. The invitation read: "All my efforts over three years to make this movie ended in vain. My sense of frustration was great. And as the facts became clear, I had to face an ugly truth that I myself had not wanted to see. What I faced was, in a way, a battle with myself."

On the other side, Aoyagi set out his position in an interview with the *Weekly Asahi*, claiming he had undertaken countless rounds of contract negotiations with Twentieth Century-Fox to make conditions favorable to Kurosawa. "Kurosawa was devoted to making the movie and did not understand any of the provisions," he said. "He didn't read English. Expecting him to understand an agreement written in English would be like asking a layman to understand nuclear physics."

In later years, Kurosawa was quoted as saying: "Tetsu Aoyagi is bad. But if I shot at him, the bullet would go round the world and hit me in the back of the head."

Contracts as Alien Culture

A copy of the Fox-Kurosawa contracts was made available to this writer through Kurosawa's nephew, the late Yoshio Inoue, and the lawyer, Jeffrey L. Graubart, who represented Kurosawa Productions, with the consent of Kurosawa Productions executives. The text was written in English; no Japanese version is known to exist. The terminology was technical and legalistic and required an explanation, which was provided by several Japanese and American legal scholars.

Twentieth Century-Fox presented a draft agreement to Kurosawa Productions on March 28, 1967. That draft was revised three times, on December 18, 1967; on June 28, 1968; and on August 12, 1968. Fox presented the final draft to Kurosawa Productions on December 11, 1968, which was 13 days before Kurosawa was fired. This "letter of agreement" is a common form of contract in the United States but is not often used in Japan. Such letters can be legally enforced in the U.S. The Fox-

ALL THE EMPEROR'S MEN

Kurosawa agreement was typed on Fox's letterhead, had 26 pages, 19 in the main part and seven in Exhibit A, and stated explicitly all of the rights and obligations of Kurosawa Productions

At first glance the agreement looks like an ordinary business letter, beginning with "Gentlemen" and ending with "Yours very truly." The first paragraph states: "This letter, when signed by you and us, will constitute our agreement regarding the possible production entitled *Tora! Tora! Tora!* (hereinafter referred to as "the Photoplay")."

The substance began in the second paragraph and went on for 22 articles. The last page said: "If the foregoing is in accordance with your understanding and agreement, please indicate your approval and acceptance thereof in the space herein below provided." Below that were two lines, one saying "ACCEPTED AND AGREED TO," and the other, "KUROSAWA PRODUCTIONS, LTD." Below that were two more lines; beneath one is typed AKIRA KUROSAWA and under the other, TETSU AOYAGI. Above the names are spaces for signatures. The final agreement kept at Fox remains blank on the lines for the signatures of the Japanese.

It is usual practice for such an agreement to have one original and two carbon copies. Kurosawa and Aoyagi were to sign all three and send them back to Fox. Fox's legal department was to examine them and send one copy back to Kurosawa Productions and the other carbon copy to Creative Management Associates (CMA), the law firm that specialized in the entertainment business in Beverly Hills and which represented Kurosawa Productions. Then the Agreement would become valid.

At a news conference in Tokyo on January 20, 1969, Aoyagi acknowledged that Kurosawa did not sign the final Agreement, saying: "Kurosawa began shooting without signing the Agreement. But this should have worked in favor of Kurosawa, not against him." Legal experts said that under common law, no problem arises about the validity of the agreement even without the signatures. Shooting could start because the two sides had confirmed the contents of the Agreement many times up to that point.

Concluding a contract is a legal act but it is rooted in culture and

279

there are basic differences between Japan and the West on how contracts are perceived. For Japanese, a contract is a pledge not to violate the relations of trust that have led to the signing of the contract. It is the proof of a pledge and is closer in nature to a written oath. Oaths are taken in the exchange of cups of *sake* wine at weddings or the ceremonial pledge of a *yakuza* gangster's allegiance to his leader. In short, for most Japanese contracts are a symbol confirming promises that have already been made.

In normal practice among Japanese companies, contracts are kept simple and in many cases do not contain details. A sentence says two sides will sincerely negotiate and seek solutions if unexpected problems should surface. It is highly unusual to include clauses that spell out what will be done if things go sour. Indeed to suggest any possibility in a contract that relations might be disrupted is unpardonable bad taste. This basic concept of contracts has been handed down through generations and is a part of Japan's culture not easily set aside.

Contracts in English-speaking cultures are based on a different set of values and ways of thinking. Before ceremonial toasts, contracts spell out what should be done if the parties fail to meet their obligations. To Japanese, this is akin to deciding on the terms of divorce before a couple marries. To an American, the idea is that if everything goes well, the contract will not be needed. If things really turn sour, a settlement can be reached in court—or the prospect of going to court nudges the parties to settle. And contracts between parties in different countries specify which jurisdiction should be used if a dispute should go to court.

The agreement between Kurosawa Productions and Fox was no different. It defined the rights and obligations of each side in detail. It specified possible disputes that might be expected. Four contractual points set the tone and substance of the agreement: the issue of credits for the movie; the right to editing and cutting; Hollywood work ethics; and conditions for dismissal.

Screen Credits

The term "credits" refers to the list of names of the cast and crew on the screen. A common practice is to show the names of the main cast, producer, and director at the beginning of a movie and a list of the entire cast and crew at the end. The size of the name on screen and the order in which the names appear indicate the importance a movie company attaches to members of the cast and crew. This affects their professional interests and their pride. Hollywood is notorious for difficulties entailed in negotiating the minefield of on-screen credits.

Kurosawa is said to have insisted, even before contract negotiations started, that his name should appear before that of the American director. This developed into a major row that was never settled. Aoyagi said Kurosawa instructed him to make sure that his demands on credit as well as his rights to cutting and editing the movie were met. But Aoyagi was not in a position to negotiate directly with Fox. Instead, Kurosawa Productions conveyed its demands to its American lawyer, Saul Pryor, who represented Kurosawa and Aoyagi. Pryor had an office in New York and was a member of CMA. Another member of CMA, Richard Shepherd, carried out the negotiations with Fox based on instructions from Pryor.

Several internal documents at Fox detail the negotiations over Kurosawa's credits. A report sent by Fox's legal chief, Harry E. Sokolov, to Richard Zanuck and 14 other senior executives on March 28, 1967, noted that Kurosawa Productions had demanded that:

...(Kurosawa's) name shall be first displayed in the production credit in Japan and in such other countries in which it can be fairly resolved that his name is more important than the director or directors engaged by Twentieth to direct the English or American portion of the picture... Kurosawa will have first billing in the United States unless a director of greater stature is hired for the English or American portion of the picture... They (Kurosawa and Twentieth) have agreed that Fred Zinneman, Robert Wise, William Wyler and even John Sturges would be considered of greater stature… Twentieth has agreed that it will give good faith consideration but Twentieth shall have final decision.

Sokolov added that if Fox planned to use Richard Fleischer as director of the American segments, then Fleischer's name should be included in the list of directors of greater stature. The directors cited as "of greater stature" were decided during negotiations with Richard Shepherd, the lawyer for Kurosawa Productions. The list apparently reflected Kurosawa's choice but why he chose them is unknown.

When the plan to produce *Tora! Tora! Tora!* was announced in April 1967, a month after the letter on credits was written, Elmo Williams said the director of the American sequences had yet to be decided. In reality, Fox had already committed itself to Richard Fleischer the previous year, a decision that was backed by Richard Zanuck. Williams knew Kurosawa wouldn't like the choice of Fleischer and refrained from divulging the name.

Williams's business diary for August 10, 1968, says Aoyagi told him of a surprise proposal from Kurosawa. Kurosawa said since Fleischer was no good, Williams should become the director of the American segments himself. Kurosawa said if Williams was the director, he would agree that both directors should receive equal credit. In his diary, Williams wrote that for him to become director was out of question and that he had rejected Kurosawa's proposal.

The question of who should be listed first in the screen credits continued for a year and seven months with no settlement. Fox's legal department claimed that Kurosawa and Aoyagi did not sign the agreement because they rejected a compromise. Compromises were on the table but apparently Kurosawa was not aware of them. The final compromise proposed by Fox called for making two different prints of the movie, one for the Japanese market and the other for world-wide distribution. It suggested credits be given differently in the two prints. Article 3 of the agreement said:

ALL THE EMPEROR'S MEN

If Mr. Kurosawa substantially completes his services as the Director of the Japanese segments, he shall receive joint credits as the Director of the segments on the screen and all positive prints of the Photoplay… Said credit on the screen and all positive prints of the Photoplay (for Kurosawa) will be on a separate card and will be the next to the last credit (for Fleischer) before the beginning of the Photoplay in all countries of the world except Japan. In Japan, said credit (for Kurosawa) will be the last credit before the beginning of the Photoplay.

In short, the credit for Kurosawa would be higher in stature than that for Fleischer only in the Japanese market. This item also referred to the rankings of credits in "all paid advertising." The agreement divided the globe into the Eastern and Western Hemispheres. It said "Mr. Kurosawa's name will be first, before the American Director, in the Eastern Hemisphere and (his name will be) second to the American Director in the Western Hemisphere." "Paid advertising" in the agreement excluded previews and highlights for theaters but included newspaper ads, posters, and billboards.

The test of contracts written in English was whether they accounted for all possible situations and defined rules to deal with them. Experts said Fox's legal department did a good job in preparing the contract with Kurosawa Productions. The last sentence of Article 3 stated: "The foregoing is subject to the provisions of Article VI of the Directors' Basic Agreement of 1964, if applicable."

"The Directors' Basic Agreement" referred to an agreement with the DGA, the Directors Guild of America. This was a union of directors, associate directors, chief production staff and others in the cinema industry. The union got its name in 1960 and in recent years more people have joined the union from the made-for-TV movie sector. As of 2007, it had 13,459 members. Most movie production companies in the United States were parties to this agreement. Under its provisions, member companies can employ only those who are members of

CROOKS AND CONTRACTS

the DGA. When disputes arise, the Basic Agreement applies. Kurosawa became a member of the DGA when he agreed to work as a director with Embassy Pictures in 1966.

Article 6 of the Basic Agreement in the 1964 version says: "In the case of a dispute between a company and a director over the credit, the DGA may mediate upon application from the parties in dispute. But the employer's position takes precedence in the final decision." Even if Kurosawa or Fleischer had not liked the way credit was given and had filed a complaint with the DGA, Fox would have had the final say. If either side brought its case to court, it would have been decided according to the law of the State of California. Kurosawa wouldn't have had much chance of winning under this contract even if he had wanted to fight it out. Fox's Vice President Richard Zanuck was a close friend of Fleischer's and never on good terms with Kurosawa.

In later years, Williams said he thought he had uncovered an unexpected aspect of Kurosawa's personality: his persistence over the issue of credit was a matter of great pride. When Williams was working on *The Longest Day*, three directors were at work, Ken Annakin for the British part, Andrew Marton on the American segment, and Bernhard Wicki for the German scenes. Their credits appeared in alphabetical order. The credits for 60 members of the cast, all of whom were big names, were given in alphabetical order. In the last group under the letter 'W' were the names of five actors. As the only exception, the name of John Wayne appeared most prominently at the tail of the screen credits, out of alphabetical order. Williams said nobody complained about this salute to a great actor.

Editing Rights

Kurosawa gave an interview to the *Weekly Yomiuri* in mid-November 1968, two weeks before the start of shooting, in which he addressed the issue of editing of *Tora! Tora! Tora!* "I will take care of everything concerning the Japanese segments from shooting through editing to dubbing," he said. "Then I will bring the completed set to the United

States. I will attend as much as possible the shooting of the American segments. And I will do the same with regard to the editing of the American segments."

Kurosawa thought he would be involved in every aspect of the movie to its completion. It appears he did not know until the very end that the movie would have differences in credits, one for Japan and the other for the rest of the world. Another major issue was Kurosawa's misunderstanding on his editing rights. The reporter who did the interview asked if the Japanese and American versions were different. Kurosawa replied, "No," suggesting a misconception on his part of his limited right to edit under the contract.

At a news conference on January 20, 1969, a month after the dismissal, Aoyagi said Kurosawa did have the right to edit the movie. On the following day, Kurosawa told a news conference: "Aoyagi was telling me I had the editing rights. My staff claimed Elmo Williams was saying he had the editing rights." Kurosawa looked baffled after having become aware of his limited rights to edit. The contract is explicit:

If Mr. Kurosawa substantially completes his services as Director of the Japanese segments, and is not in default hereunder, then, with respect only to the prints of the Photoplay released in Japan, Mr. Kurosawa shall have the right to final cut of the Japanese segments; provided, however, that Mr. Kurosawa's final cut of the Japanese segments for the prints of the Photoplay released in Japan must be done expeditiously and will not in any way delay our scheduled release of the Photoplay in Japan. Further, Mr. Kurosawa's right to make and approve the final cut of the Japanese segments for the release prints of the Photoplay in Japan shall be limited to the right to take out and delete from the Japanese segments of our final cut of the Photoplay. Mr. Kurosawa shall have no right to add to the Japanese segments or edit or change in any way the American segments of the Photoplay. Except as herein expressly provided, any cutting,

CROOKS AND CONTRACTS

editing or changing of the Photoplay shall be done by us and shall be our sole and exclusive right and responsibility.

"The final cut" is defined as the last stage of film editing before a movie's print for release to theaters is completed. This is different from the "final editing right." The right to make the final cut granted to directors is different from the "final editing right" granted to a studio that produces, releases, and distributes a feature film. To sum up: Fox had the absolute "final say" about the "final cut" of *Tora! Tora! Tora!*

1. Fox will edit common prints for worldwide release including in Japan and make the final cut.
2. Kurosawa may delete part of the Japanese segments in Fox's final cut, if he regards it as necessary, (but will not be allowed to add) and will make the final cut for prints to be released in Japan. He will not be allowed to change anything at all about the American segments.
3. Fox will have the exclusive right to the final editing of all the final prints for release including those for release in Japan.

Reports in newspapers and magazines in Japan from 1969 to 1970 made differing claims about Kurosawa's editing rights. Few were accurate. Many were indeed wrong about what "the final cut" meant in Hollywood. Kurosawa wrongly assumed he was the all-important "principal director" or "headman" of the movie production. He was equally wrong about his editing rights. In this respect, Aoyagi bears grave responsibility as he was in a position to advise and assist Kurosawa on matters of contracts, but there is a possibility that Aoyagi was uncertain as to the definition of "the final cut."

Kurosawa was an excellent film editor. He took pride in getting involved in almost every phase of film-making. He had plenty of confidence in his skill at editing and considered that to be part of the director's responsibility. Elmo Williams was also an excellent editor who won

ALL THE EMPEROR'S MEN

an Academy Award for Film Editing in 1952 for *High Noon,* directed by Fred Zinnemann. After its producer, Stanley Kramer, considered the movie a failure, Williams gave it new life by editing it with a bold hand. He produced newly composed theme music that later became a big hit. So successful was he that the phrase "Elmo Magic" entered the Hollywood phrasebook. In 1954, he was again nominated for an Academy Award for Film Editing for his work on Walt Disney's *20,000 Leagues under the Sea.*

Moreover, Darryl Zanuck took pride in his skill at editing. He was especially proud of legendary films he made with director John Ford. He believed those films were successful as much for his editing ability as for his prowess as a producer. Recent studies by UCLA and other research organizations have found that Zanuck exercised his right to decisive cuts on *The Grapes of Wrath* and *My Darling Clementine.* He is found to have added music and sound effects, edited, and even dared to direct the memorable last scenes of some John Ford classics.

Thus three men with a special talent for editing were engaged in making *Tora! Tora! Tora!* Williams wrote in his diary for August 12, 1968, that he explained to Kurosawa and Aoyagi the process for editing the movie:

1. Kurosawa is to conduct the rough cut on the Japanese segments and Williams to do so on the American segments.

2. Williams is to combine the two sets of rough cuts and to combine images of the two, if necessary. One complete set of positive prints made from negative prints is to be shown to Kurosawa and Fleischer at a Fox studio. The two directors are to be consulted and if necessary, revisions are to be made. This process is to be repeated for two weeks to make one complete set that is satisfactory to both of them.

3. Kurosawa returns home and conducts provisional dubbing on the print of the Japanese segments. Williams

CROOKS AND CONTRACTS

completes his provisional dubbing of the print of the American segments at Beverly Hills. Sound will be recorded on one-quarter-inch tapes on each side, and will be added later. Each side is to decide on the use of music. The recording of musical pieces to be composed by Toru Takemitsu and Jerry Goldsmith will all be recorded at a Fox studio.

4. Williams will conduct dubbing to combine the Japanese and American sequences. The first run will be shown to Kurosawa and Fleischer. They will be invited to express their opinions, and revisions will be made accordingly. As to color balance, Kurosawa's final view will be sought and complete preparations will be made for making the final print.

5. The print will be shown to Zanuck for his comments. Adjustments will be made, if necessary. After that, the final print will be made.

It should have been clear to Kurosawa that the key responsibility fell to Williams but it is likely that Aoyagi failed to convey this accurately to Kurosawa. Later, when Kurosawa was asked why *Tora! Tora! Tora!* failed, he replied: "Essentially, at issue was the editing. The movie dealt with a delicate subject, the start of a war between Japan and the United States. The basic plan was for the two sides to bring together the film sequences they had shot and combine them into one movie. So it would have been out of the question for me to have no right to edit. Editing can make or break a movie. In this case for example, edits could have made it appear that Isoroku Yamamoto was a bad guy who secretly started the war. If that had happened, I would have had to jump from the roof of the Fox building and kill myself. It was right and important for the agreement to say that the two sides should discuss thoroughly and in good faith but it should also have stated that I should have had the final say about editing. That was absolutely necessary. But in the final stage, nothing of that sort was included in the Agreement. This was a story about a war

ALL THE EMPEROR'S MEN

between two countries. It is a subtle story, as the United States suffered a heavy loss because of the surprise attack. Great care is needed to tell such a subtle story but as our side had no final editing rights, we couldn't do our job. That was what was behind that fiasco."

In an interview, Williams said:

> Kurosawa had the right to edit the Japanese sequences. I was to edit the American sequences. Kurosawa was to bring his edited version to the United States. Then I would combine the two sets. I would combine the images of the two sides, when necessary. The two sides would examine the work. This would be repeated within the allowable time. That was our promise. Darryl Zanuck had high hopes for Kurosawa's editing skill. I did, too. Of course, Darryl himself was confident of his own skills and he was willing to use them. But neither Darryl nor I understand Japanese. Kurosawa alone knew the details and situations in the Japanese segments. So, I thought it was only natural that we should honor his opinions.

Williams was flexible and pragmatic, as befitted a producer of his stature. Zanuck trusted Kurosawa. If Kurosawa had maintained trust until the shooting had been completed, Kurosawa might have had ample opportunity to have his say in the final shape of the movie. If the movie had been completed and the Japanese and Americans had been unable to agree on how to edit it, Zanuck would have exercised his right to the final editing of the movie.

Auteur vs. Artisan

Kurosawa at first thought that the contract with Twentieth Century-Fox must have contained a secret clause that enabled his sudden dismissal. When he finally got a copy and examined it with Matsue and a lawyer for Kurosawa Productions, the truth dawned on him. The agreement

CROOKS AND CONTRACTS

made Kurosawa a sub-contractor rather than a partner with Fox in "a co-production on an equal footing," as asserted by Aoyagi. In effect, Fox, a Hollywood major, had imposed on Kurosawa Productions, a minor independent Japanese company, a pact that set the terms for making a limited portion of a movie. Bluntly speaking, Kurosawa was to be little more than a small dispensable cog in the Fox machine. Article 10 Item (e) of the Agreement said:

> We (Fox) are the producer of the Photoplay, including the Japanese segments, and you (Kurosawa Productions), as the independent contractor, are providing us with equipment, personnel, facilities and services. You will faithfully and conscientiously follow our directions and instructions in the production of the Japanese segments.
>
> Mr. Kurosawa has been designated by us as being in charge of the production of the Japanese segments of the Photoplay; however, the ultimate supervision of the production of the Photoplay shall be exercised by our Executive Vice President in charge of Worldwide Production whose determination and decision with respect to any and all matters in connection with the production of the Photoplay, including the Japanese segments therefore, shall be final and conclusive.

Of this, Kurosawa had been unaware. Legal experts said the agreement was reasonable from an American viewpoint. In light of what Kurosawa said and did, however, the director was fundamentally wrong in his understanding of the agreement and his contractual rights and responsibilities under it. In Hollywood, the primary responsibility of a sub-contractor is to complete the production in accord with a set schedule and budget. Whether Kurosawa had seen the agreement was beside the point. Fox's position was that no excuse could absolve him from his contractual responsibilities.

One article in the agreement drew the attention of legal experts versed in movie contracts. Article 4 defined the services Kurosawa was expected to offer Fox and under what conditions:

Mr. Kurosawa shall diligently and conscientiously in a workmanlike manner perform all services customarily performed by a director of motion pictures as required by us.

"Workmanlike" conjures up an image of quiet workers who do not argue with their bosses but follow directions efficiently. Apparently Fox considered Kurosawa not an all-important auteur but an artisan, a movie director who was to work in accord with Hollywood mores. By contrast, Kurosawa took it for granted that movie directors were auteurs. This word, of French origin, refers to film directors with a strong artistic influence and who relentlessly explored their imaginations through movies. In Hollywood, however, the foremost quality of directors was the ability to be an artisan, a workman as the leader of teamwork. Darryl Zanuck and Elmo Williams may have thought of Kurosawa as an auteur, a master of cinema, but in Hollywood directors who are not artisans are rejected.

Ten Days as a Curse

Scrutiny of the Fox-Kurosawa agreement suggests that Kurosawa's dismissal was not unexpected. The decision to release him was based on provisions stipulated in the Agreement, which gave Fox grounds to do so. Exhibit (A) Article 5 said:

If, by reason of mental or physical disability, any of the Artists shall be incapacitated from performing or complying with any of the terms of conditions of this Agreement for a period of aggregate periods in excess of ten (10) days during the term hereof, we shall have the right to terminate this Agreement upon written notice to you of our election to terminate the same, unless we approve a substitute for

CROOKS AND CONTRACTS

any such Artist prior to the exercise by us of such right of termination... If any claim of mental or physical disability is made by or on behalf of any of the Artists, we shall have the right to have such Artist examined by such physicians as we may designate or approve. In lieu of the foregoing, we may require any such Artist to furnish us with a certificate of such examination by a physician approved by us.

In plain language: "You may get sick, which could happen to anybody. But if you stay away from work for more than ten days, we can sack you." Fox's man in charge of production in Japan, Stanley Goldsmith, kept a log showing that the number of lost days reached ten on December 24, 1968—the day Kurosawa was dismissed. Nobody appeared to have realized the significance of the lost days. If Tetsu Aoyagi had known, he could have alerted Kurosawa and urged him to stick to the schedule. The evidence suggests, however, that Aoyagi was either unaware of the ten-day rule or ignored it.

Corporate Methods

Not surprisingly, Twentieth Century-Fox had a corporate system for managing contracts. During negotiations, Fox had a checking procedure in which attorney Harry E. Sokolov reported developments to Vice President Richard Zanuck and 14 other executives. Everybody had heard that Kurosawa was a slow-working perfectionist. The sentence "Mr. Kurosawa shall diligently and conscientiously in a workmanlike manner perform all services..." appeared to have been inserted to forestall his divergence from Hollywood tradition.

Kurosawa Productions had no such arrangement. Aoyagi monopolized information on grounds that the agreement was a secret to which even Kurosawa and executives Ryuzo Kikushima and Sadahiro Kubota were given only limited access. Aoyagi never let anyone touch important documents related to Fox. He had a filing cabinet in the Kurosawa Productions office that was always locked. Even his secretary had been forbidden access.

Aoyagi did report to Kurosawa on progress in contract negotiations. Assistant director Yutaka Osawa said he often saw Aoyagi talking to Kurosawa about the agreement and sometimes saw Kurosawa, glass of scotch in hand, sign papers in English as instructed by Aoyagi.

Fox acted quickly after it released Kurosawa. Four days after the dismissal, Fox's legal adviser, Charles Bole, flew to Japan to clean up the situation, together with Stanley Goldsmith. Two days after Bole arrived, Aoyagi agreed in writing to cancel the sub-contractor agreement with Fox. On January 4, 1969, an agreement was drawn up to confirm the debts on the two sides and to determine ways to settle them. Bole and Aoyagi signed it. A week after Bole's arrival, the two sides agreed on a framework to handle the aftermath of Kurosawa's dismissal.

But problems emerged with disturbing frequency. Saul Pryor, an attorney for Kurosawa Productions, flew from New York to Tokyo and immediately said the two papers signed by Aoyagi were defective and that Kurosawa Productions would not abide by them. He said Kurosawa's fees as director would not be counted as part of Fox's losses. Instead, he demanded that Fox pay Kurosawa the fee he had earned in working on *Tora! Tora! Tora!*

At the same time, Kurosawa kept distance from Aoyagi and Pryor. Bole had not expected that two agreements he signed with Aoyagi would be declared void because they had not been approved by Kurosawa as president of Kurosawa Productions. Kurosawa insisted that, legally, Aoyagi was not in a position to sign on behalf of Kurosawa Productions. Bole brushed off Kurosawa's claim but began to distance himself from Aoyagi.

In a separate move, the US insurance consortium, having received Fox's claim, sent two investigators to Japan to look into the circumstances surrounding Kurosawa's dismissal.

Ego and Greed

At a news conference in Tokyo in January 1969, Kurosawa said he had seen "something in the Agreement so ugly that he didn't even want to look at it." He did not disclose which provision prompted him to say that but it probably referred to a separate agreement that said:

> Commencing as of February 1, 1967, Kurosawa Productions, Ltd. is to provide the services of the writers (Ryuzo Kikushima and Hideo Oguni) to write and deliver to Twentieth the Japanese portion of the screenplay, and the services of Akira Kurosawa and Tetsu Aoyagi to supervise the writing and delivery of the Japanese portion of the screenplay.

Little is known about the distribution of screenplay fees. The agreement said Fox would pay Ryuzo Kikushima, Hideo Oguni, Tetsu Aoyagi, and Akira Kurosawa a total of $80,000 to complete the screenplay. In addition, Fox was to pay Kurosawa and Aoyagi $25,000 as supervising editor fees upon the delivery of the revised screenplay. It was not certain, however, how much Kurosawa, Kikushima, and Oguni received. A total of $105,000 was earmarked for writing, supervisory editing, revisions, and delivery of the screenplay but no documents show who received how much and when.

One statement was on the record: sound engineer Shin Watarai said he once asked Kurosawa if he had received anything for the *Tora! Tora! Tora!* screenplay. He quoted Kurosawa as saying, "Of course, I did. I got 20,000 dollars." In those days, this was no small amount. Still, questions remain about the screenplay fees paid by Fox that was said to have been five times this amount.

Aoyagi never revealed the budget of Kurosawa Productions for the Japanese segment of *Tora! Tora! Tora!* He refused to say how the budget was negotiated with Fox. This came to light when Kurosawa read the contract. Article 6 said:

> You will prepare and submit to us a budget and shooting schedule for the Japanese segments of the Photoplay, both of which shall be subject to our approval. You represent and

warrant that the Japanese segments of the Photoplay can be produced by us with your assistance at a cost not to exceed the total of the budget therefore, approved by us.

In short, this provision says Kurosawa Productions could submit its own plan for the budget and shooting schedule but that once the plan was approved by Fox, it had to be followed. Fox made some concessions as to shooting days. Kurosawa requested four weeks in preproduction workups before the start of shooting and 18 weeks for shooting. At first, Fox was reluctant, saying this was too long but in the end agreed to Kurosawa's request.

The budget for the production of the Japanese segment was estimated to be $3.9 million, which included 20 percent of overhead that could be considered commissions for Kurosawa Productions. Williams contended that Kurosawa had not invested a single cent in the movie. Considering this, Williams said, it must have been a favorable deal for Kurosawa. Kurosawa's nephew Yoshio Inoue said that, in all probability, the director knew little about the budget. Kurosawa himself was often in financial distress. After the *Red Beard* project, Kurosawa Productions and the Kurosawa family were desperately short of money. Teruyo Nogami quoted Aoyagi as saying, "I was supposed to give the Kurosawa family money to feed them. That was my most important but difficult job as a producer of *Tora! Tora! Tora!*" One thing is certain: if Kurosawa had successfully finished this epic film, he would have earned a large sum of money, which would have relieved Kurosawa Productions and the Kurosawa family of their money woes.

The Sun and the Moon

The year 1968 marked a watershed for the film industry. In France, film makers from around the world boycotted the Cannes Film Festival to demonstrate solidarity with student protest movements. Director François Truffaut said this was no time for a bourgeois film festival as the nation was in the midst of a revolution. The Festival was canceled.

295

In the United States, the April Academy Awards ceremony in Los Angeles was postponed for two days to mourn the death of Martin Luther King, the assassinated leader of the civil rights movement. The annual ball after the ceremony was canceled. *In the Heat of the Night*, a movie about a murder in the American South, which reflected the nationwide prejudice against African-Americans, won five Oscars, including those for Best Film and Best Actor. *The Graduate* won the Oscar for Best

Director. Evincing the style of the "American new cinema," the movie depicted young people who stepped out of the traditional framework of society. *The Graduate* and *Bonnie and Clyde* caught the hearts of movie goers in Japan, where they were ranked among the ten best movies of the year by *Kinema Junpo*, a leading movie magazine.

Moreover, the year marked the start of independent film production in Japan. It began when the Japan Art Theater Guild (ATG) launched an effort to distribute artistic feature films to smaller theaters. AGT made movies jointly with small production firms led by young directors. The two shared costs equally, making movies with a budget of ten million yen ($27,000 at that time). This was one-third of the production cost that major companies considered necessary to make a movie. The directors, staff, and cast were expected to work without pay. This stimulated capable young directors and a stream of excellent films were released.

The first movie produced this way was *Koshikei (Death by Hanging)* by Nagisa Oshima. This was followed by *Hatsukoi Jigokuhen (The Inferno of First Love*, aka *Nanami: First Love)* by Susumu Niwa, and *Nikudan (Human Bullet)* by Kihachi Okamoto. This year saw a demonstration in central Tokyo by movie people protesting the dismissal of Director

ALL THE EMPEROR'S MEN

Seijun Suzuki from Nikkatsu, a movie production company. Suzuki was known for his style of esoteric beauty in B-class movies. The company's president, Kyusaku Hori, sacked him, saying his movies were "too wild for the masses." The street demonstration led by well-known directors such as Nagisa Oshima took the public by surprise.

During this year of turmoil, Kurosawa concentrated on the *Tora! Tora! Tora!* film. He declared his attempts to produce *The Runaway Train* and *Tora! Tora! Tora!* were prompted by a desire to open the way for younger film directors to advance into global cinema with funds from overseas. At a reception in Tokyo on November 4, 1968, to mark the start of the shooting of *Tora! Tora! Tora!*, Kurosawa said: "If I die before I can do something to rescue the Japanese cinema from the quagmire, I will turn in my grave."

It appears, however, that Kurosawa did not pay much attention to the rising filmmakers. In his view, the golden age of Japanese films had come and gone, lasting from the 1950s to the early 1960s. Directors such as Kenji Mizoguchi, Yasujiro Ozu, and Mikio Naruse, all his seniors, he himself, and Keisuke Kinoshita were then making good movies. Kurosawa abhorred the emergence of *yakuza* and pornographic movies. He described them as evidence of "the decline and fall of the Japanese cinema."

After he began shooting *Tora! Tora! Tora!*, Kurosawa took to writing calligraphy when people asked for his autograph. He used a traditional brush and ink and wrote a single *kanji* character on paper with the letterhead of the Japanese inn, Tawaraya, where he stayed. The character was *Akira*. In the space above it, he wrote in English 'SUN' and 'MOON.' The character for *Akira* has two elements, *hi* (sun) and *tsuki* (moon). Combined, his name *Akira* can be translated, depending on the context, as 'wisdom' or 'foresight' or 'enlightenment.' Kurosawa often said jokingly that his divine calling was hidden in the character for his name. He added that this might be a sign he was born with a duty to bring brightness to this world. It might have been a joke but, in the depths of his mind, he may have been speaking the truth as he seemed to believe that his 'mission impossible' was to bring 'light' into the world.

CROOKS AND CONTRACTS

IN THE SHADOW
OF A TIGER

Opening Night

A year and nine months after the dismissal of Kurosawa, Twenti-eth Century-Fox completed *Tora! Tora! Tora!* with the Japanese sequences directed by Toshio Masuda and Kinji Fukasaku. The world premiere was held on September 24, 1970, in Tokyo, New York, Los Angeles, and Honolulu.

Due to time differences, the premiere was held first in Tokyo. Toward evening, a large crowd began arriving at Theatre Tokyo (now Le The-atre Ginza) in the fashionable Ginza district in central Tokyo. At seven o'clock, a Maritime Self-Defense Force brass band, playing the *Warship March*, led people into the auditorium. Marching in were the movie's stars—So Yamamura (Isoroku Yamamoto), Tatsuya Mihashi (Minoru Genda), Takahiro Tamura (Mitsuo Fuchida), and Hiroshi Akutagawa (Koichi Kido). They were followed by the diplomatic corps; the widow of Admiral Yamamoto, Reiko; and his eldest son, Yoshimasa. All were welcomed with applause and cheers from the actors, celebrities, journal-ists, and photographers there.

The movie began at 7:10 P.M. and, with a five-minute intermission, ran for two hours and 27 minutes. In the latter half, the Pearl Har-bor attack itself was depicted. Images filmed in Super Panavision 70 were projected onto a wide screen by a wide-screen process known as the Super Cinerama System, with superior stereo sound. The audience was overwhelmed by the vibrations from exploding bombs.

The next day, the show was opened to the public at Theatre Tokyo and the Shinjuku Plaza Theater and was an instant hit. Both theaters

IN THE SHADOW OF A TIGER

had full houses, with a total of 9,000 people coming on the first day. Theatre Tokyo's 1,150 seats, all reserved, were taken for all four showings that began at 9:05 A.M. The Shinjuku Plaza Theater had a Dimension 150 projection system and 680 people waited in line to see the first showing at 10:50 A.M. As soon as the theater opened, all the seats were taken in an instant. The first showing began 20 minutes earlier than usual. The theater remained packed for all four showings.

At both theaters, the audience was predominantly male, in a ratio of nine men to one woman. Especially conspicuous were young men in their twenties, postwar baby boomers. At the Shinjuku Plaza Theater, some saw the 2.5-hour movie twice in succession. Many saw it standing. The theater recalls that it had poor audience turnover all day as viewers stayed for repeated showings.

New York is 13 hours behind Tokyo when it is on daylight saving time. On premiere night, also called press night, the Criterion Theatre on the corner of Forty-fifth Street and Broadway in Manhattan was filled with invited guests, journalists, and critics. At the entrance were camera crews from newsreel companies and television networks. Elmo Williams, wearing a formal business suit and a bow tie, arrived with Minoru Genda. Darryl Zanuck was not there because a few hours earlier, he had developed severe stomach cramps. His doctor diagnosed his condition as having been caused by nerves. In special seats in the balcony was a group of middle-aged men wearing badges reading "Pearl Harbor Survivors," together with their wives. They were in a festive mood, as if on a picnic, big paper cups of popcorn in hand.

At 8 P.M. sharp, the hustle and bustle in the theater subsided and the movie began. Throughout the first half, the audience was quiet. During a 15-minute intermission, people were saying things like "the Japanese officers look too smart," or "all the American officers look foolish. I don't like that."

In the latter half, when the attack began, the theater was filled with excitement. In an endless succession, Japanese bombers, dive bombers, torpedo planes, and Zero fighters swooped over U.S. warships and airfields. Then two young daredevil American airmen jumped into P-40 fighters and climbed through a barrage of fire. After they shot down Japanese bombers, the audience cheered and applauded.

Awakening a Sleeping Giant

When the movie was over and the lights came up, many Americans looked satisfied and there was modest applause. Some people wearing "Pearl Harbor Survivors" badges were heard to be saying "good," "terrific," and other positive comments to their wives but others were in a bit of a downer with audible sighs.

Overall, the audience seemed to have taken the movie's message as the Pearl Harbor attack was not a defeat but the beginning of victory for the United States. This may have had something to do with the ending, which focused on Admiral Yamamoto's words: "I fear all we have done is to awaken a sleeping giant and fill him with a terrible resolve." The words were repeated twice in the US and world-wide version. In the Fox version, Yamamoto spoke in a disheartened tone to his staff officers in the operations room of his flagship *Nagato*, saying, "According to American radio broadcasts, Pearl Harbor was attacked fifty-five minutes before our ultimatum was delivered in Washington." Afterward the admiral walked along a passageway of the battleship, mounted a ladder to the main deck and climbed it slowly. The camera followed his steps as he walked across the deck to the railing and looked out to sea. Over the close-up shot of the admiral in stern silence, his last words were superimposed with the subtitle in English: "I fear all we have done is to awaken a sleeping giant and fill him with a terrible resolve."

Some people took a dim view of this ending as a showy gimmick but many praised it as impressive and reflecting what Yamamoto, with his experience in America, could well have thought. Over the years, the "sleeping giant" speech has become a quotable quote and became more famous than the film itself. Thus, 31 years later, the supposed quotation was abbreviated in the 2001 American war film *Pearl Harbor* in which Yamamoto said: "I fear all we have done is to awaken a sleeping giant." The screenwriter of *Pearl Harbor*, Randall Wallace, admitted that he copied the line from *Tora! Tora! Tora!* but contended that nobody complained about it.

Originally, there was no closing speech by Yamamoto in Kurosawa's first draft of the screenplay (*junbiko*). In that version, Yamamoto and his staff were in the operations room of the *Nagato* anchored at Hashirajima Anchorage in the Seto Inland Sea. They had listened to the radio announcement of the successful air raid in Hawaii that was followed by a brass band playing the stirring *Warship March*. Without a word, Yamamoto abruptly stood up and walked out, alone. The scene ended with the exit of the admiral, his back to the camera.

After Twentieth Century-Fox bought the movie rights of Kurosawa's screenplay, Darryl Zanuck and Elmo Williams insisted on a wrap-up speech by Yamamoto. Kurosawa proposed to have Yamamoto say something like: "We have just stepped on the tail of a sleeping tiger." Williams and screenwriter Larry Forrester proposed the "sleeping giant" quote. Kurosawa liked the translated phrase of the quote and agreed to use it. With assurance from Williams, Kurosawa never had any doubt about its authenticity.

The source of the quote was obscure when it was written and is still ambiguous. Williams said in an interview that Forrester based the quote on a personal letter written by Yamamoto, but this claim has never been borne out. Forrester died in Northridge, California, in 1988 at the age of 63. So far, the exact quote has not been found in verifiable records in Japan or America.

For a long time, Kurosawa maintained that there was nothing morally wrong about a surprise attack on an enemy, citing the Chinese strategist Sun Tzu: "All warfare is based on deception." At the same time, like Admiral Yamamoto, Kurosawa despised the concept of a "sneak attack" as a breach of the *samurai* code of honor and insisted that Japan never sought to do that at Pearl Harbor.

There is one scene which Kurosawa described as meaningful because it would serve as the precursor of Yamamoto's "awakening the sleeping giant" statement at the end of the film. Zanuck and Williams eventually accepted Kurosawa's argument and the scene was retained in the Fox version of *Tora! Tora! Tora!*, which was completed 20 months after Kurosawa was expelled from the studio. The time of this scene was set at less than an hour before the first bomb was to fall on Pearl Harbor.

OPERATIONS ROOM, FLAGSHIP NAGATO-- INLAND SEA, JAPAN

Crowded with Staff Officers of the Combined Fleet...There is a hushed silence, broken only by the rustling of papers and the scratching of pencils... Yamamoto is sitting at the end of the room behind a big desk, his eyes closed:

YAMAMOTO
(quietly)
A samurai never kills an opponent while asleep. The samurai's code of honor is to awaken the enemy before slaying him. Our ultimatum should be delivered in Washington before the attack begins … I hope everything is on schedule …

POLITICAL LIAISON OFFICER
Don't worry sir, the Emperor insists that we follow the rules of the Geneva Convention. Foreign Minister Togo assured us that our declaration of war will be delivered at one p.m. Washington time -- thirty minutes before the attack begins in Hawaii.

Yamamoto nods in silence and goes back to deep thought, his eyes closed.

In a History Channel CATV program, *History Through the Lens* (2001), Director Richard Fleischer said Admiral Yamamoto's "sleeping giant" quote was "the knockout statement to put an end to the picture, because that's exactly what happened, so that (sic) because the end of Pearl Harbor was eventually the beginning of a great victory for us."

Speaking on the same program, Dr. Akira Iriye, professor of history at Harvard University, said: "Whether Yamamoto actually uttered the words, we never know... In any event, what he does say in the movie becomes truth."

Kurosawa always said there were no 'ifs' in history but, in the case of Pearl Harbor, there were too many 'ifs' that could have made Japan's attack a failure. He thought that if only Japan's ultimatum had been delivered on time, history could have been changed. Then what is known as "the Day of Infamy" speech by President Franklin Delano Roosevelt could have lost ground and he might have been less successful in awakening the giant and uniting his people to fight World War II.

The Box Office Speaks

In the U.S., *Tora! Tora! Tora!* did well at first. Twentieth Century-Fox hoped it would do better than *Patton*, the movie about the feisty American general in World War II that had been released earlier. In its second week, box-office income from the Pearl Harbor movie began to fall. Reviews were divided and audiences were not as impressed as Fox had hoped. The movie looked like it might be a flop even though it was doing well in Japan and Europe. "My father was tremendously disappointed," Richard Zanuck recalled. "He spent a large amount of money on the production and used much more to advertise it. I myself was confident of success. But the box office record was disappointing."

Contrary to the high hopes of Darryl Zanuck, *Tora! Tora! Tora!* failed to win any major Academy Award for 1970. *Patton* won the Best Picture and six other awards, while *Tora! Tora! Tora!* won only one Oscar, for the best Special Visual Effects.

Reviews in U.S. newspapers and magazines were generally unfavorable. Ironically, Fox's pursuit of a factual account was the main reason for negative reviews. Many critics said the film was too much of a documentary. None of the reports in the American media hinted at political messages hidden in the movie.

The New York Times, under the headline "Tora-ble, Tora-ble, Tora-ble," described *Tora! Tora! Tora!* as "a 25-million-dollar irrelevancy." The paper said: "From the moment you read the ads for this film ('The Most Spectacular Film Ever Made'), you are aware that you're in the presence of a film possessed by a lack of imagination so singular that it amounts to a death wish." The paper concluded: "The fault hasn't as much to do with the quality of the illusion, as it does with the film's aspirations. *Tora! Tora! Tora!* aspires to dramatize history in terms of events rather than people and it just may be that there is more of what Pearl Harbor was all about in fiction films such as Fred Zinnemann's *From Here to Eternity...*"

TIME magazine said: "The first half of the film is devoted to apple-pie softness and bamboo resilience...the Americans tend to blend into an indistinguishable potbellied mob. It is the Orientals who are individuals." It said: "The litany of irony and error is unending...no single man can be blamed, and no villains or heroes emerge from this foundering slipshod—and hypnotic—drama...three directors, one American and two Japanese, have managed to move crowds and planes, but not the viewer." The magazine concluded: "Originally, master director Akira Kurosawa (*Rashomon*) was assigned to oversee the Japanese sequences. He might have revealed the complex psychologies that led to the abyss and beyond. Without him, the film is a series of episodes, a day in the death. As for real men and causes, they are victims missing in action."

In Japan, reviews in leading newspapers and magazines were unenthusiastic. *Asahi Shimbun* said: "We rarely see a movie like this. It depicts the discipline of the Japanese Navy so meticulously and it was made by the United States, the target of the Pearl Harbor attack. That makes us feel a little uneasy...we become a little suspicious of the intentions. We wonder why an American movie has to give such positive recognition to Japan's military spirit."

Mainichi Shimbun said: "This is an impressive spectacle movie. But it conveys nothing about the misery of a war...we don't want the kind of movie that has no philosophy and attracts plastic-model fans alone."

Yomiuri Shimbun said: "Japan is now an important ally of the United States. If the U.S. recalls their intervention in Vietnam, they would be unable to say, with a clear conscience, that Pearl Harbor was a sneak attack. By giving what it calls an 'objective' account, the movie has gained a political usefulness that caters to a new era for Japan and the United States."

In an article for *Shukan Asahi* (*Weekly Asahi*) magazine, cinema critic Tadao Sato said: "The U.S. film industry has gone out of its way to be of service to Japan, now a military ally of the United States…everything in the movie goes too well for Japan."

At that time, Kurosawa was busy preparing for the release of *Dodesu-kaden (A Rattling Tram)*. Nearly six years after *Red Beard*, movie fans in Japan were waiting for another film by Kurosawa, still a national icon. His new movie was scheduled to be released on October 31, 1970, one month after the world premiere of *Tora! Tora! Tora!* The film was to run for an indefinite period at theaters affiliated with Toho. Expectations were running high as it was the first movie made by an independent company of four directors, the *Yonki no Kai (The Four Musketeers)*. Kurosawa and three other directors—Masaki Kobayashi, Keisuke Kinoshita, and Kon Ichikawa—had launched the initiative in an effort to rejuvenate Japanese cinema. Toru Takemitsu composed the score for *Dodesukaden*.

In an interview for *Shukan Asahi* (*Weekly Asahi*) magazine, a reporter asked Kurosawa if he had seen *Tora! Tora! Tora!* The director said he hadn't, "and I don't want to see it, either. I don't expect they've taken my advice to make that movie a good one."

Kurosawa's version of *Tora! Tora! Tora!* was never made. Fox used the costly sets with its life-size warships and elaborate stages, costumes, and art that had been designed and made to order by Kurosawa. His final shooting screenplay was cut and revised by Elmo Williams in 40 places in the U.S. and Japanese sequences, all of which had been personally authorized by Darryl Zanuck. Williams shortened the original three-hour version to 147 minutes for the Japanese market and 143 minutes for the non-Japanese market.

The four-minute difference came about because Williams and Zanuck deleted two scenes they considered relevant only to the Japanese audience. Kurosawa had insisted that those scenes were pertinent to the theme of *Tora! Tora! Tora!* and Zanuck had consented when they met in California in May 1968. One scene depicted Admiral Yamamoto's visit to the Imperial Palace to receive an Imperial Order to send the Combined Fleet to war. The other was a comic-relief scene in which two cooks aboard the aircraft carrier *Akagi* on the way to Pearl Harbor are talking about the International Date Line, which puts Japan nineteen hours ahead of Hawaii. Likewise, Kurosawa's cherished plan to open the movie with Admiral Yamamoto's elaborate "manning-the-rails" change of command ceremony was drastically simplified and shortened. Many other scenes that might have benefited from "Kurosawa's Magic" were changed or cut.

The Afterglow

Nine years after the premiere of *Tora! Tora! Tora!*, Darryl Zanuck died in Palm Springs, California, on December 22, 1979, at the age of 77. He had been a producer for 45 years from his first film, *Lady Windermere's Fan*, a silent film in 1925, to his last, *Tora! Tora! Tora!* in 1970. In all, he produced 201 films. In his later years, at least in public, he never said a word about Akira Kurosawa or *Tora! Tora! Tora!* Kurosawa did much the same, although he once said in an interview: "I feel sorry for Darryl Zanuck. He did so much for me."

For a quarter century after he had been dismissed, Kurosawa continued to make movies; seven more in his life after the fiasco of *Tora! Tora! Tora!* As if to cast off his nightmare, Kurosawa's next movie, made two years later, was different. *Dodesukaden* depicted the everyday lives of ordinary people with a humorous touch. *Dodesukaden* was adapted from Shugoro Yamamoto's novel *A Town without Seasons*. It was made on a shoestring budget, yet Kurosawa mortgaged his residence to borrow money to make the film, a determined attempt to revive his career. But the film was not well received and ended in the red. Kurosawa was unable to recover the money he had invested in it. What was left was a large debt for Kurosawa.

Bitterly disappointed, he attempted suicide a year later, on December 22, 1971. It was reported that Kurosawa had slashed himself with a razor in the bathroom of his house. Williams, having heard the news in California, said he shuddered, remembering that Kurosawa had said he would commit *harakiri* when he was informed of his dismissal. Williams said that when he saw *Dodesukaden*, he sensed the pessimism in Kurosawa's heart.

Japanese newspapers described it "a miracle" that 61-year-old director survived the self-inflicted multiple razor slashes to the neck and the wrists. His motive was never known. Many reports said that Kurosawa had apparently "got stuck with his work." Some critics said Kurosawa's career had ended. Kurosawa was aware that he was no longer bankable in Japan and elsewhere after the *Tora! Tora! Tora!* debacle. Donald Richie said: "The 'next picture' was always Kurosawa's life. When there was no 'next picture,' life had little meaning to him."

In 1975, however, four years after his attempted suicide, Kurosawa made a comeback with *Dersu Uzala*, filmed in Russia. It was the story of an old hunter guide and the rules of survival in Siberia, produced with an all-Russian cast by Soviet Mosfilm. The screenplay was co-written by Kurosawa and Yuri Nagibin. It won the Oscar for the Best Foreign Film in 1976.

Despite that success, Kurosawa continued to be a costly business risk to the Japanese film industry, which was reluctant to produce any of his projects. Then Hollywood's talented and successful filmmakers, young enough to be Kurosawa's sons, came to the rescue. His next film *Kagemusha (The Shadow Warrior)* in 1980 was made possible only after Francis F. Coppola and George Lucas, well-established Hollywood filmmakers, committed themselves to produce the overseas version. At the 1980 Cannes Film Festival, *Kagemusha* shared the Palme d'Or with *All That Jazz*.

Ran, the third film Kurosawa made after the *Tora! Tora! Tora!* fiasco, was a 1985 Franco-Japanese production. Warner Brothers agreed to finance it as a Steven Spielberg presentation.

In 1990, Kurosawa was given an Honorary Academy Award for his long-term contributions to cinema. The citation read: "For cinematic accomplishments that have inspired, delighted, enriched and entertained worldwide audiences and influenced filmmakers throughout the world." Steven Spielberg and Francis F. Coppola, who called themselves "Kurosawa's children," announced the golden Oscar at the Dorothy Chandler Pavilion in Los Angeles, California. The ceremony took place on March 26, 1990, three days after Kurosawa's 80th birthday. In a video letter from Tokyo projected on the huge screen, his grandchildren, relatives and friends produced a cake with 80 lighted candles and sang "happy birthday" at the top of their lungs. Those in the Pavilion joined in the singing and applauded. The image of a flushed Kurosawa on the stage saying, "I am truly a lucky guy" was televised live world-wide.

One of those who sang along "happy birthday" was Elmo Williams, who had received two Oscars in the past and was among those invited to the award ceremony. Afterward, Williams approached Kurosawa in the corridor to congratulate him. The moment Kurosawa saw him, however, he turned away and walked off. Tearfully, Williams said he was baffled and disappointed, as he just wanted to congratulate Kurosawa and say, "Let's forget about the past." Kurosawa left the impression on Williams that he deliberately rejected reconciliation.

Kurosawa died on September 6, 1998, at the age of 88. Some 35,000 movie industry figures and fans came to pay their respects at the final rites held in Yokohama a week after Kurosawa's death. The great golden altar was modelled on the medieval castle set for *Ran*—the film which was his interpretation of Shakespeare's *King Lear* in the Noh drama style of aesthetics. Placed on the altar was a large photo of the director in his cap and sunglasses taken while directing the film. Among the music played at the rites was the rousing rendition of Toru Takemitsu's haunting Mahleresque theme from *Ran*.

Ran in Japanese can mean varied states and conditions of human life: chaos, pandemonium, betrayal, treason, revolt, riot, conflict or war depending upon context. It was Kurosawa's last epic, which the director

IN THE SHADOW OF A TIGER

called "his best film and his last statement." Kurosawa himself described *Ran* as a series of tragic human events viewed from heaven. It harks back to his interpretation of *Tora! Tora! Tora!*

Donald Richie says: "It is interesting, if irrelevant, to read *Ran* as autobiography." Indeed, just like Shakespeare's King Lear and *Ran*'s Lord Hidetora, Kurosawa wandered many a heath—dispossessed, angered, confused, and forlorn—after he fell from grace of Hollywood, bankers and his fans.

In a career spanning 50 years Kurosawa had made 30 movies, beginning with *Sanshiro Sugata (Judoist Saga)* in 1943 and ending with *Madadayo (Not Yet)* in 1993. In the last five years of his life after *Madadayo*, Kurosawa wrote scripts and drew storyboards for two more films. But he never had a chance to direct them, mainly due to lack of funds and partly because of his declining health.

In later life, whenever he was asked about his *Tora! Tora! Tora!* experience, Kurosawa's reply was curt: "I forgot about it. Anyway, the whole truth will be out someday, somehow." Kurosawa said he had never seen the Twentieth Century-Fox film. Asked why, he always said: "simply because I do not want to see it."

EPILOGUE

Encounter

My introduction to and eventual rapport with Akira Kurosawa can be attributed to a good friend, a sad-eyed dog, and two bottles of Scotch whisky.

In the autumn of 1966, I received an unexpected phone call at home from one of my professors at my alma mater, Waseda University, the film scholar Donald Richie. He asked me if I would be interested in assisting Akira Kurosawa. At the time I was working as a journalist, and eight years had passed since my graduation from Waseda's English literature department, but Richie-sensei and I remained on close personal terms.

I was told that Kurosawa was in the final stage of preparations for the action film *The Runaway Train*, which was to have been his first experience of filming in Hollywood. Richie said, however, that the project had run into difficulty due to a difference of opinion between the Japanese and American parties over the final shooting script. To make matters worse, the American woman who had been in charge of translating the various drafts of the script had suddenly returned to the United States for personal reasons. The production was at a crucial stage, leaving Kurosawa in the lurch. They were in urgent need of a replacement and Richie wanted to know if I would be willing to accept the position.

I loved films but I had never so much as seen a screenplay before. The script in question had been written by Kurosawa himself, the illustrious and internationally renowned master and emperor of the Japanese film world. To translate this into English was a task that I felt was above my station and far beyond my abilities. Feeling completely unnerved, I declined.

One week later, however, I received another phone call, this time from the office of Kurosawa Productions. I had been recommended to them by Richie and they asked me to come to Kurosawa's residence in Tokyo's Setagaya Ward. Apparently, Kurosawa wanted to meet me in person. This came as a surprise but since it represented the fulfillment of a dream for me as an ardent fan of Kurosawa's films, I was happy to have the chance to meet him.

Thinking back now, I suppose that was the beginning of a screening process on the part of Kurosawa Productions. Blissfully unaware of that and floating on cloud nine, I was driven by producer Tetsu Aoyagi to Kurosawa's home. When the car pulled up alongside a rear entrance of the house, the deeply resonant bark of a gigantic St. Bernard boomed out from a large doghouse to my left.

When I saw the dog's face, for some reason I took an instant liking to it and walked over while calling out to it. This caused the dog to wag its thick tail and stare intently at my face with big, sad brown eyes before extending a paw through the grill of the doghouse door and emitting another single woof. This filled me with joy and I offered my hand in return. At the time I was apparently blathering away to the dog in some nonsensical tongue.

The St. Bernard was Kurosawa's beloved pet, Leo. I learned later from Ryuzo Kikushima, Kurosawa's long-time friend and screenplay writer, that the director had been watching the scene unfold from inside the house.

"I'm Kurosawa," he said as he welcomed me into his home. He was not wearing the intimidating black sunglasses that I had often seen him donning in newspaper photos, and upon seeing him up close for the first time, I was impressed by his bright smile and his gentle eyes. As he smiled, his widely spaced eyebrows drooped down, almost touching his upper eyelids, and deep wrinkles formed in the outer corners of his eyes.

My tension slipped away and I felt at ease. As soon as I had introduced myself, he inquired: "How tall are you?" When I replied that I was 5 feet 10 inches in height, he told me: "Ah, you're the same as my buddy *Sen-chan*," director Senkichi Taniguchi, who was shorter than Kurosawa by 2 inches.

After Aoyagi had left to return to his office, there were just the two of us. Kurosawa asked me what my favorite book was. I absent-mindedly responded that it was *The Brothers Karamazov*, then said to myself: "Damn it, I'm up against a Dostoevsky specialist here." I quickly calmed down and realized that it was indeed my favorite, so I continued with a straight face, saying, "My life wouldn't have been the same if I hadn't read it." Grinning, Kurosawa replied: "Good old *Dos'* (Dostoevsky) seems to have that effect on people, doesn't he?"

It was the middle of the afternoon but Kurosawa suggested we have a drink. He opened a bottle of White Horse Scotch whisky and poured a generous serving into a large crystal glass with ice in it. This was a time when the exchange rate was fixed at 360 yen to the US dollar and a bottle of imported Scotch was an expensive luxury item far beyond the reach of the ordinary Japanese man in the street.

Things became awkward from then on. The more scotch he poured into my glass, the more horribly drunk I became. I had been a cheeky little bookworm as a student, and it seems that Kurosawa out of curiosity allowed me to ramble on about my thoughts on Tolstoy and Shakespeare. It was a lively conversation but I faintly recall that it was entirely about literature and theater and that the topic of film never came up.

A second bottle of White Horse was opened and, as we reached the last few drops, the alcohol rapidly combined with my fatigue from working late the previous night and I began to feel woozy. Kurosawa's voice gradually faded into oblivion and apparently before I knew it I had passed out on his sofa.

In the middle of the night, Kurosawa and his wife lugged my unconscious self into their treasured wine-red Jaguar Mark II and delivered

EPILOGUE

me back to my home in Suginami Ward in another part of Tokyo. The following day, I was mortified to learn of my sorry state from their chauffeur, Shoji Nagamine. I had absolutely no recollection of what had happened after I became drunk and I felt deeply ashamed.

This indiscretion made me feel even less able to refuse the job offer and I eventually took on the task of translating Kurosawa's script for *The Runaway Train* into English on condition that Richie would later correct it. Subsequently, I met with Kurosawa at his residence once or twice a week to ask questions, attend meetings, and do some bilingual research work. I always looked forward to seeing Leo again, too. A bottle of Scotch appeared every time, but I had learned my lesson and never again became helplessly intoxicated in his presence.

That is how I came to assist Kurosawa with *Tora! Tora! Tora!* after the shoot for *The Runaway Train* was suddenly postponed in November 1966.

My main responsibilities were translating Kurosawa's screenplays into English and Twentieth Century-Fox's scripts into Japanese. This exchange of screenplays between Japan and the United States took place twenty-seven times. Thus I was required to translate scripts from Japanese to English or vice-versa over fifty times.

I struggled in solitude to deal with this daunting volume of translation. Without Richie's guidance and encouragement, it would have been an impossible task. Sometimes I wrote letters in English to Fox management on behalf of Kurosawa. When a reply came, I translated it into Japanese. Every time there was a disagreement between the Japanese and Americans over the script, it was necessary to analyze the relevant primary documents, meaning that I doubled as a researcher. As matters grew increasingly complicated, they became more difficult to grasp for anyone less involved than I, and my situation became ever more inextricable. The pressure of playing such a crucial role, despite being way out of my depth and suffering from a constant lack of sleep, was exhausting. Looking back on the experience, I'm amazed that I didn't collapse.

To describe what went on during that time, I borrow a phrase from Detective Sato in Kurosawa's *Nora Inu (Stray Dog)*: "In short, a lot happened." This was one of Kurosawa's favorite phrases. Although I cannot recall all of my memories from this time, some incidents I will never forget. They play back in my mind as vividly as a flashback within my favorite film. The rest, however, have mostly grown dim and don't seem real any more as if they belonged to someone else.

In front of 150 people at the press conference announcing the production of *Tora! Tora! Tora!* on April 28, 1967, I sat between Kurosawa and Elmo Williams and acted as both English and Japanese interpreter as well as master of ceremonies. I have enjoyed a close relationship with Williams ever since. I was fortunate enough to be present at the lively party held at Kurosawa's residence later that night. It felt like a send-off reception for the world-famous Kurosawa on his way to becoming a Hollywood director. He was boundlessly cheerful, keeping his guests laughing, and I remember how delighted he seemed.

I performed a similar role for the presentation of the main cast to the assembled media of *Tora! Tora! Tora!* on November 26, 1968. Apart from Kurosawa, Darryl F. Zanuck and Elmo Williams, 100 members of the press from Japan and abroad were there.

The experience that left the most indelible impression was the two-day summit meeting between Kurosawa and Zanuck in Beverly Hills in May, 1968, for which I was present along with producer Aoyagi. The record of exchanges between Kurosawa and Zanuck is based on the shorthand notes that I took as Kurosawa's assistant and interpreter. I also have memos from the meetings he held with Williams and other production and promotions people at Fox.

The most difficult part for me, however, came when my work had finished for the day. After completing his business at the Twentieth Century-Fox Studio during his one-week stay in Beverly Hills, Kurosawa returned to his hotel and had no desire to go sightseeing. Indeed, he refused to set foot outside of his suite at the Plaza Hotel. I was at a loss for what to do. Aoyagi strung together a few cursory excuses and disappeared, never to return. The trouble was that Kurosawa declined to eat out so I had to order dinner via room service. It was always just Kurosawa and me eating together for a week. His choice was always the same as if set in stone: a thick beef filet mignon, rare, with a baked potato on the side. To avoid bother, I ordered the same meal for myself. Beside the table was a one-liter bottle of Scotch and a bucket full of ice. During and after the meal, he would drink incessantly. Past midnight, we had a second bottle of Scotch and a large tray of canapés brought to his suite. Our conversations were mostly trivial but Kurosawa truly seemed to enjoy them, laughing and drinking every night until dawn when we reached the bottom of the second whisky bottle. He had no shortage of topics to talk about, all of them interesting. I have little memory, however, of what we talked about as I was in a less than sober state most of the time. About this, I am very remorseful.

The preparations for *Tora! Tora! Tora!* went on and my 'apprenticeship' eventually came to an end. On November 30, 1968, two days before filming was scheduled to begin at Toei Kyoto studios, Kurosawa and Zanuck held a four-hour meeting on the final shooting script. Williams, Aoyagi and I were present but I had to return to Tokyo immediately afterwards for business of my own. I informed Kurosawa of this before I checked out of my hotel. "I see. Thank you for your hard work," he said. He looked pallid and worn out. It would be our last farewell. In the thirty years until his death, we never crossed paths again.

Three weeks later in Tokyo, I was shocked to learn of Kurosawa's dismissal. It hit me like a bombshell. I hoped that this news was some kind of misinformation. Directly afterward, news reports hinting at sensational scandals and the witch-hunt for a scapegoat ran rampant. Then Hollywood was made the villain and Kurosawa's honor was zealously defended to sycophantic extremes. These reactions felt out of place to me. Since there were plenty of film critics and journalists well acquainted with the film world, I assumed that one day one of them would write a more accurate account of what had transpired. But it was not to be.

Eventually I came to feel that I shouldn't wait any longer. Personally, I had a craving to know the truth. My compulsion to carry out a thorough investigation, no matter how many years it took, most likely began on that rainy night of September 6, 1998, when Kurosawa passed away

ALL THE EMPEROR'S MEN

at the age of eighty-eight, thirty years after his dismissal.

I made up my mind to start from zero to research matters to my own satisfaction, to do nothing but collate verifiable facts, and to portray them objectively. For that purpose, I tried to stick to authentic, primary sources as much as possible.

This was easier said than done. For two years I searched everywhere in Japan for materials related to the *Tora! Tora! Tora!* production and tried to approach people I believed to have been involved with making the film. Most attempts ended in disappointment. Then, rummaging around on the Internet one day, I learned that materials related to Kurosawa and *Tora! Tora! Tora!* had been preserved by several universities and research centers scattered along the West Coast in the United States. In 2001, I traveled to the U.S. and began surveying them methodically. The results were more fruitful than I had expected.

One of the research facilities was the Academy of Motion Picture Arts and Sciences (AMPAS) in Los Angeles, California. Its Margaret Herrick Library housed a huge collection of film-related materials donated by Elmo Williams when he retired. I will never forget the excitement when I found Kurosawa's original *Tora! Tora! Tora!* screenplay (*junbiko*) written in Japanese, which had been presumed to have been lost forever in Japan. Besides, about 160 storyboards drawn by Kurosawa himself were found among the Margaret Herrick Library collection. When I took the timeworn script and the storyboards in my hands, I felt as if I had been led there by Kurosawa himself.

At the University of Southern California's Doheny Memorial Library in Los Angeles, I made another unexpected discovery, an English translation of Kurosawa's original screenplay that had been sent to Twentieth Century-Fox. One copy, 401 pages long, was preserved in the special collection of the Library. There was no translator's credit on the copy but it was unmistakably my work done in 1967 with the help of Donald Richie. I investigated several other leads but was convinced that the Margaret Herrick Library and the Doheny Memorial Library were the only places with those authentic copies of Kurosawa's original *Tora! Tora! Tora!* screenplay.

Following Kurosawa's ethos in making *Tora! Tora! Tora!*, I avowed to fear nothing, kowtow to no one, and face up to nothing but the facts from both the Japanese and American perspectives. I wanted to write something that I would not be ashamed to have read even by the late Kurosawa, the late Darryl F. Zanuck, or the all-knowing surviving witness Elmo Williams. This was the principle that governed my conduct. To write everything I wanted to write, I devoted myself to this project.

The objective of this book is to bring order to the facts I uncovered and to provide the reader with keys to ascertain the truth behind the *Tora! Tora! Tora!* fiasco. I will leave up to the reader any appraisal of those records and any conclusion that may be derived from them.

Reunion

The most blissful moment in the course of my research trip to America came on Tuesday, August 20, 2002, when I met Elmo Williams again for the first time in 34 years for an interview at his home in Oregon. I felt once more that I had been led there by Kurosawa, who in his life had worked so closely with Williams yet had never made friends with him. Now that both Kurosawa and Zanuck are gone, Williams is among the limited few who were involved with all aspects of *Tora! Tora! Tora!* and who may be presumed to know everything about it.

It was a hot summer day, bright with a dazzling sun, when I visited Elmo Williams's house. It stands at the end of a small bumpy road that has a tiny hand-written sign, "Iris Street." I spoke my name into the intercom at the gate. Then the 89-year-old Williams came out of the house, steadily walked to the gate, and greeted me with a broad smile. Unfortunately, his wife Lorraine was not at home on the interview day.

First he showed me around the house. Every room had large windows that overlooked the inlet. A swing hung from a crossbeam of the ceiling of the spacious living room. I wondered what it was for. Williams smiled and said that when he and Lorraine were young newlyweds with no money, they used to dream about what kind of house they would have. Lorraine wanted a room big enough to put a swing in. So here it is, he

ALL THE EMPEROR'S MEN

said with laughter.

Then he took me to his study with a window that had a view of a sheer cliff standing on the inlet. All over the walls were dozens of photo panels from the early years of his career. The largest number of them, not surprisingly, featured Darryl F. Zanuck. There were also many with legendary cinema people and actors and actresses. Among them, one showed Williams and Minoru Genda when they arrived at the theater in New York for the world premiere of *Tora! Tora! Tora!* in September 1970. There was no photograph of Kurosawa, which I took to mean that Williams did not want to be reminded of his ill-fated association with the Japanese director. I just did not have nerve to ask why.

Bookcases were filled with numerous photo collections and technical books on filming. Standing among the books were two golden Oscars. One was for Best Film Editing, for *High Noon* in 1952; the other for Best Motion Picture, for *The French Connection* in 1971.

Williams told me he respected Kurosawa as a director. He had sincerely hoped to help Kurosawa succeed in his first movie for Hollywood but all his efforts had ended in vain. He—the person who had recommended Kurosawa—had found himself in the position of having to sack him. Williams has mixed feelings and he spoke of them with some detachment. I have touched on his comments throughout the book but perhaps other personal reminiscences are worth revisiting.

By the time Kurosawa's attempted suicide was reported in December 1971, both Darryl and Richard Zanuck had left Twentieth Century-Fox, being held responsible for sharp falls in stock prices as a result of poor business results.

It was Darryl Zanuck himself who dismissed Richard as president and head of worldwide production. On December 29, 1970, Zanuck Sr., then chairman and CEO, publicly announced the decision to his son's face at the board of directors' meeting.

Elmo Williams succeeded Richard Zanuck as head of worldwide production. Zanuck winced when the board of directors appointed his arch-rival Dennis Stanfill as president. Williams served as head of production until 1973. He said his main mission was to reorganize and streamline

EPILOGUE

Fox studio production and he did his best to do just that.

Williams looked sad when he talked about Darryl Zanuck in his later years. At a general shareholders' meeting on May 18, 1971, five months after he sacked his own son, Zanuck himself was forced to resign as chairman. Immediately after that, he slipped in the bathroom of a New York hotel and hit his face hard against the bathtub. He was hospitalized. Soon after that he suffered a stroke. In 1973, he returned to his home in Palm Springs. His wife Virginia had lived there for 17 years, separate from him. He parted from his lover, Geneviève Gilles, with whom he had been living for ten years. A constant cigar smoker for years, he had developed cancer of the jaw. He was often seen in his sunny garden, alone in a wheelchair, wearing a gown and holding a Yorkshire terrier that Geneviève had left behind. He died after seven years of battling cancer.

At his funeral held at a church near his home, there were no eulogies, no sermons, and no hymns during the service. This was in keeping with Zanuck's will. Instead, the church organist played a rendition of the theme tune from *The Longest Day* over and over again. Williams says he was embarrassed. He thought it was not quite suitable for a funeral service. It was Richard Zanuck's idea.

Four hours into our interview—twice as long as first promised—we moved from the study to a spacious kitchen surrounded by large windows. I was served with a big slice of lemon cake that Williams had baked in the morning and a cup of tea. The cake was delicious. Williams had lived for a long time in London and was well versed in tea. For this day, he had chosen *Keemun* tea known for its fruity taste and hints of orchid fragrance. On the shelf were a number of cookbooks. He said he had taken an interest in cooking since his retirement and often cooked himself.

After we chatted a while, I asked him again why he chose Kurosawa as director of the Japanese sequence of *Tora! Tora! Tora!* "Because I liked his movies," he said. "He has an exquisite sense of rhythm for editing." Williams said his favorite Kurosawa film was *Ikiru (To Live)*, which was based on Leo Tolstoy's *The Death of Ivan Ilyich*. It is the story of a man

ALL THE EMPEROR'S MEN

(Kanji Watanabe, played by Takashi Shimura) who knows he is soon going to die of cancer. He thinks of his dead wife, doubts himself, and loathes his whole life as a petty civil servant. Williams said one scene was "simply unforgettable." It is a flashback in which the man remembers how he gazed through the clack clackety moving wiper of a rain-flecked windshield as the hearse carrying his dead wife is driven away. But Williams thought this film was too "low-key and sophisticated" to impress the Zanucks, who didn't know Kurosawa. Instead, Williams chose to show them *Seven Samurai* and *Rashomon* and then recommend Kurosawa. He said they immediately said yes.

But then why did everything end the way it did?

Williams said: "I think Kurosawa was basically a kind, nice man. I liked him a lot. His biggest trouble was, he didn't trust other people. He certainly never trusted me completely. Every time I tried to reach him, I found it very difficult. I know many talented film artists who are temperamental and quick to anger. Kurosawa was also known to be temperamental, but I was embarrassed to find that he was so quick to anger. I realized, though, that when top directors are being difficult with the people they work with, it is often because they are insecure and uncomfortable with themselves."

In a note dated August 1, 1968, Williams wrote to his crew: "(Kurosawa's) importance to this project is such that we would not be involved in it had he rejected our bid to make his American debut on *Tora! Tora! Tora!*" I showed Williams its copy and said: "So you hired Kurosawa because you liked and respected him and sincerely believed that his involvement would be instrumental in the making of the movie?" He replied, "Yes, sure!" But he added that, in the end, Kurosawa's involvement did "more harm than good."

Now, decades later, did the veteran producer think his choice of Kurosawa was a mistake?

"Yes. It was a mistake," he said slowly in a quiet voice. He bit his lip a little and looked serious. "It was a mistake, because it hurt him, and it hurt us. I recommended Kurosawa because I respected him and I really believed he was an excellent, talented artist. Fox hired Kurosawa because Darryl F. Zanuck also thought it would be good for us and it would be good for him as well. But it did not help his reputation. In fact, it hurt it, and it destroyed the high regard we had for him."

Williams was speaking carefully, as if each word was worth dwelling upon. Then he looked aside and gazed out the window. I followed his eyes. It was a magnificent view. The surface of the ocean was glistening in the mellow rays of the setting sun. The sound of waves lapping against the craggy rocks below was faintly heard, mingled with the distant notes of seagulls and possibly a Siren's song. Williams remained silent. I will never forget his stern profile, deep in thought.

On April 30, 2012, Williams celebrated his 99th birthday in excellent health at his home in Oregon with an open house for some 30 guests. Williams's daughter Stacy says he cooked the food himself, which included baked ham, salad, rolls and a chocolate cake with fresh raspberries. He loves being kidded and kidding back and anything that made him laugh. As always, laughter is his favorite sound.

Williams lost his wife of 64 years—Lorraine—in 2004, and since then he has been living by himself at his stately residence on the Oregon coast. In December 2008, he donated a public chapel to the city of Brookings in memory of his wife. Stacy says that her dad does his own cooking, creating his own recipes and usually starting with lots of cream and butter. He also enjoys having dinner parties for friends who come over and he prepares the meals. He still drives and does shopping.

Williams has been incredibly active in Brookings and continues to be. He lectures about his films at a local theater at least every other month. In October 2010, a poignant two-act play written by Williams titled *The Corner Pocket* was performed at the Chetco Playhouse in Brookings. Williams said, "There was no profound philosophy in it—just my observations and the humor I find in the process of aging." He did a cameo appearance at the end of each performance and said: "I want to believe in the power of smiles, hugs, a kind word, truth, justice, peace, dreams, freedom, faith in mankind, and to say 'I love you.' Goodnight." Then he threw a kiss to the audience and the cast came out to join him in taking

ALL THE EMPEROR'S MEN

their bows.

In a recent letter to me Williams said, "It still grieves me that the incident 44 years ago caused the great Japanese director personal distress." At the same time he was proud of his *Tora! Tora! Tora!* He said: "No one has quarreled with the content of the film excepting the few who felt the film was biased in favor of the Japanese. Most people recognized the honesty and integrity of the account we have given of the bombing of Pearl Harbor."

ACKNOWLEDGMENTS

In publishing this book, I must thank the many people who helped to make it a reality. Akira Kurosawa's son and president of Kurosawa Productions, Hisao Kurosawa, and daughter, Kazuko Kurosawa, both kindly agreed to be interviewed. I am deeply grateful for their understanding of the purpose of this book and for consenting to the disclosure of their father's medical certificates and other sensitive material that involved the privacy of their deceased father.

I received significant guidance from Kurosawa's nephew and Kurosawa Productions board member, the late Yoshio Inoue, and owe him a great deal especially for assisting with my investigation into the *Tora! Tora! Tora!* contracts. This would have been impossible without the goodwill and exceptional consideration of Inoue, Kurosawa Productions consulting lawyer Jeffrey L. Graubart, and Twentieth Century-Fox executive vice president Victoria Rossellini.

Many of the legal and medical specialists who kindly agreed to be interviewed regarding the technical aspects of the contracts and medical certificates had various reservations about giving their respective private opinions. Therefore, as they requested, I have not divulged their names. It goes without saying that, as the interviewer of these specialists, I am ready to take full responsibility for the contents of the book.

The massive collection of documents donated by Elmo Williams to the Margaret Herrick Library of the Academy of Motion Picture Arts and Sciences (AMPAS) was a veritable treasure trove of primary sources for tracing Kurosawa's involvement with the *Tora! Tora! Tora!* project. I am indebted to the library's veteran archivist, Barbara Hall, for her kind advice and generous cooperation that enabled me to set foot on this mountain of information and roam through it efficiently in the limited time available. Her invaluable assistance also made possible this book's inclusion of Kurosawa's storyboard sketches held by the library.

I was helped by Lauren Buisson, head of operations for the performing arts special collections of the University of California at Los Angeles (UCLA) Charles E. Young Research Laboratory. There are strict requirements for the perusal and use of the internal documents from Twentieth Century-Fox housed by this laboratory, and I was able to gain access to them thanks to the efforts of Elizabeth Albee and Robert Cohen of Fox's legal department.

Through the kind offices of film archivist Ned Comstock of the Doheny Memorial Library at the University of Southern California (USC), I was able to examine its collection of documents relating to *Tora! Tora! Tora!* that had been donated by Richard Fleischer. The bulk of its collection is made up of screenplays and, although its volume is no match for that of the Margaret Herrick Library collection, it contains rare documents that cannot be found elsewhere.

I am grateful for the assistance extended to me on my intensive fact-finding trip to the United States by Professor Reginald Rodgers of the Anderson University School of Music in Indiana and his wife, Miyoko. I owe Reg special thanks for going the extra mile in proofreading the manuscript. I was also helped greatly by lecturer Yuka Kumagai of the University of Southern California's Department of East Asian Languages and Cultures, and professional researcher Stephanie Jenz.

My research within Japan was aided by dozens of people. Prominent among them was Director Yutaka Osawa, chief assistant director on *Tora! Tora! Tora!*, who spoke to me at length about the various hardships he experienced with Kurosawa while making the film. I was also privileged to hear inside stories from Teruyo Nogami, who worked along-

ALL THE EMPEROR'S MEN

side Kurosawa for half a century from *Rashomon* to the twilight of his life. Yoshiko Miyazawa, who once worked as a secretary for Kurosawa and producer Tetsu Aoyagi, devotedly assisted with my research and the sourcing of materials. I received support concerning technical matters from Ben Nakamura, while Yoshito Yagi provided assistance with regard to interviews and research conducted within Japan.

This book is based on my original work *Kurosawa vs. Hollywood*, written in Japanese and published by Bungei Shunjusha in 2006. The reaction to it within Japan came as a surprise. It was featured in scores of reviews and interviews in national and regional newspapers, magazines, and radio and television stations, and I received many letters from readers across Japan. In addition, reviews and critiques of the book posted on the website grew to a large number, which is still increasing.

When the original book was awarded several major literary prizes, my shock outweighed my delight. The awards included the Kodansha Non-Fiction Prize, Osaragi Jiro Award, Geijutsu Sensho Award, and Oya Soichi Non-Fiction Prize. Apart from these accolades, the book was selected by the film magazine *Kinema Junpo* as their number-one film book of 2006.

Looking back, I feel as if these honors were not bestowed on me alone but represented a kind of commemoration or perhaps a requiem for the great artist Akira Kurosawa. They manifested the sense of love, respect, and compassion for the great film director held by contemporary Japanese. I was genuinely moved by the reaction of readers who had shared the pain of Kurosawa's dismissal from the *Tora! Tora! Tora!* production and had been seeking the truth that remained in the dark all those years.

This book is not a translation from the original Japanese version. It is a work of non-fiction for which the content and structure has been rewritten and rearranged for the English-speaking reader. Writing a book in English, my second language, was no easy task. It would never have been done without the help and goodwill of many collaborators.

Of them all, Donald Richie and Elmo Williams are first and foremost. Without their genial encouragement and advice, this book would never have seen the light of day. I am deeply grateful to Williams who

ACKNOWLEDGMENTS

kindly wrote a foreword to this English edition. I also offer my thanks to film scholar Peter Cowie, who wrote the introduction for the non-Japanese readers. I was assisted by many other people in the preparation for the English version of my book. I would like to express my heartfelt appreciation to Richard Halloran, an American journalist experienced in Asia, and to Fumiko Mori Halloran, a Japanese writer who was awarded the 1980 Oya Soichi Non-Fiction Prize, for their assistance in editing the text at their home in Honolulu. The same special thanks go to my good friend of thirty years and former colleague at NHK (the Japan Broadcasting Corporation) Ian de Stains. I owe my personal thanks to the late Hirotaka Yoshizaki, who encouraged me to venture into this book project. In addition, I wish to thank Marc Shultz, Don Brown, Masayuki Uchiyama, Kazuhiko Miki, and Junko Kawakami for their help and guidance. I would also like to thank Yoshiki Nishiyama of Bungei Shunjusha; my agents, Kenny Okuyama and Robert Lecker; and my editors at Applause Theatre & Cinema Books, John Cerullo, Mike Edison, and Jessica Burr for their good judgments and support. It must be said here that I, and not they, are responsible for everything in this book.

ALL THE EMPEROR'S MEN

INDEX

ALL THE EMPEROR'S MEN

ALL THE EMPEROR'S MEN